Transformative Political Leadership

Transformative Political Leadership

Making a Difference in the Developing World

ROBERT I. ROTBERG

The University of Chicago Press Chicago and London

ROBERT I. ROTBERG is the former director of the Program on Intrastate Conflict and Conflict Resolution at the John F. Kennedy School of Government at Harvard University and president emeritus of the World Peace Foundation. He is the author or editor of numerous books, among them *When States Fail, China into Africa*, and *A Leadership for Peace*.

The University of Chicago Press, Chicago 60637
The University of Chicago Press, Ltd., London

Printed in the United States of America

21 20 19 18 17 16 15 14 13 12   1 2 3 4 5

ISBN-13: 978-0-226-72898-8 (cloth)
ISBN-13: 978-0-226-72899-5 (paper)
ISBN-10: 0-226-72898-6 (cloth)
ISBN-10: 0-226-72899-4 (paper)

Library of Congress Cataloging-in-Publication Data
Rotberg, Robert I.
Transformative political leadership : making a difference in the developing world / Robert I. Rotberg.
p. cm.
Includes bibliographical references and index.
ISBN-13: 978-0-226-72898-8 (hardcover : alkaline paper)
ISBN-13: 978-0-226-72899-5 (paperback : alkaline paper)
ISBN-10: 0-226-72898-6 (hardcover : alkaline paper)
ISBN-10: 0-226-72899-4 (paperback : alkaline paper)
1. Leadership. 2. Developing countries—Politics and government.
3. Mandela, Nelson, 1918– 4. Khama, Seretse, 1921–1980.
5. Lee, Kuan Yew, 1923– 6. Atat?rk, Kemal, 1881–1938. I. Title.
JF1525.L4R68 2012
303.3'4—dc23
2011034676

⊗ This paper meets the requirements of ANSI/NISO Z39.48-1992 (Permanence of Paper).

Contents

Introduction 1

1 Political Leadership, Governance, Political Culture, and Political Institutions 6

Political Leadership 10
Governance 12
Political Culture and Political Institutions 13

2 Compelling Political Leadership: The Critical Competencies 16

The Differences Leaders Make 18
Emotional Intelligence 19
The Core Competencies 20
The Vision Thing 21
The Mobilization Momentum 23
Being Legitimate 26
Gaining Trust 34
The Enlarged Enterprise 35
Tapping into Authentic Needs 36
The Contribution of Charisma 36
The Cases 38

3 Nelson Mandela: Consummate Inclusionist 40

A Manifest Destiny 41
A Mass Leader Arrived 44
Maturing as an Activist 45

"An Ideal for Which I Am Prepared to Die" 48
"I Will Return" 52
Donning the Green Jersey 59

4 Seretse Khama: Resolute Democrat 66

A Traditional Heritage 67
"A Very Disreputable Transaction" 71
"Slow and Steady" 76
Noblesse Oblige 78
Dirt-Poor and Principled 80
"Democracy Must Be Nursed and Nurtured" 82
Prudence, Morality, and Competence 85
To Build a New Nation 88

5 Lee Kuan Yew: Systematic Nation-Builder 91

Born to Lead 93
The Singapore Express 95
"Lee . . . Is the Only Man" 97
Getting Singapore to Work 101
A First World Oasis 104
Paying a Heavy Price 107
The Coming of Institutions 112
The New Confucianism 116

6 Kemal Ataturk: Uncompromising Modernizer 119

"Victory Is Mine" 120
Only a Single Leader Would Do 124
The Forced March to Modernity 129
Off with the Fez 133
The Commanding Vision 135
Becoming Ataturk 138
The New Turkey 141

7 The Crisis of Contemporary Political Leadership 145

The Founders and Their Successors 147
The Crisis 152

Despots and Tyrants 153
Transactional Leadership 161
Leaders Making a Difference 167
Strengthening Leadership in the Developing World 173

Acknowledgments 177 *Notes 181* *Index 205*

Introduction

Recently a widely read, opinion-shaping world news magazine was bemoaning South African President Jacob Zuma's lame leadership—really his lack of anything that might be called real leadership. The magazine reminded readers that South Africa was sub-Saharan Africa's biggest economy and most influential nation. South Africa could hence guide black Africa down the path of prosperity and full freedom, or backwards. "It is largely up to Mr. Zuma to decide which way it goes," said the *Economist*. It called on Zuma to get a vision, providing it was a decent one. He has never explained, said the magazine, for what he stands.[1]

Indeed, Zuma is no visionary. But a vision, minimally, is what accomplished political leaders are meant to provide. Their followers expect even more of committed leadership—a strategy for turning visions into reality and charting a way forward to a promising future, access to improving prospects, and a program for ensuring economic growth and material and human uplift—but rarely get it. This book explores the full range of those expectations and how they have been and will be met. It portrays the competencies of gifted leadership, primarily as experienced in recent decades across the developing world, and examines those special instances in which unusually accomplished nation-builders have in fact made an impact—performing ably in political leadership positions so as to inspire and to transform their emerging countries and to deliver abundant and high-quality political goods to their constituents.

Imaginative political leadership can make a telling difference in that way, particularly in the developing world.

Peace, war, economic growth, a relief from poverty, beneficial educational and health outcomes, and a sense of belonging to a worthy national enterprise are all greatly influenced by the character and intentions of a nation's leader. This book argues that greater attention than hitherto should be paid to the critical role of leadership in the developing world. It argues that leaders are more responsible for societal outcomes in the developing than in the developed world because in the former institutions are weaker. It also argues that formative leaders help to build nations and political cultures, and that their actions help to enable institutions to take root in otherwise stony soils. Leaders can shape political cultures and therefore breathe life into institutions. Leaders in emerging or post-conflict countries help to build institutions almost from scratch. Leaders influence how governments perform—how they serve or abuse their citizens. Leaders matter.

To operate at such critical levels demands abundant analytical, contextual, political, and emotional intelligence; compassion; tolerance; integrity; and many other intrinsic leadership competencies. This book elaborates on those competencies, indicating which ones matter in the context especially of effective *political* leadership. It offers content for the prime competencies and shows how they have and have not been deployed in the varied and rough context of emerging nations. The final chapter examines a range of leadership responses to the challenges of statehood in the contemporary era. Good leaders are contrasted with bad leaders and work-a-day transactionalists with visionary transformationalists, and the various modes of developing world political leadership are compared with those of four high-achieving, founding, nation-building leaders.

Political leadership has been studied intensively in this manner comparatively little, except by biographers of presidents and statesmen. Certainly, developing world leaders have featured only occasionally in the general leadership literature and even less in the biographically based leadership literature. The dominant examination of leadership focuses mostly on corporate and organizational leadership. It is instructive, but draws heavily on the examples of successful and less successful chief executive officers and heads of industry. Much of that literature explains well how corporate managers can make the most of their opportunities, challenges, talents, and limitations. But as rich and rewarding as it is, most of that vast corporate-inspired literature captures only in part the experiences and realities of political leadership in the developing world.[2]

Notwithstanding the rather different contexts of corporate and political leadership, the former literature offers a number of helpful insights. Kanter wisely distinguishes between corporate management—"oversight of the technical or functional aspects of an organization"—and corporate leadership—"a more dynamic effort to shape the direction of an organization."[3] Her separation of the two corporate behavioral modes and responsibilities is equally instructive for this study of the varieties of political leadership in the developing world. Managers are transactionalists. Leaders are transformationalists.

A fulfilling psychological literature also exists that pertains insightfully to the family and other origins of leadership competencies and suggests the different inner qualities, even the genetic factors, that contribute to successful or unsuccessful leadership experiences. Psychobiographers have added further insights stemming from the study of individuals and groups across a variety of settings, even political settings.[4] But only a scattering of examples encompass the impact of leaders on the peoples of the developing world.

Yet, the model and experience of responsible leadership in the developing world hold lessons for political leadership everywhere. That experience also helps to explain differences within the developing world, country by country and region by region, in terms of economic, social, and conflict outcomes. This book thus examines and characterizes political leadership in the poorer half of the world and shows how some, but only some, of its most accomplished and most articulate exponents have employed their abilities to benefit and to uplift their nations and peoples.

Among the most notable and noble practitioners of those leadership arts over the past century, four (among a handful of others who might have been included) stand out. Kemal Ataturk, the creator of modern Turkey; Sir Seretse Khama, the father of modern Botswana; Lee Kuan Yew, the inventor of modern Singapore; and Nelson Mandela, the shaper of the new South Africa, were very different personalities in very distinctive settings, but each exemplified our prescriptive model of uncommon leadership. Explications of their leadership experiences, in context, constitute the combined centerpieces of this book; each was among the most skilled leaders and nation-builders of the developing world's twentieth and twenty-first centuries.

This book is about the lessons for leadership everywhere that may be learned from their telling turns as prime minister and president. How Mandela, Khama, Lee, and Ataturk led, what they did for their peoples because of their transformational initiatives, and how they managed to build successful new nations testify to their talents and what can be achieved by heads of state and heads of government who are gifted and know how to mobilize followers for good. But an examination of their lives also emphasizes the underappreciated importance of political leadership everywhere, particularly in the fragile parts of the globe that we call developing.

The four leaders examined are not perfect models. Each case contributes to an appreciation of the leadership paradigm set out in the first and second chapters of this volume, but none embodies all of the competencies outlined in those opening chapters. That would be asking too much even of masterly leaders who acted resolutely in different places and times and who confronted diverse complex and daunting obstacles.

They were and are among the best of their kind: gifted leaders and accomplished nation-builders. This book is an examination of their skills and insights more than it is a treatment of their losses and victories. Collectively, this surprisingly successful quartet offers lessons for the exercise of political leadership and nation-building in the remainder of the twenty-first century.

Among those lessons are the behavioral competencies that are revealed by a close analysis of both the extensive leadership literature and the political experiences of leaders, such as the exceptional ones detailed in this volume. The first chapter suggests that understanding competencies is critical and indicates why and how leadership greatly influences the performance of governments, the coalescence of a democratic (or nondemocratic) political culture, and the rise of durable institutions. The second chapter details the various telling components of responsible leadership competency. It sets out five categories by which leadership accomplishments can be judged within their own countries and from outside.

This book is also intended to be a how-to manual for aspiring leaders, especially in the developing world. After discussing ideal core leadership competencies, it shows how Mandela, Khama, Lee, and Ataturk used or abused those competencies during their months and years in high office. Aspiring leaders and nation-builders might do well to study and to learn from the responses of one or more of those four predecessors and founders as they themselves confront the difficult challenges of today's governance.

A concluding chapter assesses the capabilities and behaviors of contemporary and recent leaders across the developing world and compares them and their examples systematically—in terms of results—to the leadership paradigm sketched out in the first six chapters. That final chapter focuses squarely on the worrying crisis of contemporary political leadership in the developing world.[5] Political leadership is a tougher pursuit today than it once was. Today's globalized world is characterized by rapid and unpredictable changes and economic and social shifts in distant parts of the planet now reverberate in many directions and influence other regions much more speedily than in the past. Therefore, the experiences of accomplished nation-builders and forgers of unity in the developing world are still usefully contrasted to the methods of the many insufficient leaders who have brought conflict, suffering, impoverishment, and retarded growth to large swathes of today's globalized and tightly interconnected world.

ONE

Political Leadership, Governance, Political Culture, and Political Institutions

Outcomes for the citizens of the developing world depend greatly on the actions and determinations of leaders and on critical political leadership decisions. This appraisal tends to fly in the face of conventional wisdom—and to tilt against traditional emphases on the primary salience of structures and institutions. It also appears to contradict older research suggesting that little variance in corporate performance could be attributed to individuals and individual differences.[1] It may even unwittingly differ from those who prefer to emphasize structure and contingency rather than the importance of individual agency in the conduct of human affairs. Yet, after a long acquaintance with politics and political development in the developing world, especially Africa, Asia, and the Caribbean, the conclusion is persuasive and powerful that leaders matter as much as do many external influences, internal structures, and institutional constraints in shaping nation-state policy and in influencing the ways in which beneficial results are pursued across diverse national and continental cultures.

Fortunately, recent corporate and empirical psychological studies support such conclusions. Those studies show that leaders do "have a substantial impact on performance."[2] Those who have examined the role of leadership particularly in the foreign policy realm conclude that individual agency matters.[3] Leaders (not necessarily situations or structures by themselves) largely create peace and war. Leaders even help signally to guide their people into or out of poverty. For example, Jones and Olken established in a path-breaking econometric study with robust evidence that national political leaders, irrespective of institutions and context, influence economic growth attainments.[4] Leaders help to overcome geographical, climatic, and resource limitations. As close attention to the political history of independent Asia, Africa, the Middle East, Latin America, and the Caribbean will show, human agency has the capacity to strengthen or to fail nation-states, to uplift or to oppress citizens, and to unleash or to stifle the talents and aspirations of all manner of followers.[5]

Admittedly, such a conclusion allows the element of chance into the direction of human affairs. To be more precise, accidents of birth seem unusually apposite when we examine the critical early years of successful nations in the developing world. Studies of twins, identical versus fraternal, indicate that there indeed could be a genetic basis for leadership. Research shows a predisposition for and against taking up the leadership baton. Some were born to lead—born with "an innate set of skills that makes us good candidates for directing a group of people toward a goal. . . ."[6] Moreover, research reveals that genes predispose not only to leadership but also to whether the ambition to lead is achieved, and sometimes at what level.

National founders or rebuilders (after revolutions or dramatic societal breaks) have almost everywhere in the developing world helped to set a dramatic course. The influence of human agency appears at least suggestive. If Lee Kuan Yew had not been born to a Singaporean elite family, coming of age during the Japanese occupation, would Singapore have been led effectively and have developed so extraordinarily after 1959? If Kemal Ataturk had not been a radical-thinking Turkish officer under the Ottomans at the time of the empire's collapse, would there today be a powerful, modern Turkey? If a Govan Mbeki, a Walter Sisulu, or an Oliver Tambo—not Nelson Mandela—had grasped the leadership of South Africa after the demise of apartheid, would South Africa have avoided a revanchist race war or have been so peacefully, even magisterially, developed? Ambitious left-leaning nationalists could even have substituted themselves for Seretse Khama in Botswana and have ignored some of the traditional and religious foundations of what became democratic rule under Khama and his successors. If Khama had been born a Tanzanian and had risen there to political prominence, would Tanzanians now be much wealthier per capita, and much less corrupt? Paul Kagame has vigorously altered the trajectory of postgenocidal Rwandan development. So, for good or ill, have and did Evo Morales in Bolivia, Hugo Chavez in Venezuela, Meles Zenawi in Ethiopia, Yoweri Museveni in Uganda, Muammar Qaddafi in Libya, and Robert Mugabe (not Joshua Nkomo) in Zimbabwe channeled follower energies and placed an undeniable personal stamp on the remaking of their peoples and nations.[7]

What, it is also important to ask, accounts for the different outcomes in India and Pakistan after partition? Obviously, size and resources were important. So was religion, and how religion was employed to mobilize electors, a critical factor. But how the first postpartition leaders responded to the different hands that they were dealt mattered massively, too. Arguably, today's India owes its messy but secure democratic political culture and strong institutions as much to Jawaharlal Nehru's formative guidance as it does to the British Raj and the long decades of prepartition Indian Congress Party socialization to democratic norms.[8] As Huntington concludes sensibly, "Economic development makes democracy possible; political leadership makes it real."[9]

The colonial experience, like the Raj in India and Pakistan, conceivably conditioned the growth of developing world leadership. Yet, comparisons show that whether the imperial example was Belgian, British, Dutch, French, Italian, or Spanish, in modern times it has mattered little which metropole tutored and controlled.[10] Every metropole oppressed, conditioned, discriminated, and withheld opportunity and full human advancement until compelled by the rise of nationalism and changing times to respond positively. British rule, sometimes thought more benign than the others, nevertheless spawned Robert Mugabe, Idi Amin, a series of Nigerian tyrants, and many others. It also gave us excellent leaders such as Seretse Khama and his successors, Sir Seewoosagur Ramgoolam of Mauritius and those who followed him, and Lee Kuan Yew in Singapore, among others. French rule brought Jean-Bedel Bokassa, the Central African emperor; Omar Bongo of Gabon; Gnassingbe Eyadema of Togo; and many other autocratic rulers. The more positive French postcolonial examples are all in the Caribbean or in Oceania. Belgian rule, abetted by the United States, prepared Congolese for Mobutu Sese Seko's long tyranny. Portuguese colonialism preceded both the superb modern governance experience of Cape Verde and the corrupt authoritarianism of Angola. Italian colonial rule was a precursor to Siad Barre's hegemony in Somalia and what has since occurred there, and to the rise of Muammar Qaddafi in Libya. Spain's legacy is Teodoro Obiang Nguema in Equatorial Guinea, one of the worst despots in the developing world.

Idiosyncratic behaviors of individual leaders have arguably mattered more, whether in Sri Lanka, Jamaica, or Côte d'Ivoire, than whatever were those countries' received colonial legacies. Despite more representative and participatory institutions at independence in ex-British colonies than in the former dependencies of the other colonial powers, their subjects fared no better on average during the independence period than the citizens of ex-Belgian, ex-Dutch, ex-French, ex-Italian, and ex-Spanish territories. Whether a colonial experience was more or less consultative mattered little in terms of leadership and governance results. Unconscionable tyrants flourished then and now equally in common law and Napoleonic systems. Greed, and a preference for preying upon and looting, depended and depend more on the designs and integrities of a new state's first leader (or a later leader coming to power after a major crisis) than it does on any precise colonial inheritance. Likewise, excellent and reasonably good governance in Asia and Africa has flowed from leadership action, not from adherence to a colonial model or the existence or absence of ethnic plurality, geographical constraints, arbitrary borders, navigable rivers, tropical diseases, allocations of natural resources, or foreign assistance levels. Compare the two postcolonial wealthy British colonies—Uganda and Ghana—and such French outposts as Côte d'Ivoire and, say, Mali. In times of plenty and in times of scarcity, in times of ample rainfall and in times of drought, leaders help to shape the lives of their citizens and help a country to respond poorly or well to the crises and needs of their parlous states, whatever the colonial legacy.

Likewise, the quality of the political institutions that have been inherited or that exist within a given polity, its literacy and educational levels, the quality of its health care, and its overall standards of living have had and have less influence on national outcomes and leadership results than such underlying motivators as individual and group senses of what is right and wrong and what is responsible, avarice, the gaining and keeping of power, and formidable senses of entitlement.

But inadequate leadership also responds in part to the absence, especially in Africa (less so in Asia), of a large and cohesive hegemonic bourgeoisie. Most corporate leaders in Africa feed at the trough of the political class. The clashes of the Cold War may have played a role in diminishing leadership attainments, too, and high commodity prices during and after the Korean War doubtless persuaded the post–World War II leaders, few of whom were experienced, mistakenly to be optimistic about the results of what was considered very formidable Socialist instrumentalities.

Political Leadership

Political leadership is a "social construction" that acts within a particular historical and social context, as a multidimensional activation that is a peculiar mixture of contingent situation and personal intervention, and as the impact of individual style and creativity on political challenges and opportunities. Equally, "too great a focus on . . . context robs the notion of leadership of its core. . . ."[11]

In recent years the study of the leadership variable has been neglected. However, the relevance of human agency to the direction of the affairs of nations, particularly in emerging nations, is old news that nonetheless deserves to be highlighted. Such important theorists as Weber, Merriam, Shannon, Seligman, Pye, Easton, Rustow, Burns, Paige, and many others sought over earlier decades to persuade students of politics and political transformation that leadership was a central variable in the study of politics; they tried in diverse ways to emphasize its primordial centrality—to stress the significance of leadership for an understanding of how politics really worked. For Seligman, leadership was essential to the creation and maintenance of democracy. For Rustow, leadership expressed itself as the interplay between private personality and public performance. He advocated the "systematic rediscovery of leadership as a central political process." Paige suggested a reasonable all-encompassing definition: "Political leadership is the behavior of persons in positions of authority. . . ." Political leaders influence everything around them and, Paige reminded us, even external and exogenous influences come through them, being mediated by leadership decisions and determinations. In politics, leaders can often change not only the rules of the game but also how people play. "The choices they make or fail to make seemingly affect everything."[12] The average African, Asian, or Latin American worker, farmer, or voter likely would consider such insights obvious.

They would also be familiar with Burns' important but controversial distinction between power wielders and leaders. The former (Hitler, Stalin, Mao, Idi Amin, Pol Pot, Mugabe) treat people as things, the latter "may not." Naked power overrides competition and conflict, whereas leadership always is exercised amid conflict and competition—leaders appeal to the "motive bases" of potential followers. Burns' full articulation, very helpful in the context of this book, is "Leadership over human beings is exercised when persons with certain motives and purposes mobilize, in competition or conflict with others, institutional, political, psychological, and other resources so as to arouse, engage, and satisfy the motives of followers."[13] The last phrase is critical because, Burns insists rightly, that leadership is the employment largely of informal means to induce followers and citizens together with the leader to achieve mutual goals and joint purposes. Leaders do not make people do what they do not want to do. They persuade them.[14] They cajole them. They allow them to maximize their own interests by believing in and endorsing the policies and articulated goals expressed by their leaders. The genius of political leadership melds leadership drives and followership aspirations and beliefs.

Stated simply, leaders cannot exist without followers. Kellerman reminds us that there are as many kinds of followers—primarily isolates, bystanders, activists, and diehards—as there are varieties of leaders.[15] Each type of follower plays a role in the unfolding drama of political engagement and nation-building. Followers have power because should they stop following, the leader cannot achieve his or her goals, including the basic one of maintaining his or her position, unless they turn to the naked use of coercive power to eliminate competition. It is the modern political leader's task to interact effectively and successfully, preferably responsibly, with the changing cast of citizens and followers. She wins their trust. She gains legitimacy. They follow her and sometimes exert meaningful influence. The tension between leader and led, follower and ruler, remains critical to outcomes, especially and obviously in democracies, but also in autocracies.

The actions of political leaders in at least the developing world are therefore determined more by their creative interaction with (and sometimes their manipulation of) their followers than they are narrowly inhibited by socioeconomic circumstance, global trends, resource constraints, and so on. Political leaders, especially but not exclusively in the developing world, are able more than others to override structural constraints and to act largely autonomously. Sometimes, bolstered by a core of dedicated followers, they go so far as to disregard economic or global realities, big power or world order strictures, and internal public opinion. These leaders focus on the deployment both of noncoercive power (the usual mechanisms of informal power) and various kinds of co-optive and occasionally coercive power (components of formal power that many developing-world leaders use to buttress their personal power and authority).[16]

In the developing world, at least, the syllogism is straightforward: leadership begets governance, governance in turn begets political culture and, in time, begets institutions. President Obama said in Ghana that Africa "needed strong institutions," not strong men.[17] The sentiment and the intent were correct. But the analysis was incomplete. After independence, or after traumatic postconflict transitions, leaders fashion the ways in which the nation-state and its residents respond to external and internal challenges. They, either alone or together with a cohort of senior officials—and in tension with their followers—help to determine the direction of the nation-state. They govern, and the methods of governing that are chosen early create precedents and practices that shape the nature and course of a nation-state's governance. Indeed, personally influential, even inspirational leaders, or innovative leaders with transformational impulses, flourish more readily in new countries before there are institutions, in periods of extreme crisis, or before institutional safeguards have been developed and have matured except on paper.[18]

Governance

Governance is governmental performance—the delivery of essential political goods by a nation-state or some other governmental jurisdiction to the inhabitants of that place or country.[19] The essential political goods are those deliverables that every citizen everywhere, no matter the underlying traditional culture, expects of her government: safety and security, rule of law and transparency, participation and human rights, sustainable economic development, and human development (education, health services, and so on). The best leaders obviously provide the best governance. In other words, to paraphrase an early study of domestic leadership effectiveness, accomplished political leaders (and their followers) are preponderantly responsible for achieving high levels of performance for their nations and peoples—peace, prosperity, and positive human advancement.[20] The best leaders are motivated to create Locke's "common good" rather than the good just of members of their lineage or family. The best leaders are motivated neither by short-term considerations nor by staying in office. They—the rare ones—are driven by long-term fulfillment of societal goals. Burns epitomized this critical variable very well: the crucial distinction is between "the quest for individual recognition and self-advancement regardless of its social and political consequences" and deploying authority and power to "advance collective purposes."[21] This is what President Kennedy meant when he called for political leadership by "men of dedication"—men "with an honor mortgaged to no single individual or group, and compromised by no private obligation or aim, but devoted solely to serving the public good and the national interest."[22]

A polity's quality of governance correlates to the quality of a jurisdiction's leadership. It may vary a little depending on underlying resources and available human capacity at the bureaucratic level, but the main determinant of governance attainments is human agency at the top. Leaders with a positive vision (such as Nehru) create an ethos that enables and empowers good governance; absent such leadership, governance falters and political goods are not supplied adequately or well.

In Africa, where governance has been measured systematically and countries ranked accordingly, the nation-states that consistently score more highly on governance are, by definition, all better and much more responsibly led than those farther down on the list. The worst-performing countries, naturally, have been led over the years by dictators, despots, and kleptocrats. For example, the *Index of African Governance* places Mauritius, the Seychelles, Cape Verde, Botswana, South Africa, Namibia, Gabon, Ghana, and Senegal, in that order, at the top of its latest roster. Each nation-state arguably is better led than the country that follows it down the list.[23] Nothing seems to matter more than quality leadership—not literacy, not gross domestic product (GDP), not a good infrastructure, not a good location—in terms of rankings, as the *Index* has demonstrated. But, much more importantly, quality leadership improves the lives of ordinary citizens. That is, better health outcomes, improved educational attainments, and other social accomplishments all flow largely from better leadership in countries where governance ranks higher on the continental scale. (The bottom eleven African countries, according to the *Index*, were the Republic of Congo [Brazzaville], Guinea, Zimbabwe, Angola, Eritrea, Central African Republic, Côte d'Ivoire, the Democratic Republic of Congo [Kinshasa], Chad, the Sudan, and Somalia—in that order from 43rd to 53rd.)

Political Culture and Political Institutions

A national political culture—a national bundle of values conditioning the conduct of politics—evolves out of formative governmental decisions taken and not taken over years or decades.[24] The prevailing American political culture derived from a colonial war against the British, and from the new Constitution, but also from the formative leadership actions of General and then President Washington. The protean American political culture was thereafter influenced more fully by Chief Justice John Marshall, by early executive and legislative responses to Marshall and the judicial supremacy proposition, and by a gradual acceptance *inter alia* of the value of *stare decisis*, the balance of power idea, and the other rudimentary components of an American way of governance—a prevailing ethos and thus a political culture that differed significantly from its contemporaneous European models.[25]

It is from the broth of governance and political culture that institutions eventually are reduced. The U.S. Constitution sets out rules, as do other national charters, but it is the manner in which those rules are interpreted that informs political culture and sets the firmament of institutions and thus creates structure. Institutions and institutional prerogatives are specified in constitutions, but they have no meaning and no institutional power until they are nurtured by leadership actions and by the articulation of a successful agenda of governance. The experience of twentieth-century Asia and Africa, again and again, supports such a bold conclusion, as in the 1940s in Sri Lanka, the 1950s in Ghana, the 1960s and 1970s in Sierra Leone, 2010 in Kenya, and on and on. In those and so many other cases, strongly written constitutional safeguards were cavalierly pushed aside by determined, elected, political leaders. Constitutions and other written rules that specify the powers and workings of political institutions have no strength and no capacity for restraining leaders and official actions until they receive the sustained support of leaders and of the governance apparatus over time. Leaders breathe life into institutions. Founding and posttransitional leaders set the tone, inculcate values by their voice and their actions, and slowly foster a democratic political culture or some other. Many of the fifty-year-old nation-states of Africa in 2011, and a few in Asia and Latin America, still lack more than the rudiments of a democratic political culture.

Even in the 1980s and 1990s, President Robert Gabriel Mugabe's Zimbabwe inherited constitutional limitations and strong paper institutions from its British and Rhodesian colonial predecessors, but he soon ran roughshod over them, making the ruling party dominant and his own executive role thoroughly authoritarian. "The constitution is what I say it is," Mugabe famously declared in 1999. Similarly, the inherited institutions of Sri Lanka were irrelevant when Sinhalese electoral outbidding under President Solomon West Ridgeway Bandaranaike marginalized the Tamil-speaking minority and led, in time, to a bitter thirty-year civil war. Sierra Leone had putatively strong institutions after independence from Britain. Yet, when President Siaka Stevens destroyed those institutions, nothing barred his way.

Peoples in Africa, and to some extent in Asia and the Caribbean, still have every reason to believe in the relevance of "big men" and strong unaccountable leaders. Or at least they consider "big men" a necessary evil and put less faith in institutions—courts, parliaments, bureaucracies—because they assume that big men continue to control such institutions. These pernicious effects seep down through the governmental structure and influence how officials view their peoples. Even in democratic Mali, a midlevel official could disdain the views of local opponents of large-scale farming: "If civil society does not agree with the way we are doing it, they can go jump in the lake."[26]

Nation-building is a slow and deliberate process. Only when nation-states are finally strong and a sustainable national will is forged do institutional prerogatives dominate and guide governments. Then leaders become less important as human agency is subsumed under institutional safeguards. But first there is a crucial role for compelling leaders.

TWO

Compelling Political Leadership: The Critical Competencies

Good leadership separates endeavors that succeed from those that fail. Imaginative political leadership—excellent and all-consuming political leadership—is especially important, more necessary, and often more lacking in the developing world in recent decades than previously. Effective statecraft depends on consummate leadership. Careful and farsighted leadership is necessary, particularly amid dangerous or unsettled neighborhoods. Stability and peace, or at least the avoidance of cross-border or internal conflict, demands responsible leadership, especially in troubled times. Economic advances rely on skillful leadership, especially in those myriad small, fragile, climatically or geographically compromised nation-states that form so much of the developing world. Poverty can hardly be alleviated without a leadership that understands the close connections between macroeconomic prudence, increased employment opportunity, attracting foreign direct investment, and strengthening prosperity. The delivery of essential political goods—the political goods of security, rule of law, and so on that citizens expect and insist upon—is most easily achieved by the kinds of accomplished leaders who have appeared rarely in the developing world in the past half century. Where such effective leaders have gained power, they have made incomparable positive advances in terms of the material and social attainments of their peoples.

In the developing world, the critical variable of leadership makes much more of a difference in every realm, particularly in the political realm, than it does in the developed world, where value systems of democracy are fully rooted, where political institutions such as legislatures and judiciaries are independent, where the reality of good governance is taken for granted, and where open economic practices are common. In other words, the value added of responsible, enlightened leadership is much greater in those regions of the globe where political cultures and political institutions are still embryonic. Human capacity is also much more limited in the developing than in the developed world. A tiny, fully literate country such as Norway can provide innumerable potential leaders. A much poorer African country with roughly three times the population (but far less literacy), such as Malawi or Zambia, can produce far fewer potential leaders of stature. In the developing world, both the prevailing methods of political recruitment and the corrosive quality of political competition inhibit the development of broadly based leaders entering politics from the private sector or from civil society. Thus, for those and a host of other reasons, emerging as an independently minded leader responsive to national rather than sectoral or narrow party needs is exceedingly difficult in Africa, Asia, and other developing regions.

In addition, too many of the countries in the developing world are poor, fragile, low in literacy, high in infant mortality, and poor in social attainments. Indeed, in 2007, the mean GDP per capita for sub-Saharan Africa (in USD [2005] at purchasing power parity) was $3,048 and the median $1,220. For Asia, the totals were $12,400 and $3,900 (for 2008 rather than 2007). Twelve African countries had GDP per capita of less than $1,000, a few as low as $370. For essentially the same period, 42 percent of all Africans and 24 percent of all Asians lived below their own national poverty lines (usually $1.25 a day). In 2009, a UN report indicated that 100 million more Africans were living below the poverty line than in 1990; the average daily consumption in 2005 was 70 cents per day. It is no wonder that in 2010, nearly 1 billion persons in the developing world were officially classified as hungry; 30 percent of all sub-Saharan Africans were "undernourished." Child malnutrition was widespread; one quarter of all developing world children were malnourished, and 500,000 women died annually in childbirth or from complications with pregnancy. Life expectancy among women in Zimbabwe was then the lowest in the world at 34 years. Even comparatively prosperous South Africa's male and female life expectancies were as low as 48 years in 2011, having fallen from 62 years in 1990. Overall, millions of persons living in the developing world are poor and unskilled. Human resource capacities in the countries composing the developing world are accordingly limited.[1]

The Differences Leaders Make

Yet, it is precisely in those less privileged places that political leadership is more rather than less essential. In such surroundings, leadership quality matters severely and matters intensely. Who leads makes a bigger difference in the fractured, scrabbling nation-states than it does in settled, stable ones. The differing results of leadership in the same country by a Nelson Mandela, a Thabo Mbeki, or a Jacob Zuma (in South Africa) are instructive. Likewise the contrasts in governmental outcomes between a country led by a Jerry Rawlings or a John A. Kufuor (in Ghana) are notable. Or we can contrast what Sukarno did to retard Indonesia with the more developmentally and socially effective actions of his successors, especially Susilo Bambang Yudhoyono, the country's current president. Pairing in that manner dramatizes the presumed effects of good leadership and demonstrates once more that in countries where institutions are young and democratic political cultures are still being created, leadership quality is an independent variable that matters greatly to human outcomes.[2]

Responsible or effective political leaders in the developing world generally share a number of characteristics. National heads of state and heads of government like Kemal Ataturk, Seretse Khama, Lee Kuan Yew, and Nelson Mandela mostly adhered to positive methods of governing because they believed such approaches had proven or would prove more successful in uplifting and building their nations, or because they wanted to emulate successful models of governance developed in North America, Europe, or elsewhere in Asia and Africa. But those who today or in recent decades learned from Lee or Mandela, and emulated their competencies, are in the minority; too much of Asia and Africa since World War II (and since 1960 in Africa) has been led by men and women who have preyed on their citizens for private, chauvinistic gain. Even when elected freely to high office, they undermined nominal democratic procedures and, like Sukarno, Suharto, Nkrumah, Mobutu, and now Mugabe, violated all of the textbook good leadership behavioral rules. Yet, because a handful of effective leaders in the emerging world have demonstrated the principles of good leadership and good governance, and because more today are attempting to follow their positive example, it is important to specify those characteristics so as to instruct new leadership generations and to provide a theoretical context within which the careers of Ataturk, Khama, Lee, and Mandela may be evaluated.

The task of political leadership is to help citizens to "create and achieve shared goals . . . reinforce group identity and cohesion . . . and mobilize collective work."[3] Citizens are followers, of course, but followers especially in the new nations of the developing world need leaders who highlight common and collective, or perhaps more accurately *joint*, goals that go beyond narrower group, ethnic, or sectarian interests and identifications. Leadership is indeed impossible without followership, but followers remain politically inchoate without leaders who periodically emerge and offer new visions and new approaches around which to mobilize. Such leaders often employ mixtures of emotional, political, and contextual intelligence and demonstrate varieties of hard, soft, and co-optive power. They develop reciprocal dependencies with followers.

Citizens and followers seek leaders who are inspirational and appeal emotionally. They follow leaders who articulate appealing visions and who are courageous. They can be mobilized and empowered by such dynamic persons, and are comfortable with and respond more enthusiastically to leaders who exhibit high orders of integrity, inspire trust, appear to labor for all citizens (not narrow ethnic groups or lineages), and offer strong reasons to believe in the future of a new or a posttransitional state.

Emotional Intelligence

All effective leaders must possess high degrees of analytical and political intelligence. But stores of emotional intelligence are equally critical. Such leaders proceed by being empathetic. They demonstrate a "reflexive self-awareness" and are "self-actualizers" able to lead by being led.[4] They reach out and metaphorically embrace and "touch" followers or would-be followers. This sense of emotional awareness or emotional intelligence is close to what Gardner called both "self-adeptness" and "interpersonal intelligence."[5] Zupan, citing Bill George, adds that "authenticity" highly correlates with emotional intelligence.[6] Goleman argues that "self-awareness," "self-regulation," and "motivation" are crucial components of emotional and social intelligence. Below, those important competencies are called self-mastery, prudence, and intellectual honesty; they are grouped as behavioral competencies that strengthen a leader's legitimacy and thus his ability to project leadership strength and credibility.

Goleman's categories of "empathy" and "social skills" are at the heart of emotional intelligence as used herein to describe leaders, past and present, of the developing world. Empathy, to use Goleman's words, includes "sensing what people are feeling, being able to take their perspective, and cultivating rapport . . . with a broad diversity of people." Social skills include using that adeptness to persuade and to lead, and to motivate teams.[7] The importance of emotional intelligence to political leadership is illustrated by former British Prime Minister Tony Blair's acerbic commentary on Prime Minister Gordon Brown, his successor and defeated Labour Party head: "Political calculation, yes. Political feelings, no. Analytical intelligence, absolutely. Emotional intelligence, zero."[8]

Williams reminds us that "real leadership" is an interactive art that requires creativity and imagination, rather than "a singular set of well-honed practices." It is not a hard science, and prescribing specific approaches and attributes would be misleading. Real leadership requires the ability to improvise. It requires imagination and the talent to use emotional intelligence to react appropriately to shifting contextual and situational dynamics—to what some theorists have called "the environment" and others have labeled "contingencies." It demands a high order of diagnostic skill, agility, and flexibility.[9] Or, as a consummate political observer noted as President Ali Abdullah Saleh was in the final throes of his long, autocratic, skillful manipulation of the various tribes of Yemen in order to maintain the last vestiges of his hegemony, "The President's emotional intelligence is off the scale. . . . He balances all the forces, works all the personal connections, manages somehow to keep it from spinning out of control. . . . '"[10]

The Core Competencies

Successful leaders are consummate visionaries, know expertly how to mobilize followers and citizens behind their visions, and intuitively understand that in order to turn a vision and a mobilized following into a transformational force they, as leaders, must retain that difficult-to-define quality known as legitimacy. In turn, stores of legitimacy grow and shrink according to follower perceptions of leader accomplishments and talents (growing the economy, reducing unemployment, and debating well), but they mostly depend on whether followers believe that the leader is trustworthy, has integrity, is personally and intellectually honest, faces challenges squarely, and avoids even the appearance of sleaze.[11] The implied social contract between ruled and ruler is that trust once given will not be abused. But it very often is.

The relationship between performance and perception is not perfect, and neither is the relationship between leader characteristics and competencies and either performance or perception. Nonetheless, there are identifiable competencies that are the behaviors and skills that followers look for in their leaders, and what they have obtained in the emergent developing world only rarely.

The five key behavioral competencies of compelling political leadership are "the vision thing," the mobilization momentum, being legitimate, gaining trust, and the enlarged enterprise. We examine each in detail.

The Vision Thing

Effective political leaders are visionaries. That is, they have a grand but simple plan. They deal in destinies, dreams, and ultimate purposes, not necessarily in pedestrian or practical goals. They are concerned with far-reaching principles, not gamesmanship or tactics. They know what they want to achieve, in large sweeps and yet often without exact specifics, for their nations and their peoples. They also purport to know what their citizens want and value, incorporating those never-before-appreciated wants and values into a new vision.[12] Their endeavor is not to deal immediately with modalities or precise paths to greatness. Rather, their role is to articulate how and why and in what directions the nation (or the city, the group, the troop) needs to be transformed and re-energized and how citizens and followers will accordingly be enriched spiritually, and possibly materially. A successful vision "provides a unifying theme" for citizens.[13]

Effective political leadership visions, like corporate ones, are elegantly simple. "Simplicity is the strength of vision."[14] The visions that followers accept readily incorporate a citizen's sense of self into newly enunciated national goals. "The leader's identification and commitment, and the exertion of efforts to realize the idealized and shared vision, serve as a model to inspire followers to undergo a self- or inner transformation consistent with the vision."[15] That transformation binds citizens motivationally to the national project. Without projecting such a compelling and transforming vision, political leaders cannot lead persuasively. They cannot so readily mobilize followers and are reduced to presiding or governing without really leading.

The best visionary leaders are *navigators*. That is, effective leaders chart courses across the wide and fearsome seas. They have a destination and a direction, along with signs that provide guidance and metrics. Fully understanding the human desire to operate in an empyrean domain, visionary leaders take their followers there by appreciating their spiritual yearnings while surmounting mere religious genuflections. Formative, thoughtful leaders urge their citizens to join them on the farthest, most promising shores, avoiding the perilous reefs of nationalism, chauvinism, prejudice, and petty antagonism. They deploy skillful contextual intelligence.[16]

Accomplished and courageous leaders *translate* their comprehensive blueprint for the future into a vision that responds to the needs, articulated or as yet unarticulated, of their would-be constituents. They become capable of specifying why and how the content of their vision will benefit the future of the state and each and every one of its citizens. As an examination of effective corporate leadership demonstrated, "even the best vision in the world" makes little difference if leaders fail to "achieve the buy-in and motivation" of their constituents.[17] Lee Kuan Yew's genius was to be able to show skeptical Singaporeans in the 1960s how his vision of a resilient and resourceful small nation-state's future would benefit them, whatever their disparate backgrounds and aspirations. He was able to deliver results, which helped to mobilize support for subsequent iterations of his comprehensive, expanding vision. Likewise, Kemal Ataturk was able to delineate a positive, if initially hard, future for Turks, the Ottoman remnants, after they had been crushed by World War I.

When responsible leaders translate their visions into comprehensive albeit still simple programs of action, and if their followers respond, such political leaders usually operate in a manner that is called *transformational* as contrasted to *transactional*. Transformational leaders are supreme motivators. They challenge settled expectations and demand or elucidate new paradigms of performance. They "wake people out of inertia."[18] They raise their followers' "level of consciousness" about the value of proposed outcomes, encourage citizens to embrace national rather than personal self-interest goals, empower them, and enunciate high-value objectives by which citizens can be inspired. They are intellectually stimulating. A transforming leader uplifts the "level of human conduct and ethical aspiration of both leader and led."[19] Followers come to internalize a transformational leader's vision in a sustainable way. Transformational leaders enable citizens to self-actualize at an elevated level; the warm and excited response that comes from followers is almost the same as the feeling of transcendence that effective leaders engender in their constituents (see below). Such leaders offer hope.

A Leadership Practices Inventory, based on interviews with followers of supposed best leaders in corporate settings, reported that transformational leaders challenge existing processes, take risks, are open to new ideas, inspire shared visions, promote collaboration, establish trust, empower, instill values supporting their vision, celebrate achievements, and encourage high expectations.[20] Transformational leadership surmounts putting together budgets or merely passing appropriate legal bills. It operates beyond administration and bureaucracy. A transformational leader prefers to charge up distant hills rather than to call cabinet meetings to order and never ever pops up in a tank to proclaim victory or cuts a ribbon at county fairs.

In contrast, *transactional* leaders, usually incrementalists, are traditional managers within corporations and "business as usual" political leaders, often focusing on the mechanisms of statecraft and on perpetuating themselves or their parties in office. They exchange mutual self-interests with their followers and hence are primarily engaged in transactions. Such leaders act within existing frameworks; transformational leaders alter the framework. The latter inspire and uplift the lives of their followers; transactional leaders govern, sometimes well, but absent a grand design.[21] As Lee describes transactional leaders, "If you just do your sums—pluses, minuses, credit, debit—you are a washout."[22]

Ataturk imagined a Turkey transformed from a remnant of a decaying Asian empire into a neighbor capable of learning from Europe and of modernizing itself imaginatively. Lee envisaged remaking a pirate-infested swamp and distant outpost of Britain into a thriving, ordered, stable small nation. Mandela conceived of a profoundly new South Africa capable of overcoming its painful legacy of discrimination and of empowering indigenous South Africans for the national greater good. Each of these strong leaders—Ataturk, Lee, and Mandela—was a conscious motivator of followers and an ultimate nation-builder, truly transforming his country and his broad constituency by decisive actions and forceful articulations of an esteem-building design. Each also delivered on his message, providing security, stability, prosperity, and a sense of belonging to a transformative enterprise.

The Mobilization Momentum

Having a comprehensive and compelling vision is necessary but not sufficient. The most effective leaders, both in nation-states and in modern corporations, know how to sell their visions to broad internal and external constituencies and thus to engage the inner needs of stakeholders. Without that ability to activate a followership and to give it direction and urgency, leadership is moribund. Yet, mobilizing followers to accept and to support a vision of a national future is a profound and difficult task, and an adaptive exercise much more than a technical one of aligning the masses behind a new approach.[23] One successful corporate leader understood that his prime leadership task was to instruct—to communicate strategy and goals that enabled the people (citizens or workers) to take over.[24] Successful leaders instinctively connect with their followers and arouse and hence mobilize them. Otherwise, their leadership efforts lead nowhere and their enterprises, no matter how promising or innovative, become insignificant. Effective mobilization ultimately consists of a mutual investment, by leaders and the led, in new approaches to old dilemmas or in innovative solutions to problems freshly recognized or uncovered.

Successful mobilization is profoundly educative, depending on the persuasive arts. One of Lee's great strengths was his insistence on broadly *consulting* constituents (especially at election time) and making a firm intellectual case for this policy or that policy before orchestrating major shifts in political, economic, or social direction. Always, he was determined to "win them over," not to bludgeon them into acquiescence or to present them with leadership fiat by decree. Lee mentored and presented realistic options before seeking citizenry support for his own plans of action. So did Ataturk, but in a pre-electoral age. When he advised the shift from Arabic to Latin script for the written expression of the Turkish language and when he abolished the Caliphate, Ataturk took great pains to explain to a broad public how such revolutionary, transformative actions would benefit the post-Ottoman Turkish people—how such actions would "civilize" and Westernize them.

Being *inclusive* and all-embracing strengthens a leader's ability to empower his followers and, in turn, enables them to internalize his overarching vision. The most effective leaders are inclusive—their visions are national, not personal or clannish, and do far more than merely advance the aspirations of a ruling clique, a ruling party, a dominant tribe or clan, or a particular narrow point of view within a country. Thus, inclusive leaders transcend limited conceptions of high office and give all peoples in all quarters of a country the important feeling that they belong to the whole—that they are integral individual parts of a nation being constructed or of a new general community being realized.

Inclusivity brings the aggrieved as well as the satisfied into a big tent. It provides respect for those who hitherto felt rejected or marginalized. It also telegraphs toleration and fairness. Heifetz concludes that the inclusion of competing value perspectives is critical to a leader's adaptive success.[25] Mobilizing becomes much easier and more authentic if a leader is truly inclusive.

Mandela's symbolic gestures—whether taking tea with the widow of his key oppressor or donning the jersey of South Africa's mostly white rugby team—connected South Africans to each other and transcended hitherto potent racial and communal barriers. Other contemporary African and Asian leaders, unlike Mandela, have often been exclusionists; it is the rare leader (aside from those who have governed Botswana and Mauritius, and recently Ghana) who is instinctively inclusionist in the generous Mandelan manner.[26]

Mobilizing followers and citizens behind a vision works best when, like Lee, leaders know how to *listen*. That is, the best and most compelling leaders listen hard as well as instruct. They know how to spend large percentages of their officiating time—perhaps 70 to 80 percent—listening, taking in, appreciating, and empathizing. They strive to become *mwalimu*—gentle teachers (from KiSwahili) willing to instruct and to guide their fellow citizens without compelling them to obey orders. They encourage deliberation. They demand participation. Mao created the public meeting mode within Chinese communism so that cadres could "speak bitterness" and discuss personal and societal misfortunes.[27] Ideally, and at best, the policies that such leaders sponsor, advocate for in parliament and outside, and forge into laws, are founded on genuine forms of consultation with their people. The genuineness of a leader's consultation ultimately pays dividends as it helps to build legitimacy (see below). But without real consultation, and without feedback loops that are intrinsic to the overall listening approach, trust (see below) soon erodes. In other words, genuinely, "The leaders, they have to like people. They have to have a strong relationship with people, a face-to-face relationship."[28]

Lee's political campaigns were all careful models of effective consultation and strong teaching. He always knew what he wanted but insisted throughout on selling his vision by detailed consultations, by carefully articulated exercises in consensus-building, and over and over by stressing the concord between Lee as man and leader and his state's Chinese, Malay, and Tamil voters.[29]

Leaders who consult are instinctively *democratic* in their approach and understand the importance of gaining trust and winning legitimacy by noncoercive methods. Consultative leaders are democratic by design, expression, and example. Being democratic as a leader means more listening than ordering, and it also means consciously traveling the fair, not the opportunistic, road to political and electoral success. Democrats take fewer short cuts than autocrats. They endure the tedium of the hustings and acknowledge the importance of building policy support through gentle persuasion and interminable education and campaigning. Leaders as deliberative democrats refrain as much as they can from demonizing their opponents, believing more often than not in the ideal of democratic political competition. Leaders of this kind, few as they may be in today's developing world, try to foster openness, as Mandela and Khama did, and attempt never to abuse their commanding positions at the expense of democratic expression (Lee and Ataturk's prominent failings).

In the fragile outposts of the developing world, it is easier to observe democratic forms than democratic practice. The latter takes patience, it demands protracted meetings, and it requires the thick skin that too few of the modern developing world's leaders exhibit. Consummate leaders know that adhering to best practices will strengthen the state as well as strengthen their own legitimacy in high office. Khama, with abundant humility, understood best of all of his peers how a responsible leader needed to train followers and successors if legitimacy were to be translated into legacy and a democratic political culture were to be established where hitherto none had existed or had been contemplated.

It follows that consultative, democratic, effectively mobilizing leaders know how best to create, to deploy, and to maintain *power*. They can afford to minimize the use of methods that are narrowly coercive—what Nye calls co-optive power (a combination of hard and soft power).[30] The leaders discussed in the next four chapters all knew how to practice such co-optive power, albeit sometimes Lee and Ataturk, and occasionally Mandela, deployed hard power alone to achieve their goals. Effective leaders appreciate the critical ties between trust and power and between legitimacy and power. If unusually skillful, such positive leaders employ power surgically, never wantonly. They further understand that patience enhances power; being heavy-handed or rushed is the enemy of sustainable leadership power and sustainable leadership legitimacy.

Being Legitimate

Without legitimacy, effective leadership is impossible. All leaders—political, corporate, nonprofit, and informal—need to be regarded as legitimate by their followers if they are to lead strongly. Even when the leader is elected or board-appointed and therefore expresses anointed authority, her ability to lead is compromised severely by any questions about or any seeming diminution of legitimacy. In democratic polities, opinion polls reveal rising or falling levels of perceived legitimacy, as in President George W. Bush or President Obama's slumping poll numbers and consequent failures to accomplish leadership objectives. Even in less than democratic countries, nominal rulers can lose legitimacy and can be eased out by cabals of subordinates, as in Nikita Khrushchev's (1964) Soviet era and the last days (1988) of Burma's Ne Win. Zine al-Abidene Ben Ali, propelled by violently expressed popular disaffection, went the same way in Tunisia in 2011, followed by Hosni Mubarak in Egypt, Ali Abdullah Saleh in Yemen, and Muammar Qaddafi in Libya.

Legitimacy judgments are followership decisions; leaders, no matter how resoundingly elected or enthusiastically selected (by a military junta or a corporate board) can stumble in esteem and, overnight, lose the legitimacy—the respect and credibility—on which their continued leadership entirely depends. Lee understood that truism extremely well throughout his active decades in Singapore. So did Ataturk as he remade Turkey. Both looked over their shoulders repeatedly to make sure that their bold initiatives would resonate well with followers and with close associates. They each understood intuitively that remaining legitimate in the eyes of followers could never be assumed; if they once forfeited that measure of legitimacy, all would be lost. Even Mandela, possessing an aura of vast legitimacy before he assumed elected office, knew that legitimacy was his to lose; each magnanimous gesture of inclusion deftly added to followership backing and hence burnished his legitimacy. Seretse Khama's acute political sense, his evident modesty, and his moral rectitude always buttressed his legitimacy among voters and among all Batswana.

Legitimacy is hard won and easily lost because its essence is so ephemeral. Its existence is entirely subjective and judgmental. "Legitimacy," Huntington reminded us, "is a mushy concept. . . ."[31] It manifests itself as voluntary compliance with or at least acceptance of a leader's vision and objectives. As Neustadt wrote, a leader's bargaining advantages "are heightened or diminished by what others think of him. Their thoughts are shaped by what they see. They do not see alone, they see together. . . . His look in 'everybody's' eyes becomes strategically important for his influence."[32]

Writing perceptively about the U.S. Supreme Court and not about an individual leader, Justice Breyer makes the same point. Public trust in the court must be renewed regularly. "The public's acceptance is never a sure thing. It cannot be taken for granted. It must be transmitted through custom and understanding from one generation to the next." (In the context of leaders, we should substitute "a few years" for "one generation."[33])

Legitimacy can take the form of followership adulation, but the downside of adulation is always disappointment and loss. Legitimacy, derived from the aggregated feelings of arrays of followers, gives authority its source of power.[34] In democratic societies, legitimacy is based initially on performance, but those aggregated good feelings can much too easily vanish. Indeed, legitimacy almost always declines over time.

Politicians in democracies campaign to showcase their abilities to deliver good outcomes, their affinity to and empathy with voters, their good moral character, their accountability, and their stewardship. Obviously, politicians appeal to different groups of voters and to individual voters in myriad ways. But the more legitimate a candidate appears, the more likely she will be elected. Similarly, in democracies and even in some quasi democracies, the legitimacy of a real voter appeal, sanctified by a strong election, can suddenly be dashed by subsequent personal misdeeds or quirks, by misplaced hubris, by policy blunders, or by serious overreaching—failures of prudence combined with perceived misrepresentation. Even rational legitimacy, the legitimacy of elected officials, can be lost by abuses of trust or discoveries that question credibility—witness the plummeting popularity of President George W. Bush in his second term as the true facts of the 2003 Iraqi invasion became known, or the loss of legitimacy of President Thabo Mbeki when his intellectual dishonesty (over HIV/AIDs) or his refusal to be consultative (over corruption and other issues) became widely known among South Africans. In very different circumstances, to be sure, the seemingly invincible Harold Macmillan, British prime minister from 1959 to 1963, lost legitimacy in his last two years in office and had to resign. Prime Minister Margaret Thatcher, even more determined and indomitable, also lost legitimacy almost overnight in 1990 and was forced out of office by her party. Referring to Italian Prime Minister Silvio Berlusconi's intense political troubles in late 2010, one local observer explained that "the tenor is idolized until people start booing him."[35]

Legitimacy in the final analysis depends less on competency (running the macroeconomic ship of state well and/or producing real economic growth), expertise (a brilliant mind, academic degrees, previous practical accomplishments), and policy entrepreneurship (Ataturk and Lee's creation of nations from rag-tag remnants, say) than it does on stewardship: on ethical probity, moral accountability, a refusal to abuse privilege and authority, a dampening of greed, a strengthening of trust, fairness, and—in Africa certainly—a playing down of the "big man" themes of ostentation and pomposity.[36]

Too often leaders in the developing world misunderstand the fragile nature of their legitimacy and try to deploy what they have gained for personal, clan, family, or lineage benefits, and not for universal good. (There are no important cross-cultural differences regarding what is perceived as legitimate and what are universal leadership responsibilities. As the 2011 uprising in the Middle East and North Africa demonstrated, and as a close examination of African, Asian, and Caribbean responses to leadership skullduggery shows, the global village holds political leaders everywhere to the same high standards.[37])

"Big men" abuse their positions of power and confuse authority with legitimacy, and too often they enrich themselves from the public purse, distort bidding or tendering procedures, deliver special opportunities for gain to their intimates, favor relatives for appointments and jobs, and swagger constantly. Arrogantly, they regard themselves as above their followers and voters. Politically prominent persons of this kind implicitly view legitimacy as something that they hold by virtue of entitlement and that they personally can control, not as a sensibility that is entirely dependent upon the sentiments of followers. When legitimacy wanes or is threatened, leaders too often resort to coercion, corrupt practice, patronage, and electoral vote rigging.

Insofar as demonstrated competence in governing and delivering services (rare in the developing world) is insufficient to maintain high levels of legitimacy, stewardship becomes decisive. It is true that leaders can sometimes amass large sums of legitimacy by victories in war, but such triumphantly acquired legitimacy, as in Iraq, Afghanistan, or Ethiopia, quickly dissipates. Even more telling, no matter how well they may have demonstrated competence and good governance, democratic and even quasi-democratic leaders usually learn to their rapid regret that the abuse of any of the leadership stewardship attributes discussed below—integrity, prudence, self-mastery, and intellectual honesty—erodes their personal or regime stores of legitimacy. Even traditional legitimacy—the legitimacy of a monarch or patriarch—may be diminished by such irresponsible leadership actions.

Legitimate leaders display and project *integrity*. Such leaders "never [run] out on either the principles in which they believed or the people who believed in them." Leaders of integrity are never diverted by either financial gain or political ambition from the fulfillment of "their sacred trust."[38] Such leaders do the right thing at all times, often at considerable cost to themselves. Furthermore, successful leaders squarely face the moral and ethical dimensions of human affairs, even beyond their own countries.[39] Machiavelli argued that hypocrisy is valuable, even necessary, for successful politicians, and that flexibility in applying principles is a wise leadership trait, but modern political leaders succeed best when they demonstrate high degrees of integrity.[40] Machiavelli not only suggested that deceit was acceptable for leaders in the pursuit of survival and other good ends but also advocated all manner of manipulation, underhanded or not, as justifiable and purposeful. Leaders today, however, need to show their openness, their high standards and firm principles. Without integrity, leaders are vulnerable to the cynical views of their followers and easily forfeit legitimacy. Their bona fides are thus undermined, and when crises occur or perils arise, they have nothing with which to appeal for support. Integrity—a reputation for honest dealings, a reputation for morality, and seeming candor in all dealings and engagements—today trumps hypocrisy and deceit.

Legitimate leaders are also *ethical and moral*, but not moralistic.[41] Two leading students of corporate leadership suggest that there are three dimensions of ethical leadership: motives, influence strategies, and character formation. Leaders exhibit ethical behavior when they demonstrate altruistic intent, empower rather than attempt to control followers, cultivate virtues, and avoid vices. To be ethical is to be "morally right."[42] Furthermore, living transparently enables leaders to build trust more easily and to sustain whatever elements of legitimacy have propelled them to high office. Even in Europe, where personal abstemiousness has not always been common among prime ministers and presidents, greater degrees of visible morality have eased the exercise of power and have enabled political leaders to rise above the daily suspicions of their followers and the ubiquitous paranoia of the profession. A high office holder who projects intellectual honesty and prudence enhances her leadership appeal. She seemingly surmounts self-interest. She exhibits a moral purpose that can be communicated both rhetorically and by deeds.

Mohandas K. Gandhi was one such moral leader whose abilities and power to lead were enhanced by an ascetic example and were multiplied by activating a followership that literally and metaphorically trod in his footsteps. He practiced what he preached and demanded the same of his acolytes.[43] During the Salt Satyagraha in 1930, at age 60, he marched up to twelve miles a day for twenty-four days, from Ahmedabad 200 miles to the Arabian Sea, and called it mere "child's play." So, given his leadership example, was his admonition to thousands of followers to remain nonviolent, resisting civilly: "Let there be not a semblance of breach of peace even after all of us have been arrested . . . Let no one commit a wrong in anger."[44] His causes—freeing India from the "accursed" British yoke and uplifting the Indian poor—would have been difficult to realize if his personal deeds imperfectly matched his words, if his followers had not been well-instructed and well-disciplined, if civil disobedience guidelines had not been followed strictly, and if the integrity and legitimacy of his actions had been sullied by questions about his motives, his character, or his person.

Amoral or immoral political leaders get by and may do reasonably well as leaders until a crisis arises and they need every bit of available legitimacy to strengthen their position, their power, or their dealings with others. If they are of questionable morals and weak integrity, they are vulnerable and fatally weakened.

Legitimate leaders know how to *align means and ends*. The means used, the resources expended, and the opportunities foregone are then proportionate to the ends sought. The use of morally problematic means—means that use opportunistic or possibly minimally acceptable ends to justify questionable tactics—undermines legitimacy, increases resentment, and multiplies popular anger.[45] In other words, leaders who authorize torture to extract important information from prisoners or excombatants risk undermining the authority and legitimacy of their rule. So do those leaders who corruptly favor relatives or employ family members. Admittedly, it is the rare leader in the developing world who is as punctilious as Khama in refusing shortcuts and in playing politics according to strict rules.[46]

Prudence and *courage* are necessities that enhance legitimacy and emphasize good character. "Prudence requires disciplined reason—the ability to see and think clearly and not be overcome by passions or egocentricity."[47] Prudence takes account of the complexity of reality. It guards against self-deception. It calls upon diagnostic skills of a high order.[48] Emotions get in the way of responsible, clear-eyed judgments. So does ideological rigidity. Neustadt and May suggest that prudent leaders are able to understand others and that such a capacity enhances their abilities to lead effectively.[49] Prudence is the art of judgment—the judgment of balance, of reality, and of value.[50] It stresses a sense of proportion.[51] Prudence harnesses and releases emotional intelligence.

Prudence means refraining from going to war when the odds of victory are small, as in Georgia in 2008 or Eritrea in 1998. Prudence means taking on only those political or economic battles that can be won well. Prudent leaders are rarely narcissistic. They are rarely flamboyant or ostentatious, are infrequently audacious, and are politically sober. For Aristotle and St. Thomas Aquinas, prudence meant "practical wisdom"—a reasonable approximation of what good leadership always embodies.

Equally—and usefully for all leaders anywhere—prudence implies the "deliberative skills necessary to move from principle to specific action in a concrete situation."[52]

Admittedly, prudence in a vacuum would be noble but not necessarily effective. Prudent behavior also needs to be combined with *courage*, i.e., the courage to know when and when not to act to achieve good leadership outcomes. In other words, when does it behoove the skilled leader, having considered all of the available alternatives, to act in ways which are decisive and essential but risky and imprudent?[53]

Leaders of courage, President Kennedy reminded us long ago, "stand up to one's enemies" and, when necessary, stand up to one's associates, "resist public pressure," and eschew "private greed."[54]

Self-mastery is a primary moral capacity that links legitimate leaders to the real consequences of their actions. It largely corresponds to Weber's "ethic of responsibility" and incorporates courage and prudence. Adam Smith rightfully believed that persons in leading political positions were obligated to control their passions and to overcome temptations to behave irresponsibly or with partiality. Without self-mastery, which Smith called "self-command," leaders abuse power, act impulsively, and fail to reflect appropriately on the potential results of their actions. Self-mastery is akin to the best forms of self-discipline. It is "temperance," balance, managing emotions. The concept unites moral and practical concerns within consummate leadership.

Smith is even more demanding: "The man who acts according to the rules of perfect prudence, of strict justice, and of proper benevolence, may be said to be perfectly virtuous. But the most perfect knowledge of these rules will not alone enable him to act in this manner: his own passions are very apt to mislead him, sometimes to drive him and sometimes to seduce him to violate all the rules which he himself, in all his sober and cool hours, approves of. The most perfect knowledge, if it is not supported by the most perfect self-command, will not always enable him to do his duty."[55]

Self-mastery requires a focus on service delivery and not on personal aggrandizement. In many parts of the developing world, leaders substitute displays of wealth and flamboyance (lavish parties, pomp, and ostentatious circumstance) for actions on behalf their voters and constituents. They behave like "big men" without appreciating that such behavior diminishes legitimacy and erodes trust. The more democratic and prosperous the African or Asian country, the shorter the presidential motorcade and the fewer the photographs of presidents and prime ministers. Lee's visage never graced the Singaporean national currency or post offices.

Ataturk had a weakness for bronze likenesses but otherwise shunned the trappings of office. Only in Central Asia (not Turkey, Singapore, or South Africa) did rulers change the names of the days of the week to honor family members.[56] In fact, the best leaders strengthen themselves in the eyes and hearts of their constituents when they act, dress, and behave modestly and eschew the trappings of potentates.

Another component that enhances legitimate leadership performance is *intellectual honesty*. Effective leaders are clear minded, wise, and strong (without being overbearing). They exhibit the best qualities of Gardner's "intrapersonal" and "existential" intelligences. They also must be thoroughly diagnostic in the best sense, i.e., must be sufficiently tough minded to reject easy answers, wish fulfillments, pat assumptions, and the like. Prime Minister Winston Churchill's Battle of Britain speeches to Parliament and the British public were models of transparency as well as glorious morale-boosting exhortations. President Kennedy during the Cuban missile crisis bravely attempted to be intellectually honest and to hold his subordinates to that standard. He set a tone of "open, mutual criticism" within the group of decision-advisors and personally fought "groupthink."[57] Earlier, President Kennedy had enunciated an even broader standard, asking history to judge "Were we truly men of judgment—with perceptive judgment of the future as well as the past—of our mistakes as well as the mistakes of others—with enough wisdom to know that we did not know, and enough candor to admit it?"[58] President Mandela heard opinions contrary to long-enshrined African National Congress economic policy, consulted with his colleagues and followers, and decided to overturn party shibboleths and give growth a chance. President Kenneth Kaunda in Zambia in 1972 did not inquire or listen widely, and thus he disastrously nationalized the nation's copper mining industry and marginalized its main source of foreign earnings.

Being intellectually honest—Machiavelli's "constant inquirer"—is difficult for elected political leaders because so many acolytes and sycophants seek to curry favor by describing or producing favorable realities—by painting a picture of the world and the ruler's domain that is pleasing and comfortable.[59] Exceptional leaders do not want to be told that a war is being won when it is not, or that emergencies are under control when crises continue. Those gifted leaders understand that strong, effective leadership depends on understanding the world and their nation as it is, not as they would like it to be. This is what Williams calls "reality" and "hard truths."[60] Gifted leaders do not depend on rose-colored optics or on scenarios that are illusory. Indeed, such tough-minded leaders convey reality to their constituents as well as to themselves. They build trust by refusing to report results as better than they are and better than they deserve to be.[61]

Gaining Trust

The characteristics so far discussed are important in generating trust between the people, or followers, and the leader or leaders. In democracies, responsible leaders enter their political offices with a reservoir of trust, based both on their competition for followers—which is how they get elected—and on the legitimacy of the process through which they came to power. Their task as new leaders is to expand the holdings of that reservoir over time. They can build trust by dedicating themselves to their vision; by delivering meaningfully on their vision; by continuing to gain the trust of their constituents by acting consultatively, democratically, and ethically; by acting in a disinterested, self-sacrificing manner; by being "authentic"; by embracing and fulfilling the aspirations and yearnings of their peoples; and by concerning themselves with the needs of their followers rather than their own self-interests.[62] Without growing trust, the leadership enterprise succeeds only marginally and, in time, only coercively. Without trust, too, a society's capacity to act for common purposes declines. With trust, especially reciprocated trust, ruler and ruled can forge an enduring social contract and begin to amass social capital. "Trust," says Bennis, "is the emotional glue that binds followers and leaders together."[63] Trust engenders loyalty and enhances legitimacy. As even Machiavelli concluded, "It is necessary for a prince to possess the friendship of the people; otherwise he has no resource in times of adversity."[64]

George Washington understood the importance of building trust as a military commander and then knew not to squander that accumulation of trust by remaining in presidential office more than two terms. In doing so he, like other leaders early in American history, helped to set precedents and expectations that became part of the growing political culture. During the Revolutionary War, Washington strongly supported the principle that civil authority was superior to military power and that the authority of the Confederation Congress was supreme. He beat down conspiracies that would have undermined that principle and would have undercut the Congress.[65] In 1787, attending the Federal Convention, Washington reluctantly agreed to be the new American nation's first president. Then, in 1792, with equal reluctance he consented to serve as president for a second term. But in 1796 he firmly rejected a third term, and in 1797 he retired once more to his farm, defining a standard of leadership abstinence that lasted in the United States until the eve of World

War II. Washington's renunciations buttressed America's adherence to constitutional government and framed and helped to nurture an incipient American political culture of republicanism, legalism, and humility. Because of his actions and his refusals, followers trusted Washington and accorded him legitimacy. His actions also strengthened American adherence to constitutionalism.

The Enlarged Enterprise

Most of all, consummate leaders give their citizens a transcendent feeling of belonging to an enlarged enterprise—they provide a sense of purpose that enables persons throughout a nation to realize full self-worth. Presidents Franklin Roosevelt and Kennedy, Lee, and Ataturk all understood how to so ennoble their constituents. That was among their genuine expressions of genius as leaders. Recall Kennedy's inaugural presidential address, and how Americans and others in the world were excited and emboldened by his call to moral arms: "Ask not what your country can do for you—ask what you can do for your country." He went on: "My fellow citizens of the world: ask not what America will do for you, but what together we can do for the freedom of man."[66] Earlier in his speech, Kennedy said that "in the long history of the world, only a few generations have been granted the role of defending freedom in its hour of maximum danger. I do not shrink from this responsibility. . . . The energy, the faith, the devotion which we bring to this endeavor will light our country and all who serve it—and the glow from that fire can truly light the world." A great leader uplifts and inspires his people. She appeals to a high level of moral development. She is influential "by strengthening and inspiriting" her audience. Her role is to "make people feel that they are the origins, not the pawns, of the socio-political system."[67]

Under such committed leaders, ordinary constituents believe that they indeed have a real stake in their country, in their region, or in their continent—and that they are an integral part of a larger and all-encompassing global village. The most motivationally effective leaders uplift their followers in ways that are profoundly spiritual. John Gardner suggests that the best leaders "express values that hold . . . society together." Leaders revitalize shared beliefs and use them as sources of group motivation. Ultimately, leaders conceive and articulate goals in order to "lift people out of their petty preoccupations and unite them toward higher ends."[68]

If leaders can so thoroughly bring their erstwhile followers into partnership with political leadership to improve a nation, if they can construct a mutuality of responsibility, and if they can persuade citizens to believe in the motives and vision of the leaders, then the national enterprise should prosper. President Obama did just that in his first few hundred days in office. Mandela did so in his brief years in the South African presidency. It is the key task of effective leadership to give citizens a sense of larger purpose—a meaning for their lives. In the Ming era, if not before, Chinese emperors sought to convey to their people that they were together working to uphold and on behalf of the mandate of heaven. The emperors were merely the instruments of heavenly instruction and were legitimate only to the extent that the people and the emperor were joined in such an all-embracing harmonious enterprise.[69]

Tapping into Authentic Needs

Leadership is not a set of specific decisions. It is the ability to persuade followers that the leader has the interests of his followers in his heart, and that he or she will deliver from the heart to help fulfill each individual's personal aspirations. Effective leaders tap into the authentic needs of their followers and constituents, persuading themselves and sometimes their followers that they indeed are serving an enterprise greater than any individuals or groups. The best leaders do not try merely to please the lowest common denominator. Real leadership raises esteem, invigorates, inspires. That is why Mandela was such a success—the icon of Africa and of leadership. It was not because of what he delivered but of how he made people feel. "Great leaders . . . recognize that the art of leadership is to create the kind of environment where people have peak experiences, where in their excitement they become completely involved in what they are doing. . . . [and it gives them] a feeling of ownership."[70] South Africans and Africans in general were and are made proud by what Mandela said and what he did, but more so by how he embraced them metaphorically through the exercise of his political leadership skills. His inclusiveness and his generosity conveyed a moral strength of character. He was a leader for South Africans and for Africans, and he created a rich sense of almost universal solidarity.

The Contribution of Charisma

Leaders possessing all or most of the attributes already discussed are often called charismatic in popular parlance.[71] But responsible leaders need not be charismatic to succeed. Other attributes, and the various intelligences, are usually more salient. Indeed, the very intensity that infuses charismatics need not produce or describe responsible leadership. Only one kind, the "socialized" charismatic as opposed to the "personalized" charismatic, produces positive results. The first emphasizes the collective interests of followers and behaves in an egalitarian manner. The second is authoritarian, self-serving, and narcissistic, using the personalized form of charisma to intimidate and control followers. These latter charismatics are secretive, highly charged, and inclined to grandiosity and self-aggrandizement.[72] Many project "purely personal needs" onto their constituents. They are dysfunctional managers, being uninterested in administration.[73] Their sustainability as leaders is limited. Alienation often occurs. Ultimately, in the corporate as in the political world, they are destroyers, not builders.

The analytical utility of charisma is also limited because it is a social phenomenon, not an individual trait. That is, there are cultural differences influencing what attributes or traits are internalized by followers—or perhaps as accurately, projected onto individuals. Moreover, charisma as a leadership behavioral interaction with followers usually displays more affirmatively in small groups or organizations; nation-states, even less populist ones, necessarily keep followers physically and socially more distant from leaders. Size influences the ability to internalize and to act on charismatic impulses. At the nation-state level, political leaders do come along who mesmerize followers in a "charismatic" manner, but often that appeal is episodic, transient, and easily forfeited. Successful sustainable political leadership infrequently depends on charisma. More important is the ability to deliver results—growth, education, health, and national self-respect.

The use of charisma as a concept hardly helps us to explain differential political leadership success and failure at the national level. Employing the term in its loose, popular form, we can assert that Mandela possessed an iconic charisma, and that Ataturk probably emboldened followers in the same somewhat vague manner. But other attributes (see below) were more decisive. Aung San Suu Kyi, the victor in the 1990 Burmese elections but sidelined and under house arrest until late 2010, exudes charisma in the popular sense but so far has not built upon that charisma to overcome the hegemony of successive hard-nosed military juntas. Knowing that Burmans were and are entranced by her example of sacrifice and dedication—her charisma, she said, came directly from the love of her people—tells us little in 2011 about her enduring political strengths.[74]

In everyday usage, to be charismatic implies being unusually magnetic, being larger than life, being personally and spiritually attractive (but not necessarily lovable), and being compelling in vision or speech, preferably both. Often, the concept is used loosely and applied "almost indiscriminately." Kellerman puts it well: "Charismatic leaders provide their followers with more than purpose and meaning—they lend excitement as well. By holding out hope for a perfect world . . . they capture our hearts as well as our minds."[75] And Weber told us that charismatic belief "revolutionizes men 'from within.'"[76]

Charismatics are emotionally expressive, confident, and committed. They often have little self-doubt and are morally righteous. For followers, such dedicated and determined leaders fulfill unmet emotional and existential needs, especially cravings for morally enriching authority figures, for consistency and a collective mission, and for certainties instead of the usual ambiguities of workaday strivings. But many other behavioral characteristics have been more decisive in shaping and exemplifying the role of political leadership in emerging societies. Indeed, most developing world leaders are transactional in their operational modes. Thus, it is more useful to focus—as the next sections of this book do—on the positive quality of "visionary" and "transformational" leadership instead of trying to classify developing world leaders as more or less truly charismatic.[77]

The Cases

The next four chapters of this volume provide case studies and narratives showing how Mandela, Khama, Lee, and Ataturk gained their leadership spurs and gradually expressed the competencies that emerged out of their unique national and temporal situations. We generalize, as in the first two chapters, but it is important to show the fuller and markedly different contexts in which each expressed his leadership skills.

Mandela, Khama, and Lee are all late twentieth century figures, having each worked in colonial and postcolonial settings. Our fourth case, Mustafa Kemal Ataturk, created Turkey out of the wreckage of the Ottoman Empire much earlier in the twentieth century, in an era when literacy and democratic sensibilities were less fully developed than they were to become. Despite their different backgrounds, different geographical and temporal contexts, and very different accomplishments, all four of our leaders passed the most critical leadership test. In their distinctive ways, they each gave their followers and constituents a sense of belonging to a vibrant national enterprise. They enabled their followers to unite behind a national endeavor that was worthy and uplifting. Their words and deeds shaped a positive cause greater and more encompassing than any individual pursuit. They gave their people virtuous goals and profound aspirations in which the people could take pride. As President Luiz Inacio Lula da Silva said upon leaving office at the end of 2010, "Today, all Brazilian men and women believe more in their country and themselves. This is a shared victory for all of us," and a testament to the importance of Lula da Silva's leadership in transforming Brazil and each Brazilian's identity and making all Brazilians an integral part of an all-engaging enterprise.[78]

The cases could have been presented chronologically, with an opening discussion of Ataturk followed by chapters on Lee, Khama, and Mandela. But we begin instead with Mandela's example, because during his presidency and before and afterward he so fully embodied the most striking and emotionally resonant messages of this book. By analyzing how Mandela and the other three led and why each led as each did within specific (constraining and enabling) temporal and situational contexts, we can show the extent to which separately and together they offer valuable paradigms for developing world leadership performance today. Their distinctive approaches to the challenges of leadership in tough environments allow us to compare responses and to understand the manner in which ideal attributes are displayed and articulated in real circumstances.

These four developing world cases are meant to exemplify the possibility of transformational leadership across time and culture. Our four were chosen as cases to demonstrate what could be accomplished by thoughtful, forceful, exceptional leaders of the developing world. The cases show how four dedicated men chose—largely in contrast to most of their leadership contemporaries and peers—to respond responsibly and effectively, and transformationally, to difficult national challenges. In that sense, their responses are instructive. But their experiences are singular and certainly not representative. Indeed, most of their contemporaries and the successors of their contemporaries (founders and striving postconflict wannabe nation-builders alike) behaved more commonly in transactional rather than transformational modes. Very few rose to accept, much less to resolve, the tough dilemmas with which our four cases wrestled. Even more disastrously, two dozen or so rulers in modern times were positively mendacious as developing world leaders, tyrannically preying on their citizens. The experiences and operational performance of the tyrants and the transactors—the majority of examples in the modern developing world—are examined in this book's final chapter.

THREE

Nelson Mandela: Consummate Inclusionist

At the height of the vicious battles on the East Rand (now Guateng) between Inkatha and African National Congress (ANC) followers in 1993, Mandela addressed his supporters in Katlehong, east of Johannesburg. On the dais, awaiting him, was a stark message. "No peace, do not talk to us about peace. We've had enough. Please, Mr. Mandela, no peace. Give us weapons. No peace."

Mandela departed from a prepared text, just as he later did so effectively during the 1994 election campaign. "It is difficult," Mandela admitted in addressing his pent-up followers in Katlehong, "for us to say when people are angry that they must be nonviolent. But the solution is peace, it is reconciliation, it is political tolerance." Blacks were fighting each other in the townships of the East Rand. The responsibility for stopping the killings was not just the government's or the police's responsibility. "It is also our responsibility . . . If you are going to kill innocent people you don't belong to the ANC. Your task is reconciliation. Listen to me . . . I am your leader. I am going to give leadership . . . As long as I am your leader, I will tell you, always, when you are wrong."[1]

Mandela had a vision, to which he was consistent. He knew what was moral. He knew that he must win the hearts and minds of his angry followers by showing courage as well as integrity. He also needed to be intellectually honest to strengthen his existing legitimacy and to build upon it for the future of the nation and the movement. The Katlehong speech also demonstrates Mandela's finely tuned leadership instincts. He might have raised his fist and egged his supporters on, in a populist manner. He might have avoided the note and have read his original speech. But among Mandela's many competencies of consummate leadership was his ability rapidly to size up and to appreciate the seriousness of a crisis or a situation, and to turn such an event deftly into something positive. Indeed, Mandela even underlined the fact that he was speaking to the ANC in Katlehong as its leader. He was leading, not shirking responsibility, and being very explicit about his role as leader, teacher, mobilizer, and role model.

A few weeks before the 1994 South African election, Mandela, laboriously prepared by nervous international consultants for a critical television debate against Prime Minister Frederik W. de Klerk, seemed unsure and unsettled and insufficiently combative. The consultants despaired. But as soon as the debate began in earnest, Mandela ripped into his opponent as the consultants had wanted. When de Klerk accused the ANC of promising what it could not deliver, and of sponsoring violence that it could not control, Mandela said that the ANC spoke for the suffering masses who had endured being shot and killed by the racist security police of de Klerk's ruling party.

But then, after attacking de Klerk once more, Mandela paused, and with great timing and effect, said to de Klerk: "But we are saying let us work together for reconciliation and nation-building." He stuck out his hand toward de Klerk. "I am proud, he said, "to hold your hand for us to grow solid together. Let us work together to end division and suspicion."[2] What could be more inclusive? What could be more visionary, especially in the heat of an intense and bitter campaign? What could more effectively establish Mandela's transformational leadership credentials and strengthen his legitimacy in the eyes of both black and white?

A Manifest Destiny

By 1994, Mandela, once a combative pugilist and a tough-talking freedom fighter, had spent twenty-seven years in prison and four politically active years honing formidable leadership instincts that were both innate and carefully learned. He became Nelson Mandela the consummate leader by trial and error, but also as a result of a deep empathic sensitivity to colleagues, rivals, and persons of all backgrounds.

Mandela clearly possessed leadership instincts, if not necessarily leadership qualities, at least from the time of his youth in the Transkei. Even when very young, Mandela was emboldened and strengthened by a traditional sense of legitimacy. Descended from one of the key branches of the Thembu chieftaincy (the Thembu being one of twelve Xhosa-speaking chieftaincies in Transkei), he possessed status and an obligation to be responsible. The Mandela branch of the chieftaincy served within the chiefly lineage as counselors to the royal Thembu household. Although Mandela's father was a village headman near Umtata, he belonged to the Madiba clan, and Mandela has long accorded his father the role of serving as prime minister in Thembu affairs during the 1920s. Indeed, according to Mandela himself, his own youth was a form of apprenticeship leading to his own assumption someday of the Thembu prime ministership. Mandela grew up experiencing that "destiny."[3] He also grew up with more than common self-confidence. He felt himself "special" and behaved that way despite being the youngest son of his father and a son of his father's third wife.

Fortunately, Mandela's father was wealthy enough to keep four wives and thirteen children, and to provide food and milk aplenty. But that affluence ended in the mid-1920s as a result of a jurisdictional dispute with white Transkeian authorities. The young Mandela, his siblings, and his mother moved to Qunu, near Mvezo, where the young man, now named Nelson by one of his African teachers, went to a mission school. Later, after his father died of tuberculosis in 1928, nine-year-old Mandela was sent to the Thembu capital, where he was received as the ward of Jongintaba Dalindyebo, ruling Regent of the Thembu. There, Mandela later reported, he observed how to be a leader and how to project himself, being simultaneously self-contained yet articulate.[4]

Mandela blossomed as a ward of the Thembu ruler and a companion of Jongintaba's son. He also attended two elite Methodist schools—Clarkebury and Healdtown—and absorbed (even if unwillingly) the predominantly English-centered curriculum. After emerging from prison, Mandela acknowledged the profound role of the Church, and its spiritual values, in shaping his life. His innate sense of courtesy and old-fashioned etiquette stems from his Methodist years, as well as from his Thembu upbringing. A deep sense of self-restraint—prudence—and frugality and austerity may come from his schooling. So may his abiding emotional intelligence and an uncommon ability to project empathy—to reach out with a "common" touch.

After emerging from prison, Mandela said that he had learned in the Thembu Great Place and at school the importance of being a gentleman. "While I abhorred the notion of British imperialism," he wrote, "I never rejected the trappings of British style and manners."[5] But, most importantly of all, as a consummate stick fighter at Qunu and among the Thembu, and later as a boxer and team athlete at Healdtown, Mandela discovered or learned that it was best to defeat opponents without dishonoring them.[6] Humiliating one's enemies or victims was self-defeating and hardly wise.

Mandela was a prefect at Healdtown. He behaved impeccably, even self-righteously, and preached responsibility. Taking "responsibility" for one's actions was an early lesson, and one that he shared (and later imposed on Thabo Mbeki). However, if Mandela were not necessarily remembered as the brightest student in his schools, he was a leader in the dormitories and on the athletic fields. Even so, he won a Healdtown prize in 1938 for writing the best essay in the Xhosa language and passed his school certificate examinations a year early. His height, warm gaze, imposing appearance and bearing, and quiet self-assurance stood out; so did that special inner belief in a manifest personal destiny.

In 1939, in company with about fifty other emergent elite Africans, Mandela enrolled in the prestigious Fort Hare University College. He intended to study anthropology, native administration, and Roman Dutch law in order to become a court interpreter, then a reasonably lofty African career aspiration. At Fort Hare, Mandela lived in the Methodist residence, learned to play football (soccer), joined the Student Christian Association, and played the role of President Lincoln's assassin in a local drama society performance. He may or may not have joined the ANC. In any event, he himself claims not to have been more than a hesitant nationalist while at Fort Hare.

Even so, as a newly elected member of the Student Representative Council, in 1940, Mandela's sense of obligation to his fellow students compelled him to honor their widespread boycott of the election that he had just won. Fort Hare's Principal ordered Mandela to take up his position or be expelled. He chose expulsion as the honorable result, and soon found himself back at the Great Place. There, unfortunately for Mandela but fortunately for the future of South Africa, the Regent had chosen a wife for Mandela. As a result, together with Jongintaba's son (who also faced the prospect of an unwanted and premature wife), the two fled to Johannesburg. There Mandela was fatefully introduced to Walter Sisulu, a successful real estate agent and worldly urbanite. Sisulu, also from Thembuland, was six years older than Mandela, a mentor to many young potential professionals, and the chair of a local branch of the ANC. Sisulu had harbored a dream of turning the ANC into a mass movement. "And then one day . . . a mass leader walked into my office." Sisulu later recalled that Mandela had "a smile that was like the sun coming out on a cloudy day."[7]

A Mass Leader Arrived

Mandela told Sisulu that he wanted to become a lawyer. Sisulu fortunately worked with white-run law firms, including one that was known to treat African clients well and that, prevailed upon by Sisulu, was prepared to afford Mandela an opportunity to become an articled clerk—to train him in its office for a career in the law. Lazar Sidelsky, the lawyer in question, became Mandela's close friend, "elder brother," and employer. Sisulu, likewise, became a key influence on Mandela. Other formative influences were the young African intellectuals (Alfred B. Xuma, Oliver Tambo, and Anton Lembede) who met as "the graduates" in Sisulu's house. This group became the nucleus of what became the ANC Youth League, from 1944. Mandela was elected to its first executive. By 1948, Mandela was the League secretary and greatly absorbed in its work—often to the exclusion of everything else but his legal studies. He had also become a member of the Transvaal Provincial ANC executive. His early significance politically doubtless testified to the confidence others had, by the mid-1940s, in his judgment and his self-mastery. His royal status helped, too, for all of his politically connected contemporaries were commoners, lacking a patrician approach and, for many, Mandela's educational qualifications and respectable ambitions. Mandela's vast empathic gifts doubtless helped, too. "He assumed authority easily and early," writes Lodge, developing an effective "mask of command."[8]

By 1952, when Mandela successfully qualified as a lawyer after studies at the University of Witwatersrand and his articling, he was a well-known member of Johannesburg and Soweto's small but influential black elite. He was one of about two dozen black lawyers in South Africa. He was also married with two children, living in a small house in Orlando, always elegantly dressed—with a white silk scarf around his neck—and even more imposing as an adult than as a schoolboy. He ran a few miles before breakfast every day, keeping up the discipline of his youth, and boxed ferociously at a local gym.

Mandela might presumably have looked forward to a secure professional future in an increasingly prosperous, still mostly multiracial setting. Yet, from 1948 and increasingly in the 1950s, tremors in the South African segregationist ground became seismic faults. South African whites in 1948 had ousted the confused supremacists of Prime Minister Jan

Christiaan Smuts' United Party and given power to the National Party's vengeful surge to protect and to enhance white privilege. Apartheid—legalized ethnic displacement and discrimination—relentlessly attempted to reject the modernization and gradual integration of indigenous Africans into the greater, white-dominated South Africa. It tried to push Africans, except for laborers, out of the cities and back to the rural areas; sought to curtail educational and medical opportunities for Africans; legislated against cross-racial sex and marriage; banned the Communist opposition; curtailed the free media; and turned South Africa more and more into a police state and conformist redoubt where dissent would not be tolerated and skin color denominated one's place in society and in life.[9]

Maturing as an Activist

The National Party victory and the onset of apartheid transformed Mandela's world and turned gentle organizers into political activists. Mandela, Sisulu, and Peter Mda wanted the ANC to become much more militant. They wanted their elders in the ANC to sponsor a campaign of civil disobedience on the Gandhian model. The angry youth leaguers ousted Xuma as president, installing Sisulu as secretary-general. Mandela joined the national executive in 1950 and also became president of the Youth League. But his vault to national prominence and leadership stature resulted more conclusively from his managing of the Defiance Campaign of 1952.

Mandela was the mobilizer-in-chief of the widespread nonviolent protest against the growing juggernaut of Afrikaner oppression. He was its public cheerleader and arouser of popular enthusiasm. Civil disobedience began in late June 1952, in the depths of Johannesburg's winter, with curfew-breaking by hundreds of Africans. Mandela was accidentally arrested in the process but later released and acquitted. In August, with the Campaign still in process, Mandela was again arrested under the broadly written Suppression of Communism Act. He received a suspended twenty-month sentence, but at the end of the year he was banned for six months. He was constrained therefore from meeting more than one other person or from leaving Johannesburg. (During this period Mandela also was elected deputy president of the national ANC, to serve under Chief Albert Luthuli.) Mandela had gained a legitimacy in the eyes of his immediate followers and of Africans in general that he would never lose.

The high moment of the Campaign occurred in September, when there were more than 2,000 arrests (out of more than 8,000 arrested throughout the Campaign). By March 1953, the Campaign was over, with thousands still in jail and without having achieved any lessening of the yoke of apartheid. Yet, the ANC as a politically potent force had been mobilized. It had finally become more than a "talking shop." It had engaged the consciousness of rural and urban Africans. Moreover, led decisively by Mandela and others, the ANC was becoming more tightly organized, more aware of a need to prepare itself for a militant, sometimes secretive, struggle against whites. Mandela had become South Africa's uncrowned but "real" leader.

Whether Mandela was a principal architect of plans and programs, or their assembler and chief articulator, it was his leadership attributes that were widely acclaimed and widely accepted by the ANC and its followers during the 1950s.[10] Mandela's inspiration and vision was essential to ANC tacticians as it became, almost overnight, the central force of resistance to apartheid. Mandela's embrace of the ANC and its embrace of him made what once was a weak and largely muted parochial voice of protest into a sharply edged tocsin of alarm. Luthuli, principled and appealing as a symbol, was largely banned throughout the decade, immured in rural Natal, and hence unable to be an effective spokesperson or a leader of protest. That role fell appropriately and naturally to Mandela.

Militancy was increasingly the name of the anti-apartheid battle. In 1955, the government began its long-planned campaign physically to remove African families from their freehold entitlements and houses in inner Johannesburg's well-established Sophiatown, shunting them to purpose-built dwellings in distant Meadowlands, part of Soweto. Mandela had already condemned the government for its ruthlessness and publicly opted for something stronger than civil disobedience. "The time for passive resistance had ended. . . Nonviolence was a useless strategy and could never overturn a white minority regime bent on retaining its power at any cost," he said. Only violence would destroy apartheid "and we must be prepared, in the near future, to use that weapon."[11] Even so, following an incident in a crowded meeting hall shortly after his hot speech, Mandela and Anglican Father Trevor Huddleston prevented the audience from attacking policemen who had marched in and arrested a speaker. Mandela also cautioned ANC organizers against using barricades and otherwise opposing the more numerous police when the police removed the first householders from Sophiatown. He favored symbolic withdrawals of schoolchildren from classes to protest the onset of Bantu education in 1955 rather than an indefinite boycott of all schools. He also opposed picketing as a method, preferring "the freely given support of the people."[12] He favored bail instead of jail for ANC women arrested during protests. Viscerally, he was never really a bomb-thrower.

Mandela in these and other ways may have been both aroused and arousing and "tactically circumspect."[13] He may have understood, along with the Communists, that the ANC and African patriots were not yet sufficiently organized and trained effectively to oppose the apartheid machine militarily. Equally, despite what he said about the futility of nonviolence, Mandela still hoped for, or believed in, reconciliation. He was never anti-white, only anti-apartheid injustice. More than many of his colleagues, even during the Treason Trial proceedings from 1956 to 1961, Mandela affirmed the humanity of his accusers. On an individual level, he returned courtesy with courtesy, and respect with respect. On the collective or struggle level, he was unreservedly antagonistic to "racists" and "fascists."

Throughout most of the 1950s, Mandela and Tambo ran South Africa's only black law firm. They had numerous clients, many contending with interpretations of South Africa's new labyrinthine legislative restrictions. Mandela and Tambo won and lost cases in court, and Mandela developed a reputation as a clever cross-examiner. Despite his ANC activities, and his heavy involvement in the battle against apartheid, Mandela consistently took comfort in the obligations and inner logic of the law. Indeed, he was sustained then and later by old-fashioned views—or at least views unfashionable in ANC circles—of democracy, of the superiority of British parliamentary methods, and of the intrinsic fairness of British legal proceedings. He often affirmed his partiality to consultation. A chief always listened to his supplicants and his counselors before pronouncing his own decisions. Mandela, even in the heat of an increasingly bitter and heated battle against the white authorities of South Africa, remained a conciliatory, bourgeois democrat.

Mandela's path to clandestine, unbridled opposition was therefore tortured, and largely forced on him by the white state's fright and its uncompromising reactions. In early 1960, the ANC was caught off guard when Robert Sobukwe's breakaway Pan Africanist Congress (PAC) tried to surrender their hated passes at a police station in Sharpeville, near Vereeniging. The police shot and killed 69, wounding almost 200. Later, the PAC's anti-pass campaign spread to Cape Town, where its supporters marched boldly on Parliament and seriously threatened apartheid authority. Mandela soon burned his own pass in sympathy (in Soweto) and spent five months in prison. By the time of his release, the ANC (and the PAC) had been banned, and both organizations went underground. Mandela was the chief spokesman and public leader of the new ANC, mobilizing followers and attempting to raise financial support throughout the country and even in Lesotho.

In early 1961, Mandela was permitted to speak in public to the All-in-Africa Convention in Pietermaritzburg. Fearlessly, he demanded an all–South African national convention. If the government refused to meet in that way with the ANC and other opponents, then Africans should cease cooperation, invite pressure from outside South Africa, and become more militant inside the country. The government obviously refused. Not long after, Mandela—by now the unquestioned leading voice of African antagonism to apartheid within South Africa—was ordered by the ANC to go underground. He travelled in disguise throughout the country and helped to advise the ANC to stay at home rather than to strike (and to picket) the government in late May. He undertook a clever campaign to broaden support for the stay-at-home among newspaper editors and journalists, whom he met discreetly and elaborately, and improbably disguised. Mandela's moral and transformational appeal thus spread. Sampson credits Joseph Slovo with the insight that Mandela should become the new African messiah and, if necessary, the movement's martyr.[14] It was a role that Mandela, styled "the Black Pimpernel," played well, even relished.

The strike was intended to be a blow for freedom. But it largely fizzled, not least because more than 10,000 Africans were arrested on its eve. The time had come to try violence—to commence an armed guerrilla struggle, with sabotage as one of its instruments. Mandela seems to have believed that a campaign of "nonlethal" sabotage "offered the best hope of reconciliation afterwards."[15] Even as Mandela aroused his followers and opponents within the broad ranks of the ANC to accept the inevitability of the armed struggle, he (and others in the ANC) still somehow believed that the Afrikaners would listen to reason because the ANC attack was really "defensive."

"An Ideal for Which I Am Prepared to Die"

Few among the Umkhonto we Sizwe (the ANC's military wing) high command had any serious military training. Mandela had none, and little instinct for how to attack a vulnerable but formidable state from within. In hiding, he read biographies and martial texts but delegated the day-to-day control over operations and targets. Indeed, for the first half of 1962, Mandela visited thirteen countries in Africa and spent time in London, building external support and gaining funding (mostly from North Africa) for the guerrilla effort. Not long after his return to South Africa and a visit to Luthuli in Natal, Mandela was arrested while driving back to Johannesburg. The Black Pimpernel's short days of freedom were over.

First, Mandela was tried for traveling without a passport and for inciting workers to strike. At his initial trial in Pretoria, he appeared in a leopard skin cloak, which Xhosa chiefs wore on ceremonial occasions. Meaning no personal disrespect to the presiding magistrate, he said that he was not morally bound to obey laws made by a parliament in which he and his kind had no representation. The scales of justice were not "evenly balanced," he declared, when someone like himself faced white prosecutors and magistrates in a white-controlled courtroom. Sixty witnesses were called by the prosecution, many of whom were cross-examined by Mandela, serving as his own attorney. A few months later, to the same court, he delivered an hour-long plea in mitigation that deplored the government's failure to heed the democratic expression of African views; violence could result from such failure because the government, he said, seemed to understand only intemperate language. Its official actions and activities offended natural justice.

The magistrate's reaction to Mandela's sermon was swift and harsh—three years' imprisonment. Mandela responded with a clenched-fist salute to the gallery and then was bundled off to the local prison. There he demanded trousers, not the standard shorts, and protested the food that he was offered. Soon he was sewing mailbags, along with the other convicts.

Second, while Mandela was serving his sentence, the authorities raided Umkhonto's supposed safe house and headquarters in Rivonia, north of Johannesburg. They arrested many members of the high command, and others, and found Mandela's diary and incriminating documents, including a wildly ambitious guerrilla war–launching plan that had been prepared while Mandela was already on trial for his other supposed offenses. About nine white and black ANC and South African Communist Party members were, along with Mandela, charged under the Sabotage and the Suppression of Communism Acts with committing or conspiring to commit more than 200 acts of sabotage. At this trial, Mandela and the others were defended by a skilled team of lawyers, and Mandela decided that only by speaking to the world through the court—making a statement from the dock—could he regain some of the movement's lost momentum.

Mandela was already locally prominent and regarded as the spokesman, if not the unquestioned leader, of the indigenous majority in South Africa. Sobukwe and the PAC were contesting that primacy, for the

Sharpeville massacre had given Sobukwe and the PAC new visibility, but even during the preparatory phase of the trial Mandela's leadership stature and skills were acknowledged by the other accused, effectively by the state, and even by the prison warders. Even more so, it was when he addressed the court, the nation, and the world from the dock that Mandela cloaked himself undeniably and irrefutably with the cloak of legitimacy and unchallengeable leadership.

Yes, Mandela admitted, he had helped to establish Umkhonto. He had done so because the ANC's commitment to nonviolence and racial harmony had not been met with conciliatory responses from the state. So the ANC decided to sponsor Umkhonto, with the prospect of civil war only as a last resort if all else failed to persuade the apartheid government to talk to them and to halt its assault on human rights and civil liberties. Mandela explained that sabotage was intended to scare away the foreign capital on which South Africa depended and to influence the pocketbooks of white voters. Umkhonto was formed, he said, to fight for a democratic and free society. "Africans want a just share in the whole of South Africa." Under apartheid, African family life was breaking down and crime and violence were taking its place.

Mandela reiterated his patriotism, downplayed his obedience to communism, and praised the British system of government and laws. "During my lifetime," he concluded, "I have dedicated myself to the struggle of the African people. I have fought against white domination, and I have fought against black domination. I have cherished the ideal of a democratic and free society in which all persons live together in harmony with equal opportunities. It is an ideal which I hope to live and achieve. But if needs be, it is an ideal for which I am prepared to die."[16]

Sentenced to life in imprisonment along with nearly all of the other accused, Mandela was soon on Robben Island. And there he remained for the better part of nineteen years. Of the Rivonia political prisoners on the island, housed in the B block, Mandela was the acknowledged leader. Soon he was the spokesman of the other political prisoners, and later of all prisoners, gaining the grudging respect of his jailors and their distant bosses. He also became the prisoners' chief in-prison lawyer, and one of the in-prison chief educators and tutors. Mandela employed all of his legal training uncompromisingly and punctiliously to hold the authorities to account. But, despite his status and skills, he repeatedly had to strengthen his legitimacy, and thus his continued leadership, among that cohort of close colleagues, and the PAC prisoners who were housed with them. He did so by persuading challengers to accept his respectful but principled and, at times, uncompromising relations with his captors (including a number of vicious Afrikaner warders); to accept his long-term, mostly nondespairing, mind-set with regard to the struggle; to accept his and Sisulu's belief that a guerrilla war for South Africa could not be fought, Cuban style, within the country, but had to be waged from outside; in their discussions of theory and ultimate liberation to accept his eschewing of any doctrinaire Communist hard lines; and to acquiesce in a number of his tactical decisions regarding their collective attitude toward hard labor, the timing of hunger strikes, food quality, prisoner behavior toward captors, escape opportunities, and the possibility of his own early release to the Transkei and elsewhere.

Mandela knew intuitively from his early years on the island that he would also need to gain the respect and therefore maintain the followership of lesser-ranked political prisoners housed in the general area, and to gain at least some stature in the eyes of the nonpolitical general prisoners jailed in other blocks on the island. But his biggest battles, he knew, were to win over the clutch of Black Consciousness Movement adherents who were held on Robben Island from the early 1970s and the youthful, brave, aggressive prisoners who arrived after the Soweto school uprising of 1976. Both groups were initially distrustful of the much older Mandela and of his multiracial, Marxist-inspired, "more moderate" approach to the liberation of South Africa. Mandela felt it necessary to gain their committed support without altering his approach to the struggle or to apartheid. Nor was he prepared to alter his own multiracial stance. Thus, he listened to them rather than confronting or instructing them. He befriended their leaders. In the best manner, he was consultative. "I regarded my role in prison not just as the leader of the ANC, but as a promoter of unity, an honest broker, a peacemaker. . . . It was . . . important to show the young Black Consciousness men that the struggle was indivisible and that we all had the same enemy."[17] The newly arrived militants, indeed, soon pleaded for ANC membership. In prison and after, if not always before, Mandela was a dedicated political inclusionist. Gathering the flock together and keeping his legitimacy was always more important than winning ideological debates or gaining short-term advantages.

During his final years on the island, Mandela more and more was allowed to function as an elder statesman, to be relieved of hard labor, to have his own garden, and to have access to the array of nonpolitical literature in the prison's makeshift library. He managed to read Nadine Gordimer's unbanned novels about South Africa and therefore to gain insight into "white liberal sensibility," to read John Steinbeck and other American novelists, and to spend days with Leo Tolstoy's *War and Peace*. Mandela recalls that he was particularly pleased with the attitude of the widely underestimated General Kutuzov, victor over Napoleon in the novel. General Kutuzov made his decisions on the basis of a visceral understanding of his soldiers. That example reminded Mandela "once again that to truly lead one's people one must also truly know them."[18]

By 1982, Mandela was a world-renowned "prisoner of conscience." He had been awarded a prestigious human rights award in India, had been a candidate in absentia for the chancellorship of the University of London, and was the object of a widely publicized "Free Mandela" campaign in the press and by petition, with thousands of signatories. Instead of being an ordinary political prisoner, Mandela, almost unbeknownst to him and to the ANC, had become South Africa's jailor, rather than the other way round.[19] The South African authorities knew that he held many of the critical keys to the country's future. They could not afford to let anything untoward happen to him. Indeed, as early as 1981, the prison service and the ministry of justice understood that Mandela was a true liberation leader and that imprisonment had only increased Mandela's profile and his psychopolitical appeal to South Africans and world opinion.[20] The unthinkable—negotiations between the minority government and the leading representative of the majority—was also beginning to be seen by advanced members of the government as a conceivable option. As the African conurbations within the country more and more became ungovernable, and as foreign corporations and banking institutions began to back away from investments in and loans to South Africa, so the negotiating option grew more realistic. Mandela, a comparatively bourgeois elder statesman, shifted in government eyes from being an implacable enemy of the state into a possible partner. As President Pieter W. Botha later said to Kobie Coetsee, his minister of justice, " . . . we have painted ourselves in a corner. Can you get us out?"[21]

"I Will Return"

In 1982, partially in recognition of Mandela's inestimable value, his age and potential fragility, and the usefulness of having him on the mainland, he was moved from Robben Island to Pollsmoor, a comparatively modern facility near Cape Town. He soon settled into a much more gentle routine with frequent and more relaxed visits from his wife and others, with more access to a wide range of reading matter, with more time for gardening, and with better food and facilities within the constraints of confinement. Three years later, with Botha aware of South Africa's increasingly limited political and even military options, the nation's president suddenly announced to parliament that Mandela could go free if he renounced violence. Mandela, realizing that Botha was attempting to drive a wedge between the ANC and himself, understood that he must reassure the ANC inside prison and in exile, as well as the United Democratic Front (UDF) militants who were increasingly turning the African cities into places of mayhem and resistance. He needed to assure them that he remained loyal to the freedom struggle and to the new as well as the older African leadership.

At the same time, Mandela believed strongly in the efficacy of negotiation. As he told an American visitor, the ANC and the UDF realistically could make life "miserable" for South Africans, but militarily the ANC could not match the might of the government. Talks were essential, and with the enemy. To a UDF rally in Soweto, one of Mandela's daughters read out her father's dictated reply to Botha: It began by affirming his membership in the ANC and his dedication to the ANC and to Tambo, its president. "I am surprised at the conditions that the government wants to impose on me," the daughter read. "I am not a violent man. . . ." The ANC turned to resistance only when the government closed all other doors. It was incumbent on Botha to show that he was different from his predecessors as president. "Let him renounce violence. Let him say that he will dismantle apartheid. Let him unban . . . the African National Congress. Let him free all who have been imprisoned. . . . Let him guarantee free political activity so that people may decide who will govern them."

Mandela, through his daughter, continued: "I cherish my own freedom dearly, but I care even more for your freedom." He said that he owed the widows, orphans, and mothers of all of those who had been incarcerated, banned, exiled, or maimed during the struggle too much to opt for his own freedom. "I cannot sell my birthright . . . to be free." There was no freedom, he explained, when the ANC was banned and when apartheid legislation still penalized Africans. Then, with an oratorical flourish that headlined his leadership credentials and his consummate ability to mobilize followers, Mandela–still the lawyer amid a litigious society—explained that "Only free men can negotiate. Prisoners cannot enter into contracts. . . . I cannot and will not give any undertaking at a time when I and you, the people, are not free. Your freedom and mine cannot be separated." He concluded: "I will return."[22]

The long walk to freedom was almost over. Mandela, indeed, took the initiative in mid-1985, courageously initiating a colloquy with Coetsee. "There are times when a leader must move out ahead of his flock, go off in a new direction, confident that he is leading his people the right way."[23] Despite Tambo's anxiety and Sisulu's concern, Mandela had a number of discussions with Coetsee throughout the latter half of 1985, some in the presence of visiting delegations from abroad, some alone. "He was a natural," Coetsee later recalled warmly. "He was a born leader. He was affable. . . . And he was clearly in command of his surroundings."[24]

Throughout 1988 and 1989, Coetsee and a committee that he had established (including the South African intelligence chief) met forty-seven times with Mandela. By the end of 1988, too, Mandela was moved to a comfortable house on the grounds of Victor Verster prison in Paarl, forty-five miles from Cape Town. He was essentially free there to receive anyone he wished, and to enjoy life to the extent that someone in a minimum security situation could. By this time, there had been a number of meetings outside South Africa between the ANC, usually represented and led by Thabo Mbeki, and Afrikaners very close to the government. South Africa's white business leaders had talked and socialized abroad with the ANC. So had liberals from within South Africa, English-speaking and Afrikaans-speaking alike.[25]

But as thoroughly as the government and its supporters thought that Botha and the National Party remained in command of these efforts to create a soft landing for apartheid, Mandela himself—finally coming unquestionably into his own as South Africa's leader—was the man in charge. He was now fully South Africa's jailor. In many senses, he set the pace, being more aware than other ANC leaders in prison or in exile that his removal to Pollsmoor and then to Victor Verster, his conversations with Coetsee and others, and his rejection of Botha's initiative, had all strengthened his legitimacy and bolstered his self-esteem.

Mandela had always (since the early 1950s) been South Africa's most effective political operative. He had presented a more powerful vision to his fellow inmates and to the public than any other potential African leader. Unlike Harry Nkumbula in Zambia, Joshua Nkomo in Zimbabwe, Patrice Lumumba in Congo, Amilcar Cabral in Guinea-Bissau and Cape Verde, or Roberto Holden in Angola, Mandela had neither been overtaken by events nor eclipsed by a more committed, younger substitute. He had held his own in prison, strengthening his traditional legitimacy and becoming more and more self-confident and legitimate. Rarely did he make political missteps. He was prudent, with an evident self-mastery. He demonstrated unquestioned integrity, mastering rather than being overcome by his lengthy incarceration and the inhumanity and indignity associated with many of its aspects. His courage was undisputed. Everyone trusted him, even whites (if tentatively).

But Botha was a personal and a political problem. Although observers outside and a number of Botha's advisors inside were aware as early as 1985 and 1986, amid the escalating internal war led by the UDF, that the ANC was more nationalist than Marxist, that its aging leaders were bourgeois and not unfriendly, and that white South Africa and whites in South Africa had a potentially respectable future only if and when the government cut a deal with the ANC, and thus with Mandela, Botha was hesitant. Then, in 1987, South Africa's progression toward a new and more just political dispensation slowed. There was abundant evidence of a resurgence by the white far right. In the elections of that year, moreover, the implacable Conservative Party doubled its percentage of the white vote, ousting the liberal Progressive Federal Party as the official opposition. Later, the National Party lost three key parliamentary by-elections in a row. Positive change could no longer be assured through the ballot box. Hence, Botha deferred major changes to discrimination on account of color, including the long-debated reversal of some of the fundamental legislative buttresses of apartheid. Those who favored negotiations with Mandela were stilled. Early in 1988, Botha's regime was in full retreat. It even removed some lingering aspects of press freedom.[26]

Even so, apartheid had already failed. There were new demographic and economic realities: There were fewer than 5 million white South Africans and more than 26 million black South Africans. Black numbers were doubling every twenty years, white numbers every forty. About 75 percent of the nominally white cities were black occupied. The country's infrastructure was badly strained. So was its economy, suffering from limited growth, increasing unemployment, global boycotts and sanctions, and the withdrawal of international sources of short-term finance. South Africa's foreign exchange reserves were largely exhausted; capital flight was significant. White-dominated South Africa really had to talk to Mandela, but Botha hardly wanted further to alienate his constituency of extremely anxious Afrikaners.

Fate or good fortune intervened. Botha, 73, who wanted to release Mandela but did not know how or exactly in exchange for what, and did not want to be accused by his Afrikaner people of giving up on apartheid, suffered a debilitating but not fatal stroke in January 1989. He was replaced by Frederik W. de Klerk as head of the National Party in February and as South Africa's president in September. Fortunately, de Klerk, minister of national education and leader of the National Party in the Transvaal, had impeccable right-wing credentials. "Just as President Nixon was able to go to China," so de Klerk could travel metaphorically to Soweto or Lusaka. He had opposed relaxing residential segregation and dismantling the apparatuses of social apartheid. He had harassed multiracial universities. Yet, de Klerk at 53 was of a new Afrikaner generation. He was not hobbled by Afrikaner solidarity. He was ready to compromise with dogma and ideology. After studying him closely in late 1988, Mandela decided that de Klerk "was not an ideologue, but a pragmatist, a man who saw change as necessary and inevitable."[27] As a staunch member of the Afrikaner Broederbond, a secret fraternity of prominent Afrikaners similar to the Masons or Opus Dei, de Klerk knew that the organization's head had held intensive and warm discussions with Mbeki of the ANC in the United States. Most of all, de Klerk knew in his bones that Mandela, and only Mandela, held the keys to South Africa's prosperity and peaceful development. For his grandchildren, de Klerk was prepared to contemplate a reconfigured, refranchised, heavily black-influenced South Africa.[28]

Just as Nixon knew that the opportunity to create paradigm-shifting policy departures occurred only rarely, so de Klerk appreciated that only by acting boldly and decisively as a leader could he have any hope of transforming South Africa for the better, and of preserving at least some elements of white privilege and influence. De Klerk and Mandela met in late 1989 and established rapport, if without much warmth. But both men were more interested in the end game—in establishing a basis on which Mandela's freedom would unleash waves of creative energy, withstand the inevitable white backlash, and propel South Africa toward a multiracial, if black-run, destiny. De Klerk was the agent of change, but Mandela had to join him in making that change effective and dynamic.

At the December 1989 meeting in the president's residence in Cape Town, Mandela was startled to observe that de Klerk actually listened, rather than dictated. White leaders usually did not attempt to understand an African message. Mandela tried helpfully to persuade de Klerk to abandon the government's emphasis on group rather than individual rights. Insisting on group rights conveyed the message that de Klerk hoped to modernize apartheid without really abandoning its core concepts. The oppressive system must be cast aside completely, he said. The ANC, Mandela told de Klerk, had not struggled against apartheid for decades only to yield to apartheid with cosmetic changes. Finally, Mandela warned de Klerk that, if released (Sisulu, Govan Mbeki, and other leading ANC figures had already been freed), he would not be heading out to pasture. He would resume his leadership of the ANC. Hence, Mandela advised, the ANC had to be unbanned and all prisoners released and exiles welcomed back home. The mantle of leadership was fitting ever more tightly around Mandela's taut prison-endured frame.

De Klerk received the message well. On February 2, 1990, de Klerk addressed parliament. "The well-being of all in this country," he pronounced, was "linked inextricably to the ability of the leaders to come to terms with one another on a new dispensation. No one can escape this simple truth." De Klerk promised a "totally new and just constitutional dispensation in which every inhabitant will enjoy equal rights, treatment, and opportunity in every sphere of endeavor."[29] It was the season for reconciliation and reconstruction, with the ANC unbanned and its members amnestied.

A week later, de Klerk attempted to release Mandela and to fly him home to Johannesburg. But Mandela, aware of the national and international roles he was about to play, demanded a week to prepare his people and himself, and also insisted on walking out of Victor Verster on his own. Preserving dignity was critical. "Once I am free, I will look after myself."[30] And so he did, albeit several days earlier than he had hoped.

Mandela's exodus from Victor Verster to Cape Town and onward was a triumphal processional of exuberant black and white crowds and endless raised fists of solidarity. In speeches and press conferences in Cape Town, Soweto, and elsewhere, Mandela emphasized his solidarity with all of those who had struggled and who would continue to struggle against minority rule, affirmed his loyalty to the ANC, praised de Klerk, and enunciated a compassionate vision of a South Africa freed from oppression and capable of restoring autonomy to its inhabitants, black and white. He made a point of saying that he loved his enemies—he harbored no anger toward whites—even as he hated their unjust system. Indeed, Mandela impressed on his listeners the importance of all peoples to the future South Africa. "We did not want to destroy the country before we freed it," or to drive whites away. They were fellow South Africans. A new nonracial country would be a better place for all.[31] Ever the teacher, Mandela also scolded a huge throng in Soweto, urging them to go back to school, to cease thieving, and—in general—to uplift themselves now that freedom was near at hand. That was vintage Mandela.

For much of the early 1990s, Mandela toured Africa, Europe, and the United States, with reconciliation (and fund raising) key themes. At home, he visited rural as well as urban parts of South Africa as black-on-black violence, usually clashes between the Zulu-based Inkatha Freedom Party, abetted by the police, and the ANC, intensified. In between his necessary peregrinations and internal peace making, Mandela also negotiated with de Klerk the final end of hostilities and the ANC's new party political role. He and Slovo persuaded the ANC to lay down its arms in order to strengthen de Klerk's hand against recalcitrant members of his own National Party. Mandela traded this concession for a lifting of the government's State of Emergency, but Mandela also had come easily to acknowledge that a military victory for the ANC was but a "distant dream."[32]

Mandela was 71 when he walked out of his final place of detention. For the next four years he played many critical roles within the consuming struggle for South Africa's destiny. He articulated a vision of a new South Africa, black-run but with a broad welcome for whites and others who had turned their backs on apartheid and were prepared for a new beginning. Mandela over and over spelled out his compelling vision to the nation. He had to win over his exiled colleagues, particularly Umkhonto militants and Communists dedicated to taking South Africa by storm rather than by evangelical conversion.

Mandela had to exert himself to accomplish and to strengthen his vision. He also had to shape the visionary perception of his different ranks of followers, and thus to mobilize them to support the subtle embellishments of his ever-evolving vision. Indeed, Mandela proved flexible and adaptive in the service of a well-functioning South Africa. In that way, especially over such key issues as nationalization, Mandela demonstrated high degrees of intellectual honesty. Throughout, Mandela's gift of grace—his charisma—was critical. So were his bearing, his fundamental decency and courtesy, and his delivery of the common touch. Coupled with a decided refusal to abide ostentation, Mandela insisted almost everywhere on remaining "an ordinary man" despite his escalating prominence.[33] Doing so, behaving as the fundamentally warm, decent man that he was, won him even more praise and backing. He could reach out instinctively to all manner of men and women, embracing them physically or metaphorically. His integrity, prudence, and self-mastery were important at every stage in winning converts and in controlling the final stages of power transfer.

Mandela played critical tactical leadership roles as well. He kept negotiations alive with de Klerk and the National Party at various desperate points during 1991 and 1992 both through force of will and by restraining his angry colleagues and overcoming his own sense of betrayal. He was firm but conciliatory with de Klerk, eventually forging a series of critical agreements that regained the momentum of change. Along the way, Mandela importantly deflected de Klerk from pursuing the partial power transfer ploy that the president doubtless preferred, and on which the release of Mandela had presumably been predicated. Mandela also befriended the far-right white leadership, deflecting hostility from that quarter. There were many other key players on the ANC side, but Mandela gave direction. His commanding personality, his unquestioned legitimacy, and his supple as well as obvious leadership skills facilitated the peaceful transformation from a white-dominated to an African-run nation. Without Mandela's sense of himself, and his empathic intelligence, the violent struggle between minority and majority might well have resumed to the detriment of all.

Mandela also prevented Chris Hani's assassination in 1993 from destroying the entente between white and black that had been forged so creatively by persons on both sides of the main transitional fault lines. Hani was the Umkhonto leader, and much admired and respected by rank-and-file ANC personnel as well as by militants. Initially, his killing in a middle-class white suburb of Boksburg, near Johannesburg, was assumed to be yet another government-sponsored attack by a putative third force. Africans rioted. Even before the public learned that Hani's killer had been procured by the far-right white Conservative Party, Mandela knew that only he could avert disaster. He prepared a broadcast appeal for calm. A white man, "full of prejudice and hate," had killed Hani, he said. But an Afrikaner woman had in fact risked her life to identify the assassin and to bring him to justice. "Now is the time for all South Africans to stand together against those who . . . wish to destroy what Chris Hani gave his life for—the freedom of all of us." De Klerk, although still president, stayed silent. Mandela was in command and, as de Klerk knew instinctively, this was Mandela's time, not his, to exercise authority and to provide reassurance.[34]

As Kanter wisely says, "Mandela was particularly adept at the emotional dimension of leadership." She compares Mandela's instincts favorably to those of Mayor Rudolph Giuliani of New York City after the 9/11/01 terrorist attacks on the trade towers. Referring to Giuliani in words that apply to Mandela at the time of Hani's assassination and throughout his postprison years, she notes that Giuliani "healed, soothed, expressed outrage, rallied people, held hands [as in the rugby below], kept spirits up . . . and said thank you."[35]

Donning the Green Jersey

These were unusually difficult and trying years for South Africa. Mandela's release in 1990 was but the beginning of the transition, not its end. Foremost, Mandela and de Klerk had serious conceptual differences. From 1991 until 1994, they were positively estranged, frequently and publicly calling each other liars and betrayers. They and their followers stopped negotiating for months at a time. Yet Mandela also had the capacity to see that de Klerk's presidential authority was being harassed by old-guard Afrikaners; they both feared a putsch from the right, and their separate political maneuverings were often conducted so as to minimize such threats. Mandela's internal antagonists were on the left, and he had to pay them respectful heed. These symmetrical concerns were exacerbated when it was widely acknowledged that the National Party had—before de Klerk's presidency—backed a "third force" responsible for assassinating many UDF leaders, bombing ANC members and other opponents in countries surrounding South Africa, and trying to poison African officials on trips to the United States. Fortunately, de Klerk's ouster of some of his least forward-looking associates in 1992, and his decision later in the same year to break the government's covert alliance with Chief M. Gatsha Buthelezi's Inkatha Freedom Party, helped to clear obstacles strewn across the path of effective transition. In the next year, de Klerk created a race-blind single ministry of education, in a stroke scrapping separate racial educational establishments and abolishing separate educational oversight of the so-called homelands. De Klerk's most critical act of leadership in this period was to put pro-African, pro-Mandela change to a referendum in 1992. This effective political gamble—which he won massively—prevented the white right from coalescing against reform and slowing or disabling the shifting of power.

Chivvied and cajoled by Mandela, in 1993 de Klerk also abandoned the white veto in future parliamentary affairs that he had long demanded. At Mandela's insistence, they set an election date even before agreeing on constitutional provisions. Within the new constitution, both sides agreed to a justiciable bill of rights, with specific sections protecting private property and safeguarding the freedoms of religion, speech, and assembly. They agreed on the independence of the judiciary and on the formation of a high-level constitutional court with powers similar to those of U.S. judicial review. De Klerk and Buthelezi obtained a federal structure, with provincial devolution of some powers—especially over education, that both, and whites, had wanted as a form of protection against ANC rule. Mandela conceded a government of national unity (and thus a place for de Klerk and for Buthelezi) for the first five years of independence. But he also insisted on, and brought de Klerk around to accepting, the passage of legislation in parliament by simple majorities, not the two-thirds that the National Party demanded. Mandela, refusing a blanket amnesty for crimes committed during apartheid by officials, persuaded de Klerk to accept a process of transitional justice—a truth and reconciliation commission—which would be empowered to grant amnesty and also to hear testimony from victims. Those many mutual concessions ultimately enabled both the National Party and the ANC to forge a liberal constitution and an effective transfer of power. The separate visions of the new South Africa merged into one. Mandela had been able to see the big picture, and to mobilize his followers. But so had de Klerk deftly led his people to confront and then to accept the reality of black power in a democratic environment.[36]

In 1994, after many setbacks and breakthroughs in the constituent assembly, and with Inkatha-ANC violence continuing in and around Johannesburg and in Kwa-Zulu/Natal, all parties could begin focusing on the anointing elections that finally took place in April. Mandela, a tireless campaigner at 75, and a much more astute politician on the hustings than his opponents realized, was determined to bring South Africa into its new dispensation peacefully. He rightly worried about the racist right that had mobilized against de Klerk and himself. He worried equally about Buthelezi and Inkatha, with their separatist agenda and their initial unwillingness to participate in the poll. "I will go down on my knees to beg those who want to drag our country into bloodshed," he told an ANC political gathering.[37] He attempted to bring around Buthelezi, an acquaintance of decades' standing, and also employed his undoubted reasonableness and charm to acquire promises of support, or at least non-interference, from white commanding generals and police commissioners. In the end, his presence and his personality, much more than his stilted oratory or the organizational abilities of the ANC machine under Thabo Mbeki, won the day. Mandela, leader and icon, was unstoppable.

As elections go, the actual balloting was a little rough, but there were very few allegations of ballot stuffing, rigging, or malfeasance. The ANC won 62 percent of the vote, the National Party 20 percent, Inkatha 9 percent, the Democratic Party (later the Democratic Alliance) 6 percent, and the PAC and other small parties 2 percent and less. South Africa, thanks to its leaders, their visions, and their mutual ability to be persuasive and far-sighted, was finally liberated. Mandela, once the feared Black Pimpernel, was in charge. All sections of the new rainbow nation waited, by turns expectantly and anxiously, for the leadership signals that he would give, and the national direction that he would champion. There were massive hopes and demands, and massive fears. For Mandela, ever empathetic and aware, there was an immediate need in victory to be "very careful not to create the fear that the majority is going to be used for the purpose of coercing the minorities."[38]

Even with such a robust electoral mandate, a leader of unquestioned legitimacy, thoroughly forged integrity, uncommon transformational vision, and iconic charisma such as Mandela would still be tested by the rigors of pent-up expectations, of nation-building, of long-deferred integration, and of an uplift massively needed. Apartheid, the wreckage of decades, had left a difficult and impossibly taxing legacy to its successors. The nation's population, especially its African population, was growing much more rapidly than the economy. No net new jobs had been created since about 1970. Unemployment and underemployment were rife. Poverty, however measured, and crime (murder, rape, assault, robbery, etc.) had grown exponentially. Decent housing was unavailable for Africans; squalid squatter settlements or *pondokkies* surrounded all of the country's cities. They were breeding grounds for disease and criminal endeavor. In these informal slums and in the older "locations" in and near the cities, few youth were being educated. Forty years of official hostility and neglect, student-politicized boycotts of whatever schools there were, and sheer mismanagement had brought about a massive knowledge deficit. African high school graduation rates (based on the mandatory end-of-year national matriculation examinations) had fallen to 42 percent in 1990, as opposed to a white rate of 97 percent. Moreover, without that matriculation certificate, school leavers found it almost impossible to secure any but low-skilled laboring jobs, if those. None of the failures, at least 100,000 a year then, many more subsequently, could hope to enter a university or even a technical institution. Mandela's new South Africa would need technical talent, but Africans would remain for another decade largely untrained. There were lamentably few African lawyers and physicians, and hardly any chartered surveyors, chartered accountants, engineers, and other similarly qualified persons.[39] Competent black middle managers, the new government would discover, were equally scarce.

As president of South Africa from 1994 to 1999, Mandela certainly sought to overcome all of these many societal challenges. For a year or two, he ran cabinet meetings and gave instructions to his ministers. But Thabo Mbeki, his deputy president and presumed heir, more and more exercised the operational reins of day-to-day government. Mandela concerned himself less and less with the details, preferring as an elder statesman determined to serve only one presidential term to focus primarily on the larger issues of economic modernization, on harmony and peace making abroad, and on profound levels of reconciliation at home. In effect, his was an imperial presidency that for the most part attempted to frame and to motivate the new South Africa rather than to set and to accomplish specific legislative objectives.[40]

Educating himself on the go, fairly early he grasped the nettle of economic leadership. He realized that the old socialist nostrums of growth would not work; South Africa could deliver a postapartheid dividend to its struggling people only if it opened up its economy to trade and capital movements; employment creation was the answer to poverty alleviation, not the statist policies that had failed in Russia and in much of independent Africa. Mandela, intellectually aware and honest, helped to shift the ANC, and his government's policy response, from centralized market controls to a regime that approximated a freer market than his government had been expected to sponsor. The ANC had been cleansed, Mandela declared, of any "single slogan that will connect us to any Marxist ideology."[41] Importantly, too, Mandela decided to encourage a fiscally responsible macroeconomic methodology, and thus to limit white flight and to encourage new foreign investment, by retaining members of de Klerk's economic management team.

Whereas he delegated more and more detailed oversight to Mbeki, he himself kept a close eye on the nation's security and intelligence apparatus. To the consternation of his closest ANC colleagues, he retained in office many of the outgoing military officials and decided that a shakeup of the defense establishment was premature.

In the foreign sphere, Mandela's goal was to make the new South Africa welcome everywhere, to cast off the apartheid mantle in order to gain the trust of investors and tourists, and also to champion South Africa's role as a middle power concerned to advance global human rights. Mandela also exerted himself as a peacemaker, especially in Burundi, Libya, and Nigeria, and arguably also in Lesotho.

But it was as a determined inclusionist, as a fervent conciliator, as a consummate bridger of the color divides, and as a determined optimist about human nature that Mandela captured the imagination of his country and his world. By his gestures, by his symbolism, and by his actions, Mandela gave South Africans (and the rest of the globe) confidence that their novel national enterprise was worthwhile—that their nation-building enterprise was an endeavor that could be indulged in and accepted by all. Mandela gave all of his people and followers a sense of belonging, a sense of being a part of a larger project that promised to uplift them spiritually if not necessarily materially. It was Mandela's natural gift to be a leader for all of his possible followers, and to incorporate them and their concerns into his daily actions.

Fortunately, Mandela's human touch was genuine, his talent for the meaningful, heart-stopping gesture impeccable, and his pleasure in reaching out and gathering in disparate peoples—even recent enemies—infectious. He began with P. W. Botha in 1995, visiting "the old crocodile" at his home on the country's south coast. The colloquy was televised, and Botha performed as an unreconstructed diehard. But for

Mandela, bemused, the point was made in public that the former captive was paying heed to his former jailor, and respecting Afrikaners and those who still thought like Botha. Mandela also held a dinner in Pretoria for the former Robben Island commander and the outgoing head of Botha's intelligence service. He appointed another former prison chief as ambassador to Austria. He even lunched with the man who had prosecuted him for sabotage and more in 1962. He attended Afrikaans-language church services at a Dutch Reformed Church in Pretoria. Then he dutifully and systematically met both the wives and widows of veterans of the struggle and wives and widows of the previous government. In 1995, he flew to Orania, a remote Afrikaner mini-Volkstaat on the edge of the Kalahari Desert in the Northern Cape Province, to take tea with the 94-year-old widow of Prime Minister Hendrik Verwoerd, one of the key architects of apartheid. All of South Africa noticed, as they did Mandela's many other attempts to reach out and be inclusive.

Acts of conciliation were acts of courage. Forgiveness established the moral supremacy of Mandela and the new government; it demonstrated his command and his power, as well as helped to knit the country together. But it was in the sporting arena that Mandela demonstrated these approaches most dramatically. Rugby was the Afrikaner sport, and a religion in its own way. Mandela resisted demanding the renaming of the national team, the Springboks, and in 1995 startled and won the hearts of his new rainbow nation by attending a world championship match in Johannesburg between the Springboks, now back in international competition after years of anti-apartheid boycotts, and powerful New Zealand. When the Springboks emerged unexpectedly victorious after a hard, tense, overtime struggle, Mandela, already wearing a green Springbok jersey and cap, walked ecstatically onto the field to present the trophy to the astounded Springbok captain, an Afrikaner. The crowd, and the country, went wild, chanting "Nel-son" over and over.

This donning of the green jersey and walking onto the field was hardly the result of a sudden whim. From his days on Robben Island, Mandela began to understand the political power of sport in South Africa. His decision to make a grand symbolic move at the world championship match attended by 62,000 rugby-mad fans was carefully conceived strategically to help blacks and whites reconcile and to create conditions conducive to lasting peace. "The only way to beat the tiger [Afrikaners and whites more generally] was to tame him." He also had to persuade his reluctant associates in the ANC that a fraternal embracing of Afrikaner-dominated rugby, and the Springbok name, would be wise.[42]

It mattered less, afterward, exactly how Mandela ran the government and what its precise policies were. He had positioned himself as the leader of all the people, not just the ANC, and that enabled him to strengthen his nation-building endeavor and to begin to realize his vision of a united and forward-looking South Africa. He combated ANC attempts to devalue the Afrikaans language in public life, and even himself spoke in Afrikaans whenever it helped him to make a multiracial point.[43] He supported the Truth and Reconciliation Commission proceedings and actions against ANC opponents, too, and showed that so long as he were president, South Africa would be led by someone who accepted individual liberties, due process, and gradualism. Indeed, when he transferred the presidency of the ANC in 1997 to Thabo Mbeki, Mandela characteristically warned his successor, "One of the temptations of a leader who has been elected unopposed is that he may use his powerful position to settle scores with his detractors, marginalize them, and in certain cases, get rid of them. . . ."[44] Indeed, as U.S. Ambassador James Joseph noted, Mandela was a leader who elevated all of those whom he touched and met. He used power not to dominate but to distribute—to convey power to others.[45] It was not so much his saintliness as his leadership skills, carefully honed in prison and afterwards, that enabled Mandela to take a troubled, postconflict country forward in the direction of a promised land, a hallowed dispensation. Much of it was in Mandela's head; he still had daily to mobilize his ANC colleagues and successors to appreciate the depth of his vision. Paradoxically, for this quintessential nation-builder, it became easier to mobilize opponents, former critics, and non-ANC skeptics to support the outlines of his vision.

Mandela was more than a leader who emerged in a time of societal need to orchestrate the energies of his people and his nation. He grew more and more into a messianic and postmessianic role that he had gradually come to embody during the chrysalis of long incarceration. The way that he handled and capitalized on his release, and the message that he carried from imprisonment through the transitional phase and into independence all depended on the many qualities of leadership that resonated with the victors and the vanquished, with comrades and warders, with intimates and observers: legitimacy, integrity, self-mastery, prudence—all in the service of a hard-forged commanding vision.

FOUR

Seretse Khama: Resolute Democrat

Botswana has been mainland Africa's most notable outlier. Solidly democratic since its independence in 1966, with a record of economic growth that few other African countries can begin to match, Botswana in 2009 ranked fifth in the overall annual Index of African Governance rankings, ahead of Algeria, Ghana, Namibia, and South Africa and marginally behind Mauritius, the Seychelles, Cape Verde, and Tunisia. In 2007 and 2008, Botswana's rankings were equally high, as have been most of its category scores within the Index.[1] Its GDP per capita in 2011 was $15,489 (in USD [2005] at purchasing power parity), well ahead of all but three other sub-Saharan African countries; its provision of schooling and health care is exceptional for Africa, and it has known only peace and stability since 1966 despite wars on several of its borders.[2] Botswana's first three presidents transferred power according to constitutional formulas, and Festus Mogae, the country's third president, was in 2008 awarded the Ibrahim Prize for African leadership.

Botswana has been exceptional in all aspects of governance and economics since independence. Its moderate and principled methods of dealing with the common vicissitudes of developing world challenges, and its decisively singular breaks in 2009 with the African Union over Zimbabwe and the Sudan, all testify strongly to the leadership example set for the new nation and for his successors in office by Sir Seretse Khama, Botswana's first president. Deftly, gently, but persuasively, Khama created a paradigm of African leadership that was unique in his day, impressive subsequently, and formative for Botswana. Khama was a consummate nation-builder, as were Ataturk and Lee. All three, and Mandela to a lesser extent, laid down the foundations of national democratic political cultures. Ultimately, national institutions were able to rise on those scaffoldings, and, in the case of Botswana, to be cherished and expanded upon by Khama's successors as president and by his nation's citizens. No other mainland African nation now enjoys what Botswana embodies: a flourishing democracy, prosperity, good roads, a solid rule of law, an absence of serious internal strife, effective government at several levels, and a sense of pride in the national model.[3]

Botswana owes these achievements and outcomes to Khama, who carefully constructed the model and guided its elaboration and embellishment during his days as president, 1966 to 1980. His George Washington-like role is widely acknowledged and widely accepted within Botswana and beyond. But, in this case, is the role of the individual in creating and living a leadership model for Botswana and Africa overstated?

Could Khama have been but a mere product of his times and his traditional past? Might Botswana's pre-Khama experiences and its special precolonial and colonial heritages have produced or at least have enabled Khama's leadership qualities? Or did he respond to the needs of his followers? In other words, is there a Botswanan exceptionality—not a leadership example—that could explain the country's very un-African performance?

A Traditional Heritage

The Tswana-speaking peoples (five, originally eight, closely related tribes) were pushed off the lush grasslands of what is now north-central South Africa first by marauding Zulu warriors in the early nineteenth century and then by Afrikaner trekkers in the middle years of the same century. The Tswana fled westwards to poorer lands along the eastern edge of the Kalahari Desert, in what is now the Northern Cape Province of South Africa and eastern Botswana. There they attempted to find fodder and water for their cattle, and cultivated sorghum, millet, and maize. Beleaguered, they welcomed missionaries from Scotland and England who belonged to the liberal, congregational, nonevangelical London Missionary Society. John Moffat and David Livingstone were among those missionaries. Khama III, paramount chief of the Ngwato and Seretse Khama's grandfather, converted to Christianity in 1860. In good time, the chiefs of the other Tswana-speaking tribes followed the Ngwato and adopted Christianity; their peoples formed Tswana-speaking congregations.

By the end of the nineteenth century, Cecil Rhodes and the British South Africa Company had snaked a rail line across easternmost Botswana, from Cape Town, Kimberley, and Mafikeng in the Northern Cape to Bulawayo in Zimbabwe. At this time, most of the Tswana were converts and their leaders additionally had signed agreements in 1885 with Britain to create the Bechuanaland Protectorate (not a colony) west of the renegade Transvaal Republic (later northern South Africa). The imperial purpose of the Protectorate was to link Rhodes' presumed mineral-rich Rhodesia (Zimbabwe) to the Kimberley diamond mines, but a strong antislavery and protectionist lobby in Britain also sought to preserve the rights and lands of the Tswana chiefs from both the Transvaal and Rhodes' avarice.

After Rhodes' death in 1902 and the establishment of the Union of South Africa in 1910, the Tswana chiefs and their friends overseas on a number of occasions intervened to persuade the British government not to transfer Bechuanaland (and Lesotho and Swaziland) to the Union. South African segregationist policies and instincts made such a transfer unpalatable, despite the inconvenience to Britain of being compelled to continue to administer three poor African entities that were dependent on South Africa's infrastructure for all of their food and fuel imports and on South Africa's mines and industry for the gainful employment of their laborers, and thus for their national incomes and standards of living.

Within the crucible of protectorate life, the Tswana, especially the dominant Ngwato, learned to coexist alongside the South African behemoth. Britain was a largely neglectful trustee, although individual governors and district commissioners were respectful of and partial to bettering conditions for the Tswana. Nevertheless, throughout the twentieth century, the Tswana became ever stronger churchgoers. They also maintained a consensus-building governance model—the *kgotla*—that limited the arbitrary rule of chiefs. Like the *pitso* in Lesotho, the Tswanan kgotla was a gathering of all the people—in practice the influential people—around a chief for periodic consultations and the thrashing out of village, chiefly, or paramount-chiefly business. The several layers of kgotla functioned to resolve disputes, to advise the village heads or superior chiefs on how plaintiffs or defendants should be treated and their cases adjudicated, to decide and to impose collective responsibility, to enable notables and others to air opinions, and to discuss and to provide advice on threats to the village or the tribe. The kgotla could function as a parliament, a court of law, or an administrative body.[4] Botswana's indigenous leaders traditionally were supposed to make decisions after having heard their people and having considered their views.

The kgotla was a brake on arbitrary rule. So were the proceedings and spirit of the congregational church, which reinforced the notion of consensus and imbued democratic values. Masire also believes that the Tswana are by nature very process oriented, which further inhibits authoritarian tendencies.[5] Almost every Tswanan was influenced by this integrated amalgam of Western and indigenous political culture. Khama naturally was in part a product of this preindependence political culture, as were his colleagues and his constituents. Additionally, Khama was the heir to the paramount chieftaincy of the Ngwato, and had been brought up and schooled with that legacy in mind. Like Mandela, he was royal and regal, and therefore approached politics—arguably—with a greater sense of responsibility to his people than a commoner would have. A paramount chief had to be more than a politician, even as he had to prove himself an accomplished politician to win elections and to guide his party.

The tradition of the kgotla and the strength of Congregationalism helped to shape Khama (even though he was not an ardent churchgoer) and the responses to him of his Tswana followers, but the kgotla and Congregationalism cannot completely account for the ways in which he emerged as a leader and guided Botswana after independence. As a paramount chief, a Tswanan with traditional legitimacy, he might have been able after assuming postindependence power to have gone the arbitrary way of his fellow African leaders, many of whom were products of a churchly persuasion similar to his own. He could, almost without any internal protest, have joined the single-party Afro-Socialists such as Kenneth Kaunda in Zambia and Julius Nyerere in Tanzania and ruled autocratically—"for the good of his people and country." Botswana was dirt poor at independence and Khama, in order to uplift his people, explicitly could have taken decisions on his own. Few would have objected loudly. Furthermore, given the reality of apartheid-dominated South Africa next door, enfeebled Botswana had to be careful and had to maneuver skillfully. With that excuse, Khama could have abridged or limited democracy in the nascent Botswana. But Khama was never comfortable with easy answers and authoritarian postures; he was too intellectually honest to pursue such tendentious short cuts. Many of his contemporaries in Africa successfully employed specious arguments to ban opposition movements, to neuter basic freedoms, and to enrich themselves. Khama pursued a distinctly different path, and one that made him unpopular among left-leaning autocrats in the rest of Africa.

The preferred governmental model in West and East Africa in the 1960s and 1970s was either militaristic (following the dozen or so coups that had taken place by 1966) or, at best, quasi-democratic, with nominal participation but little choice. It was an era of planned economies and state centralism. Places like Côte d'Ivoire, Guinea, and Liberia, or even the new nations immediately to the north of Botswana, embraced that guided democracy model, with all of its hypocrisy and Orwellian double-speak. This was a pattern that seemed then to work for Africa, to satisfy popular aspirations, and to provide growth and the possibility of modernization. To embrace a radically different model took uncommon courage, intellectual honesty, integrity, self-mastery, an appreciation of what was and was not possible in Botswana and southern Africa (prudence), and abundant inner strength. To do so also meant that Khama must have begun to articulate a vision—at least in his head—of what would be best for a small, impoverished country like his own, and what would be best for Africa. He knew what the choices were.

As a young man, and an orphan from age 9, Seretse Khama was groomed for the paramount chieftaincy by his politically astute uncle Tshekedi Khama, regent during Seretse's minority and his late father's younger brother. Although Charles Rey, Bechuanaland's Resident Commissioner in the early 1930s, thought that the young Seretse was "an ugly little devil," and should not be schooled among potential radical Africans in South Africa, Tshekedi and other influential Ngwato believed in Seretse's educability.[6] They sent him to Lovedale School, the most distinguished mission-run establishment in the Eastern Cape Province. There he was accorded special eating and learning experiences as a future paramount chief through Standard V. At that point, in 1935, the slight, shy student was diagnosed with tuberculosis and sent home, away from the damp valley in which Lovedale sat.

After recuperating near his Botswanan home, Seretse was dispatched in 1936 by Tshekedi to Adams College, an American Congregational mission school near Durban. He spent a year there, performing very well academically and learning to box, but in 1937 he enrolled for secondary school at Tiger Kloof, near Vryburg in what was then British Bechuanaland (now part of the Northern Cape Province of South Africa). Nearly everyone spoke Setswana, which was a relief for Khama after having had to converse in CiZulu at Adams. Tiger Kloof was also a London Missionary Society School, with customs familiar to him. After three years, aged 18, Khama passed the Cape Junior Certificate examinations, became a prefect, and continued to box and to play soccer. He also developed a new talent as a versatile track performer.

Seretse Khama was known at Tiger Kloof (and subsequently when he completed his secondary education back at Lovedale and his first BA at nearby Fort Hare University College) as an underachieving but capable student; a well-liked prankster; a dedicated sportsman, excelling in the high jump, in rugby and soccer; and as an all-around athlete. He was someone who stood up against bullies, approved of controversially cross-ethnic and cross-racial friendships and even romance, and fought against white segregationist impulses when they appeared along the Rhodesia Railway line in Botswana. Even so, to the extent that he was politically involved in the emerging national consciousness of South Africa, at Fort Hare he favored nonracial or multiracial political organizations rather than the African National Congress (ANC). There is evidence that sometime during his three years at Fort Hare (1941–1944), where he studied native law and allied subjects, he became an opponent of European rule and a believer in Africa's ability to govern itself.[7]

Many of his close friends at Fort Hare were men who became nationalist leaders in their own countries—Ntsu Mokhehle in Lesotho, Charles Njonjo in Kenya, Ambrose Zwane in Swaziland, and Robert Sobukwe in South Africa—but Khama was still very much focused on his destiny as the future paramount chief of the Ngwato and successor to the regent, not as a national or regional political leader.

Had Khama spent more than a few months after Fort Hare at the University of the Witwatersrand, in Johannesburg, he might have done more than make Nelson Mandela's acquaintance. He also knew Joshua Nkomo, of Zimbabwe. But, in mid-1945, with World War II finally ended and transport overseas possible, Khama sailed to Britain, where he became a student at Balliol College, Oxford. However, what should have been a glorious two or three years in postwar Oxford, studying law amid the dreaming spires, was cut short within a year because Khama lacked sufficient Latin for the Bachelor of Civil Law degree. Moreover, his advisors had erred in devising a special compromise course (part Politics, Philosophy, and Economics) for him. He was not allowed to sit an examination in law in 1946.

"A Very Disreputable Transaction"

Khama, still determined to be a lawyer, left Oxford disgusted and for good and began eating the ritual dinners and cramming for the law at the Inner Temple in London's Inns of Court. This was a perfectly respectable method of becoming an accredited lawyer in Britain, then and now, and

Khama finally blossomed as a full-time student of torts, contracts, Roman law, and so on.

Khama's extracurricular learning and social maturing also took place in London. He lived at Nutford House, a hostel for students from the colonies. Harry Nkumbula of Zambia and Forbes Burnham from Guyana also resided there, as did Njonjo. African nationalistic fervor was in vogue in such settings, especially after India and Pakistan became independent in 1947 and it was a little clearer that the British empire was being, or could be, dismantled. It was at Nutford House, too, that Khama fatefully met Ruth Williams, a Briton, and wooed her. They married in 1948, before he had qualified at the Inner Temple. He was 27, and ready to assume his chiefly duties.

Whereas Mandela, a few years older, was assuming more and more attributes of leadership in South Africa in 1948, and making his presence felt among Johannesburg's African intellectuals and nationalists, Khama was still an up-and-coming, ethnically specific, future royal personage, little known beyond the lands of the Ngwato. His marriage altered all of that. It altered how he was perceived within the Protectorate, within southern Africa, and within the British Commonwealth and British politics. It also transformed his own view of himself and his larger societal role. The consequences for himself and his Ngwato people of the marriage proved to be Khama's first adult leadership challenge. Many of his radical responses to guiding the nascent Botswana, both before and after 1966, and to finding his rightful place in the panoply of Africa, were tempered in the fiery reactions to his marriage and his staunch refusal to renounce it and Ruth.

His uncle and many senior figures among the Ngwato and other Tswana-speaking polities were furious, being strongly opposed to a white woman coming to them as queen. For the most part, the local British administrative team was also appalled. It took Khama months of steady politicking at home, and many meetings of the Ngwato kgotla, finally in June 1949 to obtain a ringing popular endorsement from the nearly 4,000 men in the assembly, if never from his uncle and tribal elders.[8] Ruth soon joined Khama in Serowe, the Ngwato capital, while the regent made plans to exile himself from Bamangwatoland.

The British government, however, needed formally to approve Khama's accession to his paramountcy before he could officially take up the reins of command. By this point, in mid-1949 and throughout the rest of that year, local British administrators from the Serowe district commissioner through the Resident Commissioner in Mafikeng and the High Commissioner in Pretoria were satisfied that the Ngwato people wanted Khama and that he should be confirmed without delay.

Yet, the marriage had caused more high-level ideological and political consternation than the young married couple could have imagined. The new apartheid government in neighboring South Africa was about to enact a ban on mixed marriages between peoples of any color combination; legislation against white and black intermarriage had been in place since 1923. Former prime minister Jan Christiaan Smuts and his recently defeated United Party told the British High Commissioner that the Khama marriage would give further electoral ammunition to the then-ruling National Party of Prime Minister Daniel Malan. Permitting the married couple to remain in southern Africa, and with Khama as paramount chief, might drive Malan and his colleagues to take South Africa out of the Commonwealth. Prime Minister Godfrey Huggins, in Southern Rhodesia (Zimbabwe), was also opposed to the marriage and the chieftaincy on segregationist grounds. The marriage threatened white supremacy and offended those, such as Malan and Huggins, who were fighting against the presumed spread of indigenous nationalism from Asia and West Africa.

Khama was a threat, and so was Ruth. Together they were a symbolic menace to the southern African white redoubt, and to the resistance to decolonization that both the entrenchment of apartheid and the gathering movement for a Federation of Rhodesia and Nyasaland—a partnership between dominant whites and subservient Africans—signified. Clement Attlee's Labour government in Britain was thus forced to choose between either respecting the Ngwato and affirming Khama—doing what many Labour politicians knew was right—or responding to the implied threats and supposed larger political requirements of a South African and Rhodesian strategy. Labour's maneuverings and machinations over Khama, including a ruse to fly him to London so that he could be exiled relatively cleanly, and many debates in the House of Commons and the House of Lords, eventually resulted in the enforced return of the Khamas to Britain, in 1952. Khama's telegram to Ruth in 1950 said it all: "Tribe and myself tricked by British Government. I am banned from whole Protectorate." Winston Churchill, then the leader of the opposition in the House of Commons, called the whole business "a very disreputable transaction," particularly since the Labour government steadfastly denied that it was exiling Khama to appease South Africa.[9]

When a sympathetic British official visited Khama, Ruth, and their first baby (now the fourth president of Botswana) in a flat in Chelsea

(London) in early 1951, the official was impressed by Khama's lack of bitterness, by his sense of irony. He had "an honesty and directness in dealing with people, and a right judgment of them. . . ."[10] Khama refused to abdicate, or to cooperate in any obvious way with the British design. In conversations with Lords Ismay and Salisbury of the Commonwealth Relations Office, he urged them to cease appeasing South Africa. All it would do would be further to encourage South Africans in their repressive policies, "and race relations would deteriorate even more quickly."[11] He was prepared nevertheless to renounce his claim to the chieftainship, but only in exchange for the full liberty to return home to participate in Botswana's politics as a commoner.

The Conservative government that took office in 1951 was not amused. It wanted Khama instead to assume a British appointment in Jamaica and to give up his freedom to engage in the political and social life of Botswana. In early 1952, after these final conversations, it consequently barred him from ever returning home.

Fortunately for Botswana and Africa, four years later the British government, led by Lord Home, Commonwealth Relations Office minister and future prime minister, realized that its policies toward South Africa were hopelessly Pollyannish. Apartheid was more and more tightly entrenched, the National Party having trounced the United Party in 1953. Moreover, Johannes G. Strijdom, Malan's successor as prime minister, was a Hitler-adoring racist who evoked no political empathy in Whitehall. There could now be no thought of transferring the High Commission territories of Bechuanaland, Basutoland, and Swaziland to South Africa, especially since the articulation by Frederick Tomlinson of a greater homeland policy. Meanwhile, the clamor in Labour, Liberal, and some Conservative ranks for a more principled resolution of the Bamangwato crisis continued. That clamor coincided with the discovery of vast mineral deposits on the edge of Bamangwatoland, none of which could be exploited with the chiefly crisis unresolved. Moreover, as Britain was increasingly developing self-governing solutions in West Africa, especially in Nigeria, it appeared illogical and inconsistent not to let the Ngwato and other Tswana-speaking peoples themselves evolve politically in a democratic direction.

Fortunately, Tshekedi and Seretse became more reconciled to each other just as these southern African realities made themselves obvious in London. Together, in mid-summer 1956, the former regent and the former heir apparent visited Lord Home and in a jointly signed statement renounced the Ngwato chieftainship for themselves and their children.

They both now wanted to live freely, as Seretse had indicated in 1950, in the Ngwato Reserve with their families. They sought to help the Ngwato and other Tswana create representative institutions (and a post-Imperial political culture). They both wanted to "be allowed to serve [their] people in any capacity. . . ."[12] Seretse Khama arrived home in early October 1956, having told reporters that he sought to help his people "to develop a democratic system, raise the standard of living, and establish a happy healthy nationhood."[13]

It is unlikely that Seretse Khama knew at this stage exactly how he would establish democracy and a healthy nationhood. He had not devoted his years of exile to manifesto writing or political agitation. Nor had he consorted with nascent nationalists in exile. He had not even resumed his legal studies. But his enforced absence from Botswana and the loss of his traditional inheritance obviously concentrated his mind. Some of the stirrings that had arisen at Fort Hare and all that had happened to Britain and her colonies since World War II were part of the consciousness that accompanied Khama home, just as Britain and France were humbled by Gamal Abdel Nasser and Egypt over Suez. Khama after all had, fortuitously, been influenced more by the British and the world than by parochial African politics. He returned home with broadened horizons and a personal mandate rather more extensive than that of African nationalists in adjoining territories.

Khama very much wanted to be accepted by the Ngwato as their leader on the basis of merit, not on chiefly prerogatives. When area councils were introduced in 1957 and elections held (in village kgotlas), Khama welcomed this long-overdue acceptance of indigenous governance. Representatives of the area councils formed a tribal council in 1958 and Khama became its vice-chairman, later tribal secretary. In the next year, he attended the all-Botswana Joint Advisory Council and African Advisory Council as the Ngwato delegate. In these councils, both Seretse and Tshekedi advocated the creation of a territorial Legislative Council, as in neighboring Zambia, and in Tanzania and Kenya. Seretse also promoted leadership that was democratic and based on ability, not race. In both councils, and in his political speeches from about this time, Khama emphasized the rightness and timeliness of Africans making their own political decisions. Particularly, Botswana should find its own participatory path. Botswana should offer lessons to others, not copy the solutions developed farther north. Indeed, from 1959, Khama voiced definite ideas about writing a constitution that would recognize Botswana's unique circumstances. Khama also spoke firmly against discrimination, against multiracialism of the Rhodesian kind, and against holding Botswana back from the tide of nationalism that was about to create a number of self-ruled or independent countries to the north.

"Slow and Steady"

Khama became a national leader and a likely national prime minister during the early and middle 1960s. G. Mennen Williams, the new American Assistant Secretary of State for Africa and former governor of Michigan, recognized such talents as early as 1961, when he passed through Bechuanaland on his way to Madagascar. Few Africans in the protectorate were "progressive or modern minded," Williams reported back to Washington, but Khama was an exception. He was intelligent and able, and the territory's chief nationalist. Moreover, Williams complimented the future Botswana and praised its satisfactory "slow and steady progress from tribalism to legislative council–type government. . . ."[14]

Williams was more prescient than analytically correct about Khama's standing in 1961. Six months before, a small group of talkers and radicals had formed the Protectorate's first serious political party, the Bechuanaland People's Party (BPP). Kwame Nkrumah's Ghana had quickly acknowledged the BPP as a vanguard nationalist movement akin to the South African ANC and Nkomo's Rhodesian African National Congress; it even supplied funding for Land Rovers and spread the word that the BPP was Bechuanaland's "authentic" freedom movement. Khama, however, derided their leaders as hotheads full of empty rhetoric, "promising everything and yielding nothing." In late 1961, he proposed the creation of the Bechuanaland Democratic Party (BDP) to "expose the falsehoods" of the BPP and also to enable "proper leaders" to advise the government on future political progress.[15]

From 1962, when the BDP held its inaugural congress in Gaborone, Khama slowly grasped the reins of national political leadership, despite bouts of illness and occasional fits of indecision. He was ably assisted by Quett (later Sir Ketumile) Masire, a well-known journalist and agrobusinessman from southern Botswana. Already, South Africa had become a republic and left the Commonwealth, and Britain had made it clear that it would never transfer the High Commission territories to South Africa. Their future was as self-governing polities, although how rapidly the territories would progress was, even in 1962, not clear. But in Botswana there would soon be a Legislative Council, as in other British dependencies, and the BDP demanded "one man, one vote" from at least 1962. It committed itself to independence through cooperation with Britain, not confrontation, and Khama and his associates, and as a result, his party, consequently were for many years regarded as "sellouts" and "stooges" by newly emergent politicians farther north. Fortunately, Khama had abundant self-mastery; he did not seem to care what others thought of him, focusing instead on constitutional and economic advancement within Botswana.

In the 1960s, the future Botswana, with fewer than 600,000 people along the railway line and scattered inland across a country the size of Texas or France, was among the poorest territories in Africa, with an estimated GDP per capita of about $50.[16] Although the Roan Selection Trust was about to develop copper and zinc deposits at Selebi-Pikwe, near Francistown, Botswana otherwise had no known sources of export income other than that derived from the export of cattle, which numbered more than 1 million. There was no public hint of diamonds, little tourism, no manufacturing, and but limited returns from the remittances of local workers on the South African gold mines. Selling large quantities of beef depended upon the long-term health of Botswana's vast cattle herds, subject as they were to periodic bouts of hoof-and-mouth disease, rinderpest, anthrax, cattle lung disease, and East Coast fever. Migrating wildebeest and buffalo sometimes infected local cattle with these and other epizootic diseases. The path to prosperity in Botswana in the 1960s appeared to Khama and others to depend on improving the health of their herds, constructing larger and more modern abattoirs, seeking new markets, and strengthening the country's pathetically weak infrastructure. It also depended on that scarce and variable commodity—rain sufficient to make the pastures bloom.

In the 1960s, the only paved roads (12 km in total) were inside the border towns of Francistown and Lobatse. Everything else on which wheeled traffic progressed consisted of little-improved or unimproved dirt and sand tracks either across the marginally fertile lands abutting the Kalahari Desert or across the desert (two-thirds of the country's land mass) itself.[17] Seeking a World Bank loan in the early 1960s to transform the Francistown to Maun track into a gravel road was a major initiative of the Legislative Council. Indeed, one of the reasons why Britain finally favored self-government for Botswana was financial; until independence the territory remained a constant charge on Her Majesty's Treasury.

Botswana, admittedly an unusual British dependency because of its impoverishment adjacent to comparatively vast South African wealth and abundant social services, had weak educational and health systems and hardly any skilled local professionals; even by 1972, only 30 percent of the top administrative and professional positions were held by citizens. In 1966, there were only twenty-two university graduates and about 100 secondary school certificate holders. Throughout the Protectorate there were fewer than 1,000 secondary school pupils, mostly boys, in 1964. In that year, only 27 passed the Cambridge Overseas examinations at the conclusion of their secondary schooling. And of the 27, only 13 had marks high enough to win them entrance to what was then the combined University of Basutoland, Bechuanaland, and Swaziland. Of secondary school teachers, 80 percent were noncitizens. Forty percent of primary school teachers and some secondary school teachers were untrained. Only one child in ten who finished primary school found a secondary school place.[18] Khama and his team therefore fostered a major expansion in every aspect of schooling. By 1980, primary school enrollments more than doubled, to 170,000, and 85 percent of eligible children were in school. Within ten years of independence, secondary school enrollments had reached 9,500 (and by the end of the century had reached 140,000). By the late 1970s, too, Khama and Masire had created a University of Botswana, in Gaborone, to replace the tripartite university with its base in Lesotho.

Botswana on the eve of independence was a calm and deliberative place. BPP agitation had excited a limited following. The future of Botswana, it seemed to Khama and the colonial officials with whom he dealt, depended on educating the broad mass of the people and on the local intelligentsia and the cattle owners—the nation's bourgeoisie. Khama may not have realized that twelve percent of Tswana owned sixty percent of all cattle in the country or that thirty percent of Tswana owned no cattle and were employed by wealthier cattle owners like himself and Tshekedi.[19] Even if he had realized the extent of existing social and economic disparities, he and others could have argued that social stability and the possibility of prosperity could come only through a measured devolution of power from Britain to the cattle people. Khama and others like him wielded local political influence and power and were therefore effective custodians of a nascent popular will.

Noblesse Oblige

That was one of the underlying political bases of Khama's leadership—that he knew cattle and the cattle issue thoroughly enough to advocate for more and better access to water, veterinarian services, and marketing opportunities (and an expansion of the abattoir in Lobatse). But he also was a champion of the rights of the ordinary Tswanan citizens. As a leading member of the Legislative Council before independence, Khama's other crusade was against racial discrimination. That meant ending segregation along the Rhodesia Railway and in the border towns like Lobatse and Francistown, which were run by and for white farmers and traders. It also meant integrating the schools and seeking equal pay for equal work in the civil service. Some of his colleagues urged consumer boycotts, as in Zambia and in Francistown, to end the practice of Africans being served from segregationist hatches, but Khama wanted demeaning practices to change without confrontation so as not to drive whites from his fragile country. He favored nonracialism, not multiracialism and affirmative action. (Much later, when his presidency was secure, Khama still fought strongly against what he called anti-whiteism—attacks usually directed at senior civil servants whom Khama had retained in his administration.)[20] As a result of Khama's skillful politicking in the Legislative Council, in 1963 and 1964, Botswana approved these measures and accelerated the process of real integration of services and opportunities.

By the middle of 1963, Khama and Masire had decided that they must transform the BDP into a popular party by broadening its reach and making it more democratic. Soon Khama was on the campaign trail, giving speeches and meeting villagers across the Protectorate. He and Masire also were well prepared with their own proposals and drafts when the Protectorate's British officials convened a constitutional conference in 1963 and immediately conceded full adult suffrage and an end to white and chiefly privileges. Khama then insisted that the country move rapidly to the installation of a prime minister and a cabinet—the essence of a parliamentary system—and not to a lesser and intermediate stage of responsible government.

Khama's quiet and credible leadership had brought the transfer of power to this point. Thereafter, it was a matter of strengthening his already broad popularity and legitimacy as the territory's obvious leader and assisting the outgoing administration fully to prepare for complete devolution. A major step forward was the removal of the territorial capital from Mafeking (Mafiking) in South Africa to Gaborone, a mere railway halt until 1964. Another was Khama's insistence in 1964 that the new Botswana should pride itself on a nonpoliticized, not necessarily a prematurely Africanized, civil service. It was from about this time that Khama, aware that he would soon be running the country, suggested that "A wise man is one who can make use of the wisdom of others."[21] Masire could do much of the detailed preparations, in other words, and senior advisors, some employed from outside through special foundation grants, would assist. Khama also told an American visitor in 1964 that

Botswana's destiny in Africa was special, even unique. "Our role is not one of violence. We will achieve our independence without it. Our mission [and transformational vision] for Africa will be to demonstrate for our neighbor South Africa that we have a stable African government in which no man is discriminated against on racial grounds and in which the living standards of all are being raised."[22]

Botswana's first of many peaceful parliamentary-style elections took place in early 1965 with the BDP trouncing the BPP and the new Bechuanaland Independence Party. (Subsequently, at elections held at regular intervals, the BDP maintained its parliamentary majority throughout Khama's presidency. But the several opposition parties always won some seats.) Khama swiftly became prime minister within a British- controlled final phase of colonial rule. Later that year, he persuaded the legislature to vote for independence, and the British acquiesced at a constitutional conference in early 1966. In September of that year, Botswana became officially independent, with Khama as president and Masire as vice-president and finance minister, and with the remainder of the cabinet consisting of former headmasters and other Tswana of what Khama would have called good character.

Dirt Poor and Principled

There were acute economic concerns. The rains had failed and famine had spread across parts of southern Africa. Botswana was dependent upon food aid. It also still relied on British budgetary and developmental support, which had to be negotiated and secured.[23] South Africa controlled Botswana's import and export routes and locked Botswana into customs and currency unions that prevented much economic maneuverability. Ian Smith's Rhodesia had recently declared itself independent, and political refugees and potential insurgents had fled across the border, causing acute difficulties then and until 1980 for the new regime in Gaborone.

Khama remained a calm and steady leader, conscious of self-mastery, always prudent and democratic, with growing rational legitimacy and some understated inspirational abilities to add to his traditional abundance of legitimacy. He was pleased when Kaunda and others in Zambia appreciated that the delicate problems posed by Botswana's unusual political geography—Rhodesia and South Africa—could be dealt with only in a statesmanlike manner, not emotionally.[24] That was vintage Khama. In many ways, Khama was a cautious traditionalist, conscious like Mandela of appropriately royal ways of behaving and of achieving a forward-looking political movement. In the successful run-up to independence, few could fault him for achieving too little by moving deliberately and considerately. The BPP, still backed by the Organization of African Union, could not have obtained independence so painlessly, so rewardingly, and so rapidly. Khama did so by demonstrating a quiet vision, by gaining support for that vision among his party and his peers and followers throughout the territory, and by a series of principled political maneuvers that slowly made loyal followers of potential opponents, whether local or colonial. He worked closely with Masire, as he did throughout the remainder of his life, slowing Masire down when necessary and leading in ways that Masire could not. "Seretse and I worked together very closely," Masire recalled. "Seretse and I were extremely candid and honest with each other. If I differed with him, he would reconsider his position. From the beginning, there was simply a fund of trust between us. . . ."[25]

Khama was also more aware than almost anyone of the obligation—the responsibility—of nation-building. He shared Masire's genuine belief that "The essence of a democracy is an informed public."[26] Both were determined to act in a national manner, to emphasize the importance of unifying Botswana's peoples, and to eliminate tribalism. Without their mutual vision and Khama's careful efforts, the young Botswana might have remained a collection of tribal fiefdoms or a purely cattle economy controlled by barons like himself. Instead, from before independence but certainly from the onset of independence, Khama knew that knitting the country together and giving it and its people a central purpose was the main charge of his administration. To do good, he declared following Thomas Paine, was his real religion.[27]

Khama took himself and his secular religion seriously. (He was otherwise distinctly nonreligious, despite his background and schooling.) But he also did so by rejecting the panaceas and easy nostrums of many of his fellow African presidents. The construction of a modern Botswana could be accomplished only by refusing the convenient notions that were being advanced elsewhere and that seemed wrong and dangerous to him, with his deep experience overseas and his regal view of the world and his role in it. At the inauguration of Botswana's parliament, Khama declared that he and his new administration would "not tolerate autocracy of any kind." Much later, after visiting North Korea and China, Khama declared that "Dictatorships and tyrannical systems of government are hatched in the minds of men who appoint themselves philosophers, kings, and possessors of absolute truth."[28]

"Democracy Must Be Nursed and Nurtured"

In his talk to the first legislative assembly, Khama pledged that together they would foster a national spirit, so that the peoples of the country would think of themselves as one, not as members of this or that tribal group. He promised not to localize the civil service too quickly, being aware, he said, that precipitate and reckless action would be the antithesis of sensible economic development. His government's foreign policy would be dictated by reason and common sense, rather than by emotions or sentiment. Botswana, he promised, would be non-ideological: The "histrionics and fulminations of extremists outside this country will not help Botswana achieve its destiny." Indeed, Khama took the unusual step of declaring that his nation would be aligned, not non-aligned as was the fashion almost everywhere in the developing world. Whatever would benefit Botswana would be done. Botswana would be a good neighbor even to South Africa, providing that it reciprocated. More so, as he later told the United Nations, Botswana's unique position as a majority-ruled state on South Africa's border would effectively challenge South Africa's racial and homelands policies by presenting a strong case for contrasting nonracial harmony and growth. Khama made it clear that anyone could be considered a Botswanan citizen if he or she accepted the new nation's ideals of nonracialism and democracy. Botswana was not a "Tswana-stan," and it was defined by ideals, not by "narrow ethnic criteria."[29]

Increasingly, during the 1970s, Khama also exerted himself to lead the "front-line" struggle against white Rhodesia. There were three components to the struggle: (1) to strive to unify the various African contenders for nationalist primacy in the future Zimbabwe: Robert Mugabe, the most intractable; Joshua Nkomo; Ndabaningi Sithole; and Bishop Abel Muzorewa; (2) to prevent the white Rhodesians from overrunning northern Botswana in pursuit of the insurgents; and (3) to encourage and assist the negotiation efforts with Smith by Britain and the United States, and eventually by the Commonwealth and even South Africa. Despite Botswana's lack of national heft in these arenas, Khama's quiet leadership was felt, usually in partnership with Kaunda, Samora Machel of Mozambique, and Julius Nyerere. He was even prepared as a mostly peaceful president to combat racist violence with African violence, as in the Rhodesian civil war and the battle against apartheid, but without ever inviting an attack on defenseless Botswana. To try to keep the Rhodesians at bay, he even condoned, reluctantly, the establishment of a small defense force for Botswana, replacing a poorly armed Police Mobile Unit. Without taking the sides of any of the rival Zimbabwean African movements, Khama was often an initiator of the several rounds of talks that eventually, at the end of the decade, led to a ceasefire and transfer of power from Smith and Muzorewa to Zimbabwean nationalists under Mugabe.

In his unassuming way, Khama was also responsible for forging a unified stand among the African states from Tanzania to Angola in favor of what became the Southern African Development Community. Khama's role was to nudge, and sometimes to pull and push his fellow presidents, but always to do so with a smile and a conciliatory word. He took the lead in this area almost by default, when Kaunda and Nyerere were at loggerheads and others among the community trusted only Khama. But he also saw the Community as an economic and political amalgam that would help keep South Africa at bay, especially after Zimbabwe's independence in 1980.

Compelled by circumstances to carve out a careful role for Botswana in the context both of apartheid and the freedom struggle, Khama understood that among its roles and his roles was a leadership without easy answers. He also was explicit about creating an ethos—an embryonic political culture—on the basis of which Botswana could grow enduring political institutions. He called them "structures by which national objectives could be achieved."[30] Before the legislative assembly could operate effectively, the chiefs could appreciate the new national dispensation and the loss of many of their prerogatives, and the courts could function independently, the people had to notice that the executive never acted arbitrarily and always respected the separation of powers into the other branches of government.

Khama was also sensitive to being inclusive, embracing Tswana constituencies other than his own, and the powerful and talented Kalanga minority. His early diplomatic posting and senior civil service promotions were widely noted and largely applauded. So was his emphasis on talent, not tribe or family. Khama appreciated the delicacy of his presidential role, intuitively understanding that he could forfeit the legitimacy that he brought to it by behaving with partiality. But he was a natural teacher and consensus builder. He was instinctively consultative. Moreover, tolerance was his watchword. His commitment to a thoroughly open society was genuine, and rare in Africa in the 1960s and 1970s.

From his youth and his boarding school days, Khama had always been a democrat. "Seretse was a democrat through and through," wrote his successor.[31] Being democratic was natural for leaders in at least higher Tswana society, and the BDP was established with democracy for the territory as its goal. But comparable political parties in African states to the north, or even Lesotho, had also espoused democracy in their earlier days, before expediency ("developmental needs" or "primordial African respect for authority") turned democrats into autocrats and rulers of one-party states. Khama could have followed Kaunda and Nyerere, or even Hastings Kamuzu Banda of Malawi, in exerting a heavy-handed rule over his party and his government. But, constrained by his heritage, by his marriage, by his long years in Britain, and, most of all, by his sense of what was right—by his integrity, Khama insisted on repeated democratic responses to the trials of Botswanan governance. Toward the end of his life, reflecting on what he had seen elsewhere and on how Botswana, rightfully, was following a different drumbeat, Khama opened a National Assembly meeting by admitting that "democracy, like a little plant, does not grow or develop on its own. It must be nursed and nurtured if it is to grow and flourish. It must be believed in and practiced if it is to be appreciated. And it must be fought for and defended if it is to survive." Even a nation at peace, he went on, must be vigilant since democratic institutions will not perpetuate themselves on their own.[32]

Khama was unusually aware of "the mess" that Africans elsewhere had made of their postindependence political decisions. A state visit to Malawi, where Banda acted every inch the potentate, disturbed him. So did the coming to power of Idi Amin in Uganda, and even the comparatively gentle but still one-man rule of Kaunda in Zambia and Nyerere in Tanzania. Africa's political problems discouraged this intellectually honest leader. "The time has come," he said, "when we should sit down and look very closely at ourselves before we condemn, before we accuse, and try to determine where the fault lies, whether it is really due to the interference of external powers or to our own mishandling of our own affairs."[33]

Khama considered himself an educator. He also recognized Botswana's poverty and its enormous shortage of homegrown skilled persons. For that reason, he turned his back against a liberal education and compelled Botswana's ministry of education to lean more and more toward "purposeful" education that would contribute to national manpower development. Fortunately, much of this thrust in the direction of polytechnical training also coincided with Botswana's new wealth from diamonds. That unexpected bonanza allowed Khama to preside over a great expansion of primary and junior secondary schooling, and to foster a strong national spirit of learning at the senior secondary level and then at the new local university. Often, as in this case, Khama eased into a problem, grasped what was needed for his people, and then set in train procedures and mechanisms that would deliver to the people what he and his experts believed that they needed.

He operated in that manner in governing Botswana from within his cabinet of ministers. Preferring decisive advice and disagreement, he always favored open and free-ranging discussion. Indeed, he never liked to dictate policy, preferring to guide his ministerial colleagues in the direction that seemed best but that might not have been initially obvious. He also protected the autonomy of his chief political and nonpolitical advisors, whatever their ethnic or racial backgrounds. Sometimes his more impatient advisors and ministers felt that he dithered, and Masire frequently sought to move faster. But the final decisions often were seen as wise and as exercises of careful leadership that took Botswana's delicate international position, say, or equally delicate domestic considerations, fully into account.

Prudence, Morality, and Competence

Among Khama (and Masire's) signal accomplishments in the early years, and one that made Khama particularly proud, was infant Botswana's ability by 1972 to balance the national budget. This may seem a minor achievement in retrospect, but it showed that fiscal discipline, duties derived from a new customs agreement negotiated cleverly with South Africa, the collection of taxes from an emerging middle class, income from beef exports, and the first returns from diamonds at Orapa would enable the former Protectorate to cease begging Britain for continued ordinary support; Botswana could now stand on its own financial feet. Moreover, Khama could demonstrate tangible economic returns to his constituents, with the promise of more. A few years later, in 1976, Botswana astutely created its own currency, the pula, and broke with the South Africa rand. Doing so gave Botswana much more control over its monetary and macroeconomic prospects; it also thus avoided importing South African inflation and deflation through the rand.[34] Although not Khama's own idea, he quickly saw its value and how it added to the strengthening of Botswana's independence from its bullying neighbor.

Nothing advanced Botswana in the earliest years of independence, and demonstrated Khama's consummate leadership abilities, more than his capture for his nation and its people of substantial revenues from diamonds—the country's only significant source of real income and potential for growth. Prospectors from De Beers Ltd. discovered diamonds at Orapa in Ngwato territory in 1967 after spending twelve years tracking down the source of a set of small diamonds that had been found in a dry river bed in 1955. By 1969, the size and quality of the diamonds in the

Orapa pipe had been proven, and a joint Botswana-De Beers company (Debswana) was created with the government holding only a 15 percent stake and De Beers 85 percent. Subsequently, two smaller diamond properties were located south of Orapa, and, farther south, the great mine of Jwaneng was discovered by De Beers in 1973.[35]

Khama and his advisors took a strong position regarding this wealth. It belonged to the nation, but Khama was also conscious that he desired and valued De Beers' managerial skills and industrial acumen. Hence, instead of nationalizing or otherwise demanding total control of the diamond mines, Khama decided to seek a full partnership with De Beers. The 1969 agreement was inappropriately stingy as far as Botswana was concerned, given the vast and unexpected mineral bonanza that lay under Botswana's sandveldt. It took four years and much tactical leadership by Khama and Masire, but ultimately De Beers and Botswana agreed in 1975 to split the ownership 50–50 and the revenues from all diamonds more favorably for the nation at about 70–30. Later, in 1978, Botswana and De Beers concluded difficult negotiations over Jwaneng; that mine reached full production in 1982 and became the most profitable diamond property in the world, at one point producing about 12 million carats of gem diamonds a year.[36] The solid partnership between the company and the country has since operated on the basis of complete unanimity and mutual trust, with De Beers chairing the board of Debswana and a leading Tswanan minister being deputy chair. Few other African nations and leaders would have been able to renegotiate an original weak agreement so effectively and without ultimate rancor. Khama and his advisors did so, to the benefit of the people of Botswana.

Once there was national income from mining, Khama could afford to attempt to narrow the urban-rural divide, and to generate more and more employment. He knew (better than other contemporary African leaders) that creating jobs was critical if the people of Botswana were to prosper. The balanced budget also showed once again that Botswana was distinct. It did not permit extravagance and the kind of wild spending that characterized other African nations. Neither Khama nor Botswana ever favored ostentation, not even during their travels abroad or during their state celebrations at home. Khama in Pyongyang startled his North Korean hosts by playing billiards with his traveling entourage, at one point stretching full length on the table to deal with an awkward shot.[37] Botswana, led by Khama, was true to its modest roots.

Indigenous Botswana before its independence had never known much corruption. Afrikaner-dominated South Africa was much more corrupt, and some of its petty corruption may have crossed the border with white police or the staff of the Rhodesia Railway. But Khama early knew (like Lee) that he could not afford to diminish his country's image when South Africa was adjacent or to mortgage his nation's prospects for growth and prosperity by explicitly or implicitly condoning practices that could be construed as corrupt or nepotistic. As early as 1974, Khama noted that Tswanan civil servants and officials were likely to be as tempted to pilfer as their counterparts elsewhere in Africa. But no level of corruption would be permitted. Khama was very clear that politicians and civil servants were not to view independence (as they had elsewhere in Africa) as a route to personal enrichment. He insisted that his cabinet ministers pay their debts promptly and cover their bank overdrafts. He was even tough on Masire when his close colleague was slow in repaying a large agricultural borrowing.

As the diamond industry grew and the second and third of the country's mines were opened, additional opportunities for smuggling opened up. The cabinet ministers responsible for mines could invent special ways to profit from the growing national largesse, especially when they could arrange permits and other nonofficial methods of sharing the new wealth. Foreign businessmen and technocrats were often accused of such illicit profiteering, and the nation's minister of natural resources committed suicide in 1976. Khama tried to exert himself against any and all persons who were rumored to be tainted by corruption. For him, as for Lee Kuan Yew, corrupt practices undermined the nation-building enterprise.

As Masire, Khama's vice president and successor as president, later wrote, corruption wrecked "whole economies" and benefited the few at the expense of the majority. "We worked hard to avoid" corruption, he wrote, and then punished it severely if discovered. "In the beginning we were a poor country with a very simple administration and few resources." It was therefore very easy, he reported, to operate transparently. From the British, Botswana inherited a legacy of "properly accounting for things." From traditional society, it inherited a custom of open discussion in the kgotla, so citizens could complain easily about abuses.[38]

Khama lived modestly, with limited motorcades and absent forced adulation. That approach—rare in Africa—helped to strengthen and to make effective the overall anticorruption message. No cabinet minister traveled by first class air, unlike his peers in the remainder of independent Africa. During the initial years of an independent Botswana, cabinet ministers drove their own automobiles. There were few of the usual perquisites that came with office in the developing world. Masire, as vice president, traveled in the rear of an aircraft to an important meeting in Ethiopia. By the time that he had exited the aircraft, the red carpet had been removed and the welcoming party had decamped.

Of practical importance for anticorruption activities was Khama's canny and very un-African decision to refrain from giving too much power to any individual. Ministers could make no major moves on their own. They had to involve or at least to consult the heads of other departments, thus spreading and collectivizing responsibility. For example, when Botswana decided to grant mining leases for diamonds or coal, a number of ministries had to be canvassed and a final decision taken by the entire cabinet and the president. Khama specifically instructed an early minister of mines who wanted to exercise the authority that had been invested in him by the Mines and Minerals Act that he could not. "No, this is not something for one man on his own; it is too important. Even if you think it is right, if anything goes wrong, you must share the responsibility with your colleagues . . . And if the people later think it is wrong, then you will have others to help you defend why it was thought to be the right thing to do."[39] Khama insisted that ministers should reveal all implications of any official decisions taken by them, whether administrative or financial. Full transparency was necessary at all levels.

Khama and Masire also saw to the prosecution of the few prominent Tswana cabinet ministers and officials who misappropriated funds or benefited illicitly from their positions. One of those was Khama's cousin, a senior civil servant. Another was a senior officer in the ruling BDP. Allegedly, a third was Masire's younger brother. In that case, the report of a high-level commission that examined the accusations was published for all to read. In a fourth case, Masire terminated an assistant minister in and the permanent secretary of the Ministry of Local Government and Lands, even though the assistant minister's criminal conviction in the case was later overturned on appeal.[40]

To Build a New Nation

What Khama and his administration, and successive presidents in Botswana, communicated so well to their constituents throughout the vast country was that he and they were not in politics to gain wealth or power. They were in office to build a new nation more singular than anywhere else in Africa. For Khama, being the first president of Botswana provided an opportunity to implant alternative African values, to create an open society, and to develop a political culture of democracy. For him, responsible leadership meant guardianship, on behalf of the people. He was in office to provide a strong moral and practical compass for the nation, and that meant the elimination of any germs of corrupt practice.

Khama's refusal to condone corruption helped to make Botswana the well-governed and minimally corrupt place that it is. His successor presidents, emboldened by his leadership example in these and all other areas, continued his and the nation's antagonism to corruption, no matter where it arose. Given his and their actions, Botswana for at least a decade has been the least corrupt country in Africa. In 2010, it ranked first in Africa and thirty-third in the world, according to Transparency International's Corruption Perception Index, placing it just ahead of Puerto Rico, Taiwan, Bhutan, Malta, Brunei, South Korea, and Mauritius.[41]

A searching inquiry by Acemoglu, Johnson, and Robinson into the reasons for Botswana's "spectacular" economic success concluded that the country was rich because it had good institutions, especially institutions of private property. Its success was not an immediate consequence of its natural resource wealth. Institutions mattered more, but why, they asked, did Botswana have such good institutions? Cattle owners were influential; they favored solid property rights and good institutions. The political elites were largely the economic elites, and no one opposed or felt threatened by the process of rapid economic growth and increasing prosperity. The political elites, moreover, were constrained by informal and formal political institutions. Finally, they concluded, the structural factors about which they wrote were assisted by "agency"—by the decisive manner in which Khama and Masire led the infant Botswana. They credit Khama with particularly insightful actions.[42] Indeed, Khama created the political culture that made positive institutions, and the institutional climate about which the three authors wrote, not only possible but also plausible and desirable. Without Khama's ability to have created the context and drive for good outcomes, corruption might have hampered Botswana as it had new nations elsewhere in Africa. Without Khama's astute leadership, there might well have been no effective political institutions and little opportunity to harness diamond wealth for the benefit of all of Botswana.

Khama was ill periodically throughout the 1970s. A diabetic, he also contracted cancer of the abdomen and died in mid-1980, shortly after his fifty-ninth birthday. By his death, the ethos that he had talked about and worked so hard to achieve was mostly a reality. By setting an example of responsible, democratic, incorruptible, national leadership and by implanting in the Botswanan political consciousness a right way and a wrong way of gaining and exercising power, Khama launched the new nation onto Africa's most successful trajectory. Creating a nation that prized good governance, Khama (and diamonds and tourism more than beef) ensured steady economic growth and indigenous prosperity. With the establishment of the tone and the reality of a democratic political culture, democratic political institutions could flourish, and the executive could take its place in the minds and actions of his successors as but one of the poles of national power. Botswana's stability, its freedom from internal division, and even its prosperity follows from Khama's methods, values, and sense of integrity, and from the commanding quality of his vision. In some ways undynamic, he was courageous, principled, and clear sighted. Less popularly inspirational than Mandela or Ataturk, and less energetic and clever than Lee, Khama nevertheless still provides a role model for leadership competency in Africa and the developing world.

FIVE

Lee Kuan Yew: Systematic Nation-Builder

Along with the preceding two leaders, Lee Kuan Yew has demonstrated many of the leadership competencies in the broad range set out in the beginning of this book. Few leaders, however, have been as successful as a visionary and as a realizer of visions as Lee has been. Few have been so effective as a nation-builder. Few have been so thoroughly transformational, so capable of boosting Singaporeans' ability to prosper economically, and so determined to remake an entire (albeit small) society along modern lines.

A phalanx of impressive numbers testifies to Lee and Singapore's successful odyssey of fifty-plus years. Across a range of governance-type indexes, Singapore ranks very high, and often well ahead of every other developing and many developed nations. According to Transparency International's annual Corruption Perception Index, Singapore in 2010 was the least corrupt country in the world, joined in first place by New Zealand and Denmark, and well ahead of the United States, which was ranked twenty-second.[1] The Index of Economic Freedom and the OECD have always ranked Singapore highly, as does the World Bank's annual *Doing Business* surveys and the World Economic Forum's annual competitiveness reports. But the most telling number is Singapore's GDP per capita. In 2009, that figure was $45,997 (in USD [2005] at purchasing power parity), more than triple the GDP per capita of Botswana and South Africa. Moreover, Gini coefficient ratios showed that Singapore's prosperity was comparatively egalitarian. Educational and medical facilities and accomplishments were among the world's best; life expectancies were high, schooling results strong, corruption almost absent, and crime rates very low. Despite its historic legacy as a consummate part of and contributor to the developing world, in 2011 Singapore was more and more listed and discussed as a developed country. It is now widely regarded as among the ten most nurturing nation-states in the world despite (or because of) its limitations of individual free expression and its curbs on pure forms of participation. Under Lee's direction, and, indeed, largely due to the heavy hand of his leadership guidance, Singapore made the great leap forward out of the developing world by at least the 1990s, remaining ever since an exemplar of societal advancement globally.

The Singaporean renaissance hardly happened by chance or by accident. It is largely the result of one man's consummate leadership and one man's ability to articulate a persuasive and politically saleable vision to a mixed mass of unruly and undisciplined immigrants in the years after 1959, but most pointedly, after 1965. "I do not think you learn leadership," said Lee. "This attribute called leadership is either in you or it is not." Nevertheless, Lee agreed that "A leader without the vision, to strive to improve things, is no good." Furthermore, political leaders "must enthuse [their followers] with the same fire and the same eagerness that pushes you along." Leaders must also have idealism, Lee believes. "You must have that vision of what is at the bottom of the rainbow you want to reach." Again, Lee said in 1989, "to build a country, you need passion. If you just do your sums—pluses, minuses, credit, debit—you are a washout."[2]

In an interview at Harvard's Kennedy School in 2000, Lee said that his most important character trait was consistency. "I don't say one thing today and another tomorrow." Another was determination, and a third was the ability to persuade people, if not the first time, then on a second, third, or fourth try. Building trust between the prime leader and his key associates was also critical. Lee said that a leader must be energetic and have the ability to project himself and his ideas. Leaders must provide hope, never despair. Lee (echoed later by Tony Blair) said that leaders whose emotional intelligence was limited would not last long.[3]

Today's robust Singapore is a result of leadership decisions made by Lee (and his associates) in those early and desperate years. It is the creation of a political culture that flowed in early Singapore from Lee's actions and teachings, and the gradual implantation into Singapore of political institutions made possible by the development of a firm, largely (but not fully) democratic political culture. According to one acute observer, Singapore uniquely has always placed "national interests, albeit narrowly defined by a narrow elite . . . ahead of any particular benefits for the rulers."[4]

Born to Lead

Lee argues that he was born (in 1923) to be a leader, and always assumed that his destiny was to lead. His parents, convinced of Lee's call to greatness, were long-settled inhabitants of the British-ruled Straits Settlements of Penang, Malacca, and Singapore, and members of its wealthy *baba* class. That is, although Lee's accomplished paternal great-grandfather was of Hakka ethnicity, and an émigré from southern China, his doting and accomplished grandfather was Singapore born. His immensely nurturing and influential mother was also Chinese from another wealthy local Hakka-derived family. The baba, as the Straits Settlements Chinese were affectionately known, were an elite colonial creation—an amalgam of English-speaking Chinese and Malayan cultures with a British overlay. Lee learned Mandarin Chinese only as an adult, and grew up in an English- and partly Malay-speaking household.

Lee was a firstborn, and the son of an adoring and attentive mother who was determined that he should succeed in the British colonial world of the 1920s and 1930s. She enrolled him at an early age in an English-medium primary school. Later he attended the prestigious and immensely competitive Raffles Institution for his secondary training. It was at Raffles that Lee was introduced to and became imbued with the idea that ensuring progress and thus overcoming historical obstacles to societal advancement was to be his personal contribution to the remaking of Singapore and of Asia. It was at Raffles that he became a formidable debater, researching his topics and preparing his arguments rigorously. Lee was precociously bright and driven, always almost effortlessly emerging at the top of the rankings on competitive school examinations. In 1939, Lee wrote the best Cambridge Senior Examination in all of Singapore and Malaya. Already, the principal of Raffles had suggested that he was sure that one of the students in Lee's class would become a prime minister of Singapore.[5]

After topping the Cambridge examinations, Lee enrolled in Singapore's Raffles College to study mathematics, economics, and English literature. There, as a student politician and embryonic leader, he developed an intolerance of and contempt for inefficiency and incompetence that he subsequently honed finely. A task was not worth doing unless it was done well and thoroughly. This intolerance was noted by the British teachers in the College and became among the prized contents of the Lee legend.[6]

Lee's studies at Raffles were truncated radically after a little more than a year when the Japanese in 1942 began their brutal occupation of Singapore and Malaya. From the Japanese and from the manner in which the local population accommodated the despised Japanese, Lee learned lessons that would influence his life and his political career: "I understood how [raw] power operated on people."[7] Lee became a clerk-typist in two commercial firms, and then a transcriber in the local Japanese Propaganda Department, working with Allied news notices. He also learned Japanese. Later he speculated successfully as a trader on the black market. After the war, he ran a construction labor supply operation.

The Japanese invasion transformed Lee from a devotee of British imperial life into a jaundiced protonationalist. For three days at the beginning of the occupation, 90,000 British, Australian, and Indian troops tramped into captivity down Singaporean streets past Lee's home. The troops were bewildered and lost, and Lee's belief in the impregnability of the British imperial might, and in the strength of the British navy, was shattered. The Japanese invasion, Lee wrote, made him into a fighter of freedom "against servitude and foreign domination." From the time of the occupation, Lee "decided that our lives should be ours to decide." He was not going to be a "plaything" of a foreign power.[8] After the war, when the British returned, Lee resented the fact that the British believed that they could and should rule Singapore even though they had betrayed the colony and its citizens. Later, Lee said, "I saw no reason why [the British] should be governing me; they're not superior. . . . I was going to put an end to this."[9]

In late 1946, Lee nevertheless set sail on a British troopship for London. There, in the anonymous city, he was lonely. Within six months he managed to wangle a place in the University of Cambridge's newest noncollegiate hall, Fitzwilliam House, and thus a place to study law at Cambridge. There he soon dazzled fellow students and tutors, combining an active social life with vigorous study. A contemporary remembered him as displaying a very fine "legal brain."[10] Lee took a series of prizes and graduated with a starred first degree, being the best of the brightest. By this time Kwa Geok Choo, his future wife, whom he had known since she obtained higher grades than his own at the Raffles Institution and with whom he had worked during the Japanese occupation, had come up to Girton College in Cambridge, also to study law. She graduated with him in 1949, also with first class honors. Secretly married, after Cambridge they both traveled to the Middle Temple of the Inns of Court in London (and to Cornwall) to cram for their English law examinations, and then home to Singapore in 1950. Before their return, Lee also found time to give speeches for a Labour Party candidate in Devon; he explained how votes in Devon could affect the future of Malaya and Singapore, and why that mattered to the British electorate.

The Singapore Express

Lee's future was bright professionally, but he also had acute political aspirations. Quick, alert, unusually talented, strategically and tactically astute, politically naive, and personable if touchy are all descriptors of the young Lee. An anticolonialist of Fabian Socialist persuasion in Britain, a cerebral anticommunist, a keen and accomplished debater, and in his middle 20s already someone to whom other students from the colonies looked for direction and persuasive arguments, Lee had leadership potential that was always evident and keen edged. But sheer ability often fades when confronted with the sordid realities of gaining and keeping power.

Lee knew that the British would soon be willing to leave their Asian colonies. He also knew that Singapore would then have to be wrested away from the communists, who had fought valiantly against the Japanese occupation and had consequently gained a wide measure of respect and following among working-class Singaporeans at a time when their compatriots were in open rebellion against the British on the Malayan peninsula and Mao Tse-tung's long march was culminating in glorious victory on the Chinese mainland. Partially to counter the communists and partially because it seemed a logical progression, Lee had begun by 1950 to envisage a postcolonial Singapore as an integral part of a new union of the Malayan states. He saw himself as a nation-builder; the task of a leader in an embryonic nation was to provide or to create "a strong framework within which [the people] can learn, work hard, be productive and be rewarded accordingly." Lee added, "And this is not easy to achieve."[11]

Lee and his wife quickly obtained employment with a prominent legal firm in what was now the Crown Colony of Singapore, separated administratively as it had been from peninsula Malaya, now a federation of states, and destined soon to be self-governing. Ostensibly, a small handful of English-educated Chinese and European members of the local elite, mostly lawyers, were guiding the Singapore colony's political evolution through the Progressive Party. But they were gradualists, not populists, and, as Lee quickly discovered, no match for the local branch of the Malayan Communist Party. After World War II, the Malayan Communist Party had led successful strikes against the colonial authorities. Lee flirted at first with the "feeble" Progressives, but soon realized that he would have to find a better political vehicle with which to outwit or outmaneuver the communists.

Fortunately for Lee, in 1952 the Postal and Telecommunications Uniformed Staff Union asked him, an inexperienced lawyer who had only recently joined the Singaporean bar, to represent them against the government in a salary dispute. Guiding the union through a well-organized and well-conducted strike action, Lee produced an unexpected victory through negotiation and advocacy. "We . . . exposed the stupidities and inadequacies of the colonial administration," said Lee.[12] As a result, Lee vaulted into prominence throughout the city-state, encouraging a number of other local unions and many opponents of the government to employ his undoubted talents, pro bono. "We had found the way to mobilize mass [noncommunist] support," Lee later commented bravely.[13]

But he and like-minded, educated, anticommunist nationalists in fact lacked ways of appealing to popular opinion until communist-led Chinese secondary and tertiary students protested violently against the state. Lee represented them and won a series of political (not legal) victories. Those triumphs in turn led to clandestine conversations initiated by the communists with Lee, and a decision in 1954 to forge a tactical political alliance with local Chinese communists to establish the People's Action Party (PAP) and together to contest the 1955 legislative assembly elections. Lee understood only later how dangerous it was to ally intellectual, politically callow, English-speaking returnees like himself to committed, much better-organized communists. Yet Lee, having just turned 30, was supremely self-confident and saw no other tenable and relatively rapid method of achieving his political aspirations. He also had to break cleanly with the existing dilettante politics of people like the Progressives. Even at this early stage in politics, Lee exhibited self-mastery and clear vision.

Although the new Labour Party, led by David Marshall, captured the most legislative assembly seats in the election, Lee won a dockworkers' constituency overwhelmingly, alongside the victories of two of his PAP colleagues in neighboring areas. The Progressive Party was thoroughly defeated. As the de facto leader of the opposition, Lee was to play a commanding role in the political development of the colony, hampered somewhat by the confrontational tactics of his nominal communist allies. He was bitterly to learn how the Chinese communists attempted to use and to manipulate him and the PAP, and how they drastically limited his available policy choices. In the communists' determined battle to gain control of Singapore's labor movement by fair means or foul, Lee gained an appreciation of their discipline and their tactical ability to mobilize schoolchildren and workers. He understood, which Marshall never did, that premature independence would mean a Chinese communist takeover of the island. He therefore attempted to develop a space within which to establish an effective noncommunist government "in the people's interest," but with ultimate British control as a foil to the communists.[14] Fortunately for Lee, this was the British position as well. It needed its big naval base in Singapore to protect Malaya, still in the grip of a hard-core communist insurrection. Later in 1956, when Marshall's Chinese successor presided over a crackdown on striking and rioting Chinese communists, Lee prudently stood aside. "Marshall had taught me how not to be soft and weak when dealing with the communists. Lim Yew Hock taught me how not to be tough and flat footed," Lee later glossed his learning.[15] Lee also insisted that the voters in Singapore's next election, when the city-state would be self-governing under the British, should include an expanded electorate of 300,000 newly enfranchised Chinese immigrants, up from 75,000 "British subjects." And he quietly acquiesced in the British disbarment of candidates for election who had been detained for subversive activities. He also calculatingly promised the public that the PAP would not take office without its detained (communist) comrades. "We understood the values and social norms of our people and we had to be seen to have acted honourably."[16] During this early period of a very difficult political apprenticeship, Lee was always charming, impressing the outgoing colonial rulers with his probity and leadership potential, and gaining influential friends at the top of Singapore's police apparatus. He masterfully employed British anticommunist intelligence and security policies to his own advantage; nothing demonstrated Lee's leadership talents more than his skillful outwitting of the better-organized communists, both those within his own party who sought his ouster, and outside, underground.

"Lee . . . Is the Only Man"

By the next legislative assembly elections, in 1959, Lee was ready to rule. Inspired by Lee's overtures overseas and at home, and by the Malayan Federation's independence in 1957, Britain was prepared to devolve effective self-government. It was also willing to detain many of Lee's communist rivals. Lee first outmaneuvered his supposed communist associates within the PAP and then led a PAP dominated by himself and his close allies to a striking triumph over Marshall's renamed Workers' Party. The PAP won 43 of 54 seats in the Assembly.

Now the PAP had to govern, and to end colonial rule. But Lee, prudent, was reluctant to take the Crown Colony to independence outside of a merger with Malaya—its hinterland and only sizable potential domestic market. He was not yet confident of Singapore's future as an independent polity. He also continued to fear the local communists, with their hold on the port city's workers and their strong support from China. As the head of a free city-state, Lee would be called upon to curtail the liberties of his sometime allies, and to invoke draconian security legislation. For that reason, and because of his own inexperience and insecurities, Lee began in the 1950s to advocate a merger of Singapore with an independent Malaya, now led by his old London colleague Prime Minister Tunku Abdul Rahman. The Tunku resisted those overtures until 1961, when he suddenly decided that Singapore should join Malaya as part of a newly proposed Malaysian Federation (incorporating Sarawak and Sabah as well as Singapore, the other Straits Settlements, and the states of peninsula Malaya). Lee regarded this volte face as an answer to prayer, and managed initially to persuade the communists within the PAP to agree to such a merger. But when it came time to begin negotiating with the Tunku, Lee lost the communists, who split from the PAP to form a rival socialist front.

Lee's political leadership, somewhat scattershot until this point, became more effective and sustained as he campaigned within Singapore for the proposed merger. He both consulted with and attempted to educate Singaporeans about the advantages of joining the Federation. His dozen or so radio broadcasts, in a mélange of languages, proved very influential. For him, and in realization of his developing vision for Singapore, security considerations were paramount. The communists understood that logic as well because, given the anticommunist emergency on the peninsula, they would be detained the moment Singapore and Malaya were joined. Lee could also explain the economic advantages of linking his island with the peninsula, particularly once the British withdrew from their vast naval base.

Lee's intellectual hegemony and his unsurpassed ability to overcome opponents logically and rhetorically were demonstrated in 1961 and 1962, during the run-up to a tactically effective referendum on the merger in late 1962. The purpose of the referendum was to gain political legitimacy for the decision to join the Federation. But the more significant use of the referendum exercise was to isolate the new communist political front. Obtaining a positive response was somewhat easy since Lee made sure that all of the choices a voter might select affirmed the merger. Even spoiled or blank ballots counted affirmatively. Indeed, Lee's side received a smashing 71 percent of the votes in the referendum, having once again outmaneuvered the communists.

By force of intellect and will, and by declaring in visionary fashion that Singapore's future prosperity depended entirely on joining wider Malaysia and the Malays who would dominate, Lee overcame the hesitations of Singapore's electorate. From late 1962 through mid-1963, Lee further campaigned relentlessly in four languages to shore up his support for merger and to strengthen his position against the Tunku and the Malayans, many of whom were reluctant to abide by the agreements that had been negotiated regarding Singapore's role within the Federation. Lee also won a striking endorsement of his approach in the Singaporean elections of September 1963, again strongly defeating the communists and winning even the local Malay constituencies. "This was a famous victory," Britain's representative in Singapore cabled home, "and the crowning achievement to date of Lee Kuan Yew's career. . . . We have always said . . . that Lee . . . is the only man who can run this city and that the Malaysian government would either have to do business with him or to put him in jail."[17]

Despite these vigorous and strategically astute victories by Lee, the Federation was established in September 1963 largely on Malayan, but not Malaysian, terms. Lee had battled robustly, but the Tunku held too many of the trump cards. The Tunku and his compatriots compelled Singapore and Lee to enter the Federation on sufferance. The Tunku and his team wanted Singapore inside the federal system, but only according to its dictates. They never wanted an energetic Chinese Singaporean cancer to eat away at Malay domination of the body of the Federation. Their political agreement was designed to further, not to marginalize, Malayan aspirations. Nor did the Tunku want someone as clever and articulate as Lee to become a rival for power within the Federation.

Lee, surprisingly, may not have fully understood this Malay power dynamic. As a supremely forward-looking modernist anxious to build new nations, Lee may have overlooked or refused to see the Tunku as a traditionalist with visions different from Lee's own. Or, confident of his own intellect and abilities and greatly disdainful of Malays and their accomplishments, and of Malay culture, Lee may have thought that, in time, he would find a way to lead the Federation despite his Chinese ancestry. Lee himself believes that the Tunku never really wanted a merger, so Lee, desperate for it, was unable to negotiate a favorable basis on which Singapore could enter the Federation. "I did not understand," Lee wrote later ruefully, "that their objection was basic; they did not want the Chinese to be represented by a vigorous leadership that propounded a noncommunal or a multiracial approach to politics and would not confine its appeal only to the Chinese."[18]

The federal experiment had deep flaws and worked neither for Singapore nor for Lee. Indeed, Singapore's two years under Malayan rule were almost the undoing of Lee as a consummate, successful leader. He lost control of the taxes imposed on infant industries. And then he lost control of security. To his chagrin, he had too little power to prevent and then to cope with racial riots that broke out inside Singapore in 1964. Lee's party's foray into peninsula politics against the Malays also backfired badly. The putative economic advantages of the merger were unrealized, thwarted by Malay governmental rivalries and jealousies. Moreover, he himself was effectively sidelined, limited by the Tunku and others to a political role only in Singapore, a mere administrative unit within the Federation. Had he not emerged from the terrible trials of the failed partnership wiser, if not immediately stronger, little would have been heard internationally of Lee, and Singapore might have remained the Chinese gang–infested, Communist-embroiled swamp that observers saw and experienced during the early 1960s. "There were strikes about nothing. There were communist-inspired riots almost every day. . . . The general opinion was: Singapore [was] going down the drain, it [was] a poor little market in a dark corner of Asia."[19]

After two trying years, Lee and his closest associates knew, all previous anxieties to the contrary, that they had no future as substate chiefs in a nation-state—the Federation—organized for and ruthlessly dominated by determined Malay nationalists. Lee, in contrast, sought a Malaysian Malaysia where he and the 42 percent of the Federation's population who were of Chinese origin (about 40 percent were Malays) could play a significant rather than a subordinated role. Lee and his colleagues feared being arrested or otherwise cast aside permanently. They thus realized by early 1965 that they had to remove themselves from the Federal arrangement, and without displeasing Britain, and without the rupture appearing internationally and locally to be of their own making. Moreover, if seemingly expelled from the Federation by an angry Tunku and his colleagues, Lee could present to Singaporeans a stark set of limited options—to survive as a city-state on its own or to "go down the drain." In August 1965, the Tunku largely agreed with Lee: "You go your way, we go our way. So long as you are in any way connected with us, we will find it difficult to be friends because we are involved in your affairs and you will be involved in ours." When Singapore was no longer in Malaysia, and no longer an obstacle to a fully Malayan Malaysia, "we'll need each other," the Tunku told Lee, "and we'll cooperate."[20] The Tunku had earlier emasculated the non-Malay political leaders of Sabah and Sarawak, but Lee was too strong and too representative of Chinese political sentiment within the Federation. Thus "disloyal" Singapore was "expelled" and Lee, his hand seemingly forced by circumstances, could calibrate a new vision for a Singapore that would show the Malays and show the world how determined, skillful leadership could build a new nation.

Getting Singapore to Work

Lee retroactively assessed Singapore's circumstances in characteristically candid and explicit terms: The entrepôt did not yet have the "basic elements" to become a nation. Singapore lacked a common ethnic identity and a common language. "How were we to create a nation out of a polyglot collection of migrants from China, India, Malaysia, Indonesia and several other parts of Asia?" Lee asked.[21] Moreover, to forge a Singaporean nation, its people (and Lee) needed to have been exposed to the "sharp lessons of . . . communal intimidation." Malay racial domination transformed Singaporean attitudes. The Chinese in Singapore would otherwise have "stayed mesmerized, trapped by Marxist slogans and Chinese chauvinist chants."[22] They would never, Lee recalled, have faced reality or have come to grips with the harsh facts of national identity construction. Lee suggested that despite overwhelming odds, he and his colleagues succeeded ultimately in transforming the jettisoned Crown Colony into a strong nation-state by making "survival"—"a matter of life and death"—both a necessity and a virtue. "I was to spend the rest of my life," Lee commented, "getting Singapore not just to work but to prosper and flourish."[23] *A fortiori*, Lee forcibly articulated a vision that mutated disadvantages into advantages and challenges into opportunities. The collapse of Lee's Malaysian dream made possible the Singaporean miracle.

But the miracle depended in turn on levels and kinds of leadership that had hitherto been lacking, on unusual strategic insights, and on Lee's steely determination to give Singapore the kinds of government and governance that would soon make it the envy of Asia. In 1965, Singapore consisted of 224 square miles and about 2 million people, 75 percent of whom were Chinese—a tiny minority in a South Asian sea of 100 million mostly Muslim Malays and Indonesians. Malaysia controlled Singapore's sources of potable water and was linked to Singapore across a causeway from the Sultanate of Johor, thus enhancing Singapore's vulnerability. Furthermore, Indonesia under President Sukarno had been engaged since 1963 in a low-level war of sabotage and terrorism against Malaysia, and now Singapore. Britain, the retreating colonial power, was responsible through its large air and sea bases for 10 percent of all employment in Singapore and about 20 percent of its GDP; there were few assurances at independence that Britain would continue to maintain its critical involvement in Singapore and continue to defend Singapore, as it had Malaysia, against the Indonesians. Lee had to create his own security forces, as well as to gain control over the plurality of his new nation's citizens. By 1971, when the British were ready to depart, Lee and his colleagues, with Israeli assistance, had created a large national defense establishment of seventeen battalions filled by men and women completing their required national service obligations (another innovation), backed by fourteen battalions of reserves. Lee had also purchased tanks and armored cars ahead of the Malaysians, which helped his campaign of shock and awe. His air force was small, but a deterrent, and he had begun equipping a tiny navy.

In 1965, trade was at a standstill; unemployment was at 14 percent and rising. The island's GDP per capita was a modest $500. The Malayans were going to cease grading and shipping their rubber, copra, and pepper exports through Singapore. The Indonesians were determined to avoid sending commerce through the city-state. Lee realized that Singapore, shorn of its hinterland, had to reimagine itself as an economically independent small emporium, surviving on its wits and on the new investments that it could attract. Admittedly, Singapore still had a first-rate harbor located athwart one of the world's busiest sea-lanes. It also had a determined government and a willingness, under Lee, to cast aside postcolonial shibboleths and ideological phobias if they interfered with development. "My strategy," wrote Lee, "was to create a First World oasis in a Third World region." Singapore "had to be more rugged, better organized and more efficient than others in the region."[24]

There were social and developmental deficits. The British colonial government had educated Straits Chinese (like Lee) and Malays, but had not devoted resources to the training of Chinese-speaking immigrants. Educational and literacy levels in Singapore were therefore much lower than in other parts of East Asia. Moreover, as Lee remembered, the Chinese majority included at least twelve separate, self-identifying, and linguistically distinct groups. Fifteen percent of population were Malays, and seven percent Indians, mostly Tamils but not united by caste or regional origin.[25] Nearly all of the parents or grandparents of these Singaporeans had arrived as laborers or traders.

For all of these reasons, but mostly because Lee did not wish to cede hegemony to the communists, whose Chinese ethnic and political base of support largely came from the ranks of the non-Straits Chinese, he painstakingly (and with deviations and some backtracking) forged a Singaporean identity. Such an endeavor made Singapore (and Lee) more palatable to the Malayans and the Indonesians.

Lee employed at least four primary methods of creating a new national identity and a new nation. First, after initially giving pride of place linguistically to Malay, he and his government gradually elevated English and Mandarin to positions of primacy, thus over time turning speakers of Chinese home languages into Singaporeans by privileging what for 90 percent of Singaporeans were effectively foreign tongues. Opponents who made their antagonism known in the Chinese press were jailed. Second, Lee's educational policies favored English-medium schools. In terms of social engineering, teaching more and more students in English enabled the city-state to compete effectively for foreign direct investment. There would be trained workers for the new manufacturing firms from Europe and America. Forty-three percent of pupils were enrolled in English-medium schools in 1965, and 82 percent were enrolled in 1980. (By 1980, however, the most popular television programs were all in Mandarin.)[26] Third, Lee merged the Chinese-medium Nanyang University in 1981 with the English-medium University of Singapore to create the National University of Singapore. Admission to it was based on competency in English and teaching was in English. By 1984, at all levels of education, the primacy of English was established, and Lee had in fact successfully shifted an embryonic state from its traditional tongues into an English-dominated Asian nation.[27] Fourth, Lee built great, tall blocks of attractive, publicly financed flats for 85 percent of his fellow Singaporeans, eventually giving a sense of ownership to the great mass of Singaporean families. Home or apartment ownership would be a stabilizing force and a method of encouraging national solidarity. But Lee, the consummate social engineer, insisted on integration rather than ghettoization. There were quotas. The citizens of the young country would become part of a new nation by living in close proximity, apartment complex to apartment complex, with families whose home languages might be mixed, but who were all being transformed by Lee's nation-building endeavor into Singaporeans. His housing scheme also eliminated the old ethnic neighborhoods and cleavages between communities while simultaneously avoiding the growth of slums and strengthening the sense of nationhood.[28] The housing blocs had their internal leaders and group accountability, but organizing Singaporeans in this manner also meant that Lee could easily disseminate a sense of citizenship and develop a civic spirit based on his notions of how Singaporeans should behave and comport themselves in their complexes. As benign as Lee's housing policies might have been, they also enabled him to regiment, and to instill conformity—what Lee often referred to as necessary "social discipline."

Widespread apartment ownership, an innovative state-sponsored medical insurance plan, and a broad-based contributory pension scheme—all essential elements in Lee's paternal system of social provision (not welfare) for Singaporeans—would not have been possible without the uniquely thought-out Central Provident Fund. The Fund and its workings are yet another example of Lee's ability as a leader to size up a problem (whether how to pay for home ownership, for medical services, or for pensions), to investigate solutions developed elsewhere, to adapt or to reconfigure the best of those solutions to suit Singapore, and personally to micromanage the experiment until the results proved acceptable to the government as well as to the people at large. The Fund, with very high mandatory contribution rates (from wages and salaries) enabled Singapore to afford out of the forced savings of its citizens necessary national infrastructural improvements (which benefited the citizens) and also facilitated individuals to employ their contributions to the Fund for housing, medical, and retirement costs. From Lee's social engineering point of view, the Fund enhanced political stability, "the foundation upon which Singapore grew."[29] He also made both the Fund and stability work by mandating low inflation rates and a sound currency, so personal savings did not vanish. It was Lee's ability to focus with unrivaled intensity on these and similar innovations, and to deliver results for the common good (but not necessarily with sufficient consultation over the details), that distinguishes Lee as a leader from so many of his contemporaries in small and big states.

A First World Oasis

Another example of Lee's attention to detail was his very early realization that Singapore would be a better city-state in which to live, and more attractive to investors, if he sponsored its greening and also cleaned up polluted waterways. It would be a "First World oasis." Moreover, a green

Singapore would help the water-short island create its own reservoirs of water. For all of these, as well as for aesthetic, reasons, Lee from the 1970s presided over the planting and maintaining of new grass, shrubs, and trees throughout the city-state, even under and around freeways. He imported varieties of greenery that might grow in tropical Singapore. A few decades later, Lee's obsession demonstrated how a determined leader could with followers' approval transform even the contours and looks of an embryonic nation.[30]

These environmental, linguistic, and housing policies went hand in hand with Lee's decision to create a tightly controlled, but democratically inspired, self-reliant and meritocratic governmental machine on the ruins of his crumbled Malaysian ambitions. There was little room in the early years of modern Singapore for backroom or ward politics, as played out in Chicago or Malaya, for those kinds of politics would have provided too many openings for the Chinese communists and for their aboveground Barisan Sosialis party. It would also have detracted from Lee's reliance on a newly conceived mandarinate—the young Singaporeans, all educated overseas in Britain, who had joined him to battle the communists, to separate from Malaysia, and then to chart a determined survival course for the new Singapore. With them, he was largely a consensual leader, prevailing for the most part by logic and the force of his powerful ideas. He was the conductor and his ministers the principal orchestra players.[31] But for the mass of Singaporeans, during electoral campaigns and in between each election, as prime minister, Lee was an articulator of a vision, and an educator, explaining why it was better, indeed essential, for Singapore to follow transformational Path A rather than Path B. One commentator compares Lee favorably to France's Charles de Gaulle.[32] Lee consulted with the people, but on his own terms. He was prepared to allow choice, but only within set limits. As a member of parliament later explained, referring to his constituents, "We will allow feedback . . . but we don't accept all their concerns."[33] Lee as leader always knew what was sensible. Indeed, Lee unwittingly but successfully established an administrative state, albeit with political trappings and procedures and the construction of a broad consensus of conformity. He prized passivity on the part of his people, and was content to have created a sterile rather than a deliberative ground of political discussion.

"There is little doubt that the PAP leaders" were elitists. "They admire the power of the intellect, and they believe that only a few of the best and brightest are capable of leading well." They, Lee foremost, were rationalists, pragmatists, extreme meritocrats, and believers in scientific and technological problem solving.[34]

Careful analysts of the Singaporean state further suggest that the administrative state gradually, in the 1980s, became the inclusionary corporatist state. That implied a "genuinely consensual partnership between state and society," together with restrictions on populist participation, leaving a technocratic elite to oversee economic development pragmatically.[35] In this model, the state tries to achieve both legitimacy and control, and imposes sacrifices on citizens in exchange for rapid modernization. This is the model that Lee, more unconsciously than consciously, elaborated during the second half of his prime ministership.

The executive was supreme. In practice, parliamentary activity and questions were largely cosmetic. Significant governmental decisions were not subject to judicial review. The meritocrats knew best, especially in the early years, and each decisive departure from past practice was deftly and decisively arranged in the best interests of an evolving Singapore. Moreover, meritocracy "creates an aura of special awe for top leaders and provides a basis for discrediting less meritocratic opposition almost regardless of the content of its arguments." Vogel goes on to suggest that the first generation of Lee and his close colleagues established a "macho-meritocracy." But Lee dominated and his personal style set the tone for debates and political combat: "It is the style of a fighter who is willing to pursue the battle until his opponent . . . is disgraced or dismissed. . . . It is the style of justice without ambiguity, decisiveness without hesitation, rationality without human softness, and flamboyant, obvious integrity without thought of personal gain."[36] An observer with strong local ties was even more pungent: Lee was "bloody-minded and ruthless with his adversaries. He stomps them into the ground."[37]

Governing well was not the same as being popular. "If you want to be popular all the time," Lee asserted, "you will misgovern. . . ." Taking unpopular decisions from time to time was an unavoidable necessity. The real test was whether, at the end of an electoral term, the leader had brought about "sufficient benefits" so that the people would vote for him or her again. "That is the basis on which I have governed," Lee affirmed. In addition, people want a government that they can trust to look after them and their families, that is fair, that refrains from looting the public purse, and whose leaders do not live in luxury.[38] Lee always knew that he could gain the people's trust only by deeds, not by mere words—by exuding what he termed a "sense of purpose."

Lee believed strongly that good government depended on good men, not necessarily good institutions. In that sense, Lee understood that he and his fellow political meritocrats would be creating a political culture capable of allowing Singapore to grow, to prosper, and to succeed. "To get good government, you must have good men in charge. . . ." In innumerable former colonies (such as Burma, Pakistan, and Sri Lanka), there were good constitutions and institutions, he observed, but no leaders "who could work [or respect] those institutions." Coups and riots occurred in many former colonial countries where "the leaders who inherited those constitutions were not equal to the job. . . ."[39] Lee was giving birth to a consciously democratic political culture, leading to strong institutions. The others were tearing down their inherited institutions.

Singapore as an effective administrative state owes much of its success and its triumph over adversity to Lee's insistence, from 1965 and 1966, that the PAP and the government must recruit members and civil servants systematically, must educate them to appreciate the Singaporean vision, and must promote only the best of those very bright persons, especially those who combined intelligence and dedication with what Lee called character. A major part of Lee's legacy, and a major contributor to Singapore's emergence as a developed nation, is this carefully honed, elaborately developed and run, system of recruitment and deployment. Lee argued that his city-state was too small for talent to arise spontaneously. It had to be spotted, nurtured, and channeled. Lee understood that careful attention had to be paid to political succession, a detailed process in which Lee justifiably takes great pride. It flowed naturally from leadership executed well and responsibly and from his thinking explicitly about strengthening the young state and its emerging political culture. In this way, as the meritocratic approach to governance grew out of his commanding vision, so it flowed from his interpretation of self-mastery, prudence, and intellectual honesty.

Paying a Heavy Price

The international entrepôt of Singapore under British colonial rule and after, within Malaya and Malaysia, was widely acknowledged to be a permissive, wild city where corruption was customary and crime rampant.[40] Ten thousand members of 360 Chinese gangs (triads) specialized in extortion, kidnapping for ransom, and other endangering criminal pursuits. It could easily have become a peninsula version of wide-open Macao. Lee knew that he had to tame the city to survive politically and to provide an underlying platform for rapid growth. The meritocratic, administrative state could not deliver good governance and its appropriate rewards if the new city-state remained unsafe and permissive. Government was responsible for ensuring fundamental freedoms, especially personal security.

In Asian society, Lee contended, the people looked to the authorities to establish order, and good rulers were ones who could do so effectively and fairly. Lee was personally offended, too, by poor discipline. The law could not function without order, and Lee used his parliamentary majority, leftover British laws, and his immense personal insistence to impose that sense of order and decency. For him there were clear and distinctive rights and wrongs and goods and evils. To avoid chaos and anarchy he promoted the use of extraordinary powers of detention without trial, sometimes for years, and for both political and gangster offenders. Out of his Japanese and his Malayan experiences came an appreciation of raw power, and its exercise. "You know," he told the Singapore Advocates and Solicitors Society in 1967, "we have paid a very heavy price. We have departed in quite a number of material aspects . . . from the principles of justice and the liberty of the individual . . . in order to maintain . . . standards. . . ."[41] From his early legal practice days, when he managed to acquit criminals by swaying juries, he learned to distrust open trials and a strict adherence to the laws of evidence and discovery. Very early, he also understood the value of severe punishments for minor offenses, such as spitting in the streets or urinating in high-rise elevators. "We were determined that they should behave to First World standards. . . ."[42] It would deter more dangerous crimes, he believed, and severe physical retributions, such as caning, would prevent all manner of recidivism. Whether or not such harsh approaches to deterring crime found justification in the West, Lee was persuaded from the beginnings of Singapore that they would work in Asia, especially in "his" city-state. And, for whatever combination of reasons, draconianism did contribute mightily to Singapore's intrinsic safety and stability. Crime rates in 2011 were very low, especially compared to those of Kuala Lumpur, Jakarta, or Hong Kong.

Lee also knew that he could not hope to grow a successful city-state without ending the sway of corruption. He had to demonstrate that corrupt practices would not be tolerated at any level—there could be no deviations from an absolute jihad against corruption for fear that every minor mishap would undermine both the overall anticorruption crusade and the entire, imperiled nation-building enterprise. Lee's task was difficult since his administration (from 1959 and, especially, after 1965) battled deeply engrained expectations of corruption locally and throughout Southeast Asia.

To quote Lee, "The percentage, kickback, baksheesh, slush, or whatever the local euphemism is a way of life in Asia: People openly accept it as a part of their culture. Ministers and officials cannot live on their salaries. . . . The higher they are, the bigger their homes and more numerous their wives, concubines, or mistresses. . . ."[43] Lee also cites the enormously high cost for candidates of winning elections in Taiwan, Malaysia, Indonesia, and Japan as another contributor to corruption. Winners had to recover their expenditures, so they naturally exploited their official positions for private gain. In Singapore, Lee outlawed driving voters to the polls; subsequently, campaign expenses have always been minimal.

When Lee's Singapore was removed from the Malaysian Federation in 1965, he knew that his battle for political hegemony against the nearby external forces of Malaysia and Indonesia; the comparatively distant external influence of China; and the more dangerous internal communists, triads, and other local opponents could not be won if the legitimacy of his new administration or of himself was fatally sapped by real or perceived charges of corruption. Nor could his imperiled nation-building effort afford to be compromised by charges of corruption. Otherwise, his intrinsically difficult enterprise would fail to capture the political support of the then–wildly divided and linguistically fractured Chinese, Malay, and Indian populations of Singapore. It would fail to attract the foreign direct investments that were essential if the city-state were to prosper. Corrupted, Singapore would not thrive and it would remain a haphazard enterprise adrift in the backwash of Malaysia and Indonesia.

Lee's is the toughest and best modern example of a leader who understood the dangers to society and governmental accomplishment of corruption. His was not a moral or ethical critique, but his strict puritanical stance against practices that were corrupt or appeared corrupt was fully political. In the 1950s, in Singapore, idealistic students and others had become communists, disgusted with the "venality, greed, and immorality" of many Asian leaders. Fighters for freedom had become the "plunderers" of their new societies. Students in Singapore and elsewhere saw the communists as dedicated, selfless, and noncorrupt.[44] Lee diagnosed, further, that corruption must be dealt with from the top down and by example. If the probity of the top leadership were exemplary, lower ranks less often would be tempted, and certainly rarely would feel entitled, to cheat. He thus chose to confront the scourge of corruption head on, by declaring zero tolerance for elected or appointed officials who were inclined to act inappropriately on behalf of friends or clients (or their kin or cliques) and thus to accept illicit favors.

"It is easy," as Lee admits, "to start off with high moral standards, strong convictions, and a determination to beat down corruption. But it is difficult to live up to these good intentions unless the leaders are strong and determined enough to deal with all transgressors, and without exceptions."[45] Indeed, few of the leaders of the nation-states of the developing world had those high moral standards, much less a determination to beat down corruption. Many talked the talk, piously, but few did more than establish mostly ineffectual anticorruption commissions. Few had Lee's gimlet-eyed approach. Few disciplined their closest associates and thus translated the lofty rhetoric of promised integrity into effective action.

Tan Kia Gan, Lee's close friend and one-time minister for national development, was a director on the board of the then-national Malaysian-Singaporean airline in 1966 when he was unceremoniously removed by Lee from all of his appointed positions and ostracized. Lee suspected that Tan had accepted cash to favor one aircraft supplier over another, but there was insufficient evidence to prosecute him. Nevertheless, Tan was ousted and shamed.

Wee Toon Boon was minister of state in the ministry of the environment in 1975 when he accepted a free trip to Indonesia, an expensive bungalow, and loan guarantees—all from a housing developer who could benefit from government contracts. Lee sacked Wee, but in this case the evidence was strong enough for the courts to hear his case and to sentence him to more than four years in jail.

In 1979, Phey Yew Kok, president of the National Trade Union Congress and a Member of Parliament for Lee's ruling party, was accused of taking funds from the Congress and investing them for himself. Phey jumped bail and vanished to Thailand before Lee could press charges.

Teh Cheang Wan was minister for national development in 1986 when he accepted two large cash payments, the first from a development company that wanted to retain land that had been earmarked for compulsory acquisition and the second from a developer who wished to purchase state land for private purposes. After his bribe-taking was discovered, Teh committed suicide rather than face disgrace.

Lee's gloss on Teh's disgrace was: "The purpose is not just to be righteous. The purpose is to create a system which will not be compromised. . . . But if I had compromised, that is the end of the system."[46]

Because these instances of Singaporean high-level corruption were treated in an exemplary fashion, similar breaches of trust became remarkably rare. Singaporeans quickly appreciated that the governing elite were not routinely (as elsewhere) taking advantage of their official positions to enrich themselves and that Lee and his associates meant what they said when promising a "clean administration." That Lee punished his colleagues for stepping out of line was remarkable in Asia and in the developing world. That robust message had its impact on lesser officials as well as on the ruling cadre.

It also helped that in 1995, Prime Minister Goh Chok Tong ordered an investigation of properties that were purchased at a discount by Lee's wife and son (subsequently, the prime minister). Lee's brother was a non-executive director of the publicly listed company, and the developer had apparently offered the same discount to others. When property values rose, the property that Lee (through his wife) and Lee's son had purchased appreciated, casting suspicion on the transaction. Parliament, investigating, and the Monetary Authority of Singapore, doing the same, exonerated the Lees, presumably demonstrating that the country's top leadership (Lee was then Senior Minister) continued to be incorruptible.

In earlier times, Singaporean police were renowned for scandal. As late as 1971, 250 mobile squad police took money regularly from truck drivers to overlook infractions. Hawker license inspectors and land bailiffs were also on the take. But once Lee's administration jailed them, and demonstrated that their superiors were not themselves equally on the take, incidents of corruption at middle and low levels in Singapore receded.

Lee's government refused to rely on example alone. It tightened regulations and also loosened evidentiary restrictions. It published very clear guidelines, so that those tempted to take advantage of their official positions (and the public) would have no illusions regarding the exact consequences of improper behavior. Continuing to use the British-created Corrupt Practices Investigation Bureau as the instrument of enforcement, Lee had it report directly to him in the prime ministerial office. In order to ease the possibility of convictions in questionable cases, Lee persuaded Singapore's Parliament to tighten various laws in stages. The definition of gratuity was widened to include "anything of value." Investigators, under the amended laws, could arrest and search suspects and family members, scrutinize bank accounts, and obtain income tax returns. Judges could fully accept the evidence of accomplices. Indeed, other legal changes compelled any and all witnesses who were summoned by the Corrupt Practices Investigation Bureau to give testimony.

Along the way, Lee's government greatly increased the fines for corruption and for misleading testimony. Later, the courts were permitted to confiscate all benefits that were derived from corruption.

Lee was particularly pleased that he had enabled the courts to consider as corroborating evidence of corruption that a suspect was living "beyond his means" or owned property that could not be afforded on his or her nominal salary. The government thus gave increasing powers to the Corrupt Practices Investigation Bureau; it was the watchdog and in a society as tiny and tight as Singapore, persons with ostentatious life styles were quickly suspect. (Even before he strengthened the Corrupt Practices Bureau, Lee sacked a government chief fire officer when, at a reception, the officer's "stunningly attractive wife" appeared "bedecked with expensive jewelry." Unfortunately for the fire officer, "her scintillating adornments caught the practiced eye of the prime minister. . . ."[47] The fire officer was promptly dismissed.)

All of these legal shifts, together with the immense leadership demonstration effect, greatly helped Lee to keep Singapore "clean." Lee also argued that the strongest deterrent was "a public opinion which censures and condemns corrupt persons . . . in attitudes which make corruption so unacceptable that the stigma of corruption cannot be washed away by serving a prison sentence."[48] Imbuing a profound sense of shame, in other words, is and was critical to keeping Singapore free of rampant corruption (as was inviting Singaporeans to implicate persons suspected of giving and taking bribes).

But many Singaporeans would argue that it was more the pegging of official salaries to corporate earnings that enabled policemen on the beat, accountants in government service, and even cabinet ministers to avoid accepting bribes or other inducements. After the 1970s, when Singapore had begun to grow robustly and Lee was sure that he and his associates had brought both prosperity and integrity to the emerging city-state, he spearheaded a drive to create for Singaporeans perhaps the highest civil service salaries in the world. Salary improvements were instituted in 1972, and again in 1985, when civil service and political salaries were pegged to commercial market rates. In 1994, ministerial and senior public officer salaries were set at two-thirds the level of comparable private sector earnings, with automatic annual increases without parliamentary approval. Senior officers in the police force, for example, were soon earning far more than commissioners and chiefs in large American municipal systems. Excellent emoluments obviously helped to keep Singaporean officials on the straight and narrow.[49]

The Coming of Institutions

It is possible to argue, as many have, that institutions, not leaders, combat corruption. The experience of Singapore and Botswana and the emerging case of Rwanda (plus almost all of the positive American, European, and other Asian cases) support that proposition. But leadership actions greatly determine the kinds of political cultures that arise in newly emergent or postconflict nation-states, and it is only from the establishment of political cultures that enshrine values antithetical to corruption that effective institutions of accountability and oversight emerge. Additionally, leaders beget good governance, and the practice of good governance nurtures and enables robust institutions and strengthens rules of law. The latter do not emerge in a vacuum but only as a result of early and careful leadership attention or core values. Leaders create a positive ethos by force of will or example, as Lee did, sometimes drawing on preexisting mores or distilling traditional values (as Khama did). Only then can institutions and a workable institutional framework emerge.[50]

Lee had to mandate and then ensure rule of law regimes that were fair and perceived to be fair. He had to equip his regime with a judiciary that was evenhanded and not controlled by state house. This he did, in the critical sphere of contractual observance and property rights. Singapore's reputation in this arena remains impeccable. But in terms of political rights, Lee's state tolerated nothing that would threaten the hegemony of Lee and the PAP. Jurists understood their very limited room to maneuver in this sphere, and so did nearly all Singaporeans. Lee's actions, and the signals that he sent to his close associates, were carefully monitored by emerging publics. If those signals had been found wanting, rule of law even in the property rights sphere would have been as compromised as it has been in most developing-world countries. It would have undercut the nation-building endeavor and vitiated the national attack on corrupt practice. Efficient allocation of resources had to occur as well. Otherwise, corruption would have been a necessary instrument to fulfill goals—as in Thailand and other nations.

But was and is Singapore really free from the taint of corruption—thanks to Lee's vision, tutelage, leadership, legal shifts, and salary improvements? The city-state has always ranked high on Transparency International's lists. Even skeptics and critics, including early pundits, accept that Singapore has been "virtually free of corruption."[51] Compared with African countries other than Botswana and Mauritius, and Asian nations and the Oceanic island-states, Singapore has, since the 1970s, if not before, been in a class of its own because of its early focus on the dangers to the state posed by corruption and because of its success in creating a conformist society that has long favored stability and prosperity over open political participation and the enjoyment of broad civil rights and liberties.

Despite Singapore's high anticorruption reputation and its appropriate rankings near the top of all such listings, nepotism—a form of corruption—ostensibly seems to be rife in a small country where Lee remained in charge or nearly in charge until he could safely pass the prime ministership on to a handpicked successor and then on to his son and main heir. Lee's defense, naturally, is merit. His wife and son gained their prominent positions because of their talent, not through Lee. In that sense, Lee enabled family members to enrich themselves. At the same time, there have never been accusations that either Lee or his family otherwise used their positions for illicit profit. And, like Lee, his son and wife are inordinately competent.

Critics such as Francis T. Seow, however, argue that Lee used his position to abuse power and to punish critics. Seow, then solicitor general, instances (among others) a case in which Seow agreed to hefty bail for a legal advisor to the then-Malaysian Singapore Airlines—someone who was suspected of a minor criminal breach of trust and indiscreet political interference. Lee—with whom Seow anyway had a testy relationship—strongly objected and hastened Seow's departure from government service.[52]

Lee, in other words, is hardly a paragon of virtue. Nor is he tolerant of incompetent adversaries or criticism. But he and the institutions that he has built have kept modern Singapore free from the taint of corruption as it is commonly understood. That is a unique achievement in Asia and the developing world.

Even so, Lee has often been accused by political opponents of being corrupt. His response to such criticisms or, indeed, to unsupported criticisms of any kind has been to sue. He is proud of his use of "brass knuckles" to defend himself and the state. "When any newspaper pours a daily dose of language, cultural or religious poison, I put my knuckle-dusters on. Do not believe that you can beat the state," Lee told the Singapore Press Club in 1972.[53] Lee and his government have won innumerable libel and slander cases against publications and individuals. They have bankrupted local critics and forced many media (even international media) operations to curtail their operations and their sales or to shut down.[54] These methods have emasculated opponents and cowed protesters. Lee's view of the role of the press and the media in an emergent nation like Singapore is, however, in complete harmony with his overall view of the meritocratic nature of Singaporean politics: "Freedom of the press, freedom of the news media, must be subordinated to the overriding needs of Singapore, and to the primacy of purpose of an elected government."[55] In Lee's day, the local press knew enough to practice self-censorship and, if it wanted to prosper, to support Lee and his programs positively. Despite the interlocking complexity of the meritocratic state, Lee further rejects the notion advanced by his critics that Singapore's judiciary is captive or partial, or that the PAP stayed in power with little competition because it (and Lee) were hard on its opponents as well as on the local and overseas press.[56] Michin suggests with ironic understatement, however, that the energy of Singapore's judiciary for many years was devoted to "creating precedents for [Lee's] distinctive theories of law and order"—a "thankless" exercise.[57]

When Lee was 87 and a self-confessed political street fighter in "decline," he reflected to a visiting reporter that not everything he had done was right. "But everything I did was for an honorable purpose. I had to do some nasty things, locking fellows up without trial."[58]

Creating a well-governed, stable, corruption-free Singapore enabled Lee to attract foreign (at first mostly American) multinationals, and to transform the old transshipment entrepôt and British sea base into a sizable electronics manufacturing center, a petroleum refining base for the region, a massive container port, a banking and insurance headquarters for Asia (and later a world financial hub), a tourism mecca, and a great transportation and services emporium. Lee knew that job creation was paramount. Within the first ten years, unemployment fell from 14 percent to 5 percent. He and his colleagues performed an unexpected economic overhaul, giving Singapore astonishing economic growth rates and enviable annual improvements in GDP per capita, by avoiding xenophobia, by empowering a very energetic economic promotion board, by never worrying about being "exploited" by foreigners, by abolishing exchange controls and ensuring financial integrity, by sensible tax policies, by currency stability, and especially by using the instrument of the state to invest in a range of critical commercial endeavors (Singapore Airlines, the National Iron and Steel Mills, Neptune Orient Lines, etc.) and commercial infrastructure, such as the industrial park in Jurong and Changi airport. Under Lee, an impatient pragmatist with a compelling vision, the city-state rapidly moved into skill-intensive activities, investing heavily in education, especially that of a technical nature. Singapore also tightly regulated and directed local entrepreneurial activities, held to prudent and open macroeconomic practices, and was willing to take necessary economic risks. As early as 1973, the state completely owned twenty-six major companies and partly owned another thirty-three. Through the Development Bank of Singapore, it wholly owned another seven major entities and had hefty investments in fifty additional corporations. Intraco, a state trading corporation, controlled twenty more. Statutory boards, such as the Housing Development Board, had subsidiaries and investments.[59] Critical new trade union legislation, a National Wages Council, and other national policies co-opted and neutered the labor unions; learning from its strike-prone 1950s and 1960s, Singapore produced a docile but well-trained, English-speaking work force with moderate wages well through the 1970s. Industrial peace was Lee's goal, and he obtained it by a combination of clever incentives and tough sanctions. Lee's insistence on turning hot, humid equatorial Singapore into an air-conditioned mecca of trade and tourism also helped. By these and similar means, Lee was able by the late 1970s, anyway, to deliver on his vision. Singaporeans had jobs, were well housed, and were growing wealthy and middle class in their aspirations.[60] Twenty years later, after Lee had himself stepped down as prime minister, Singapore was indeed a First World oasis.

The New Confucianism

Singapore's developmental model, one astute local commentator explained, was "a total systems approach." For example, its modern success as a functioning port was "based not only on its suitable waters and strategic location, but also the use of hyperefficient information technology and business-friendly policies" that made it worthwhile for shipping companies to pay higher fees to operate through Singapore. Lee's greening approaches and his environmental cleanup also required civil reengineering on a massive scale and the relocation of vast numbers of slum-dwellers—actions that were possible only in a controlled economy and society.[61]

Lee himself understood all of the policy and governance innovations that contributed to Singapore's rapid economic development. But he knew, too, that he was the key mobilizer who taught and exhorted the mass of Singaporeans to work hard for themselves and their families, and thus for the new nation-state. That made the difference. "The greatest satisfaction in life comes from achievement," he told the nation in 1973. "To achieve is to be happy."[62] Lee was determined to transform the city-state's economic base. He created or sanctioned an acquisitive community. "You cannot have people just striving for a nebulous ideal. They must have that desire to improve, whether it is the scooter, the minicar, the flat, the fridge . . . or better homes." People want "equal chances in order that they can show how one is better than the other. This is a fact of life. . . ."[63] Lee wanted old-family business mentalities to be converted into modern management. He oversaw the flattening of class differences and a new emphasis on social mobility through gainful employment. He wanted to reward learning and hard work. Then, capital and new knowledge could be employed by skilled workers to produce profitable, exportable goods. For him, the unhappy alternative to such progress was misery and poverty. Lee relentlessly pushed his fellow countrymen to achieve, to be purposeful, to reject sensual pleasures as ephemeral, and to join him in fashioning a new kind of what he called Confucian society. But it was really a society in the founder's own image.

Unlike Mandela and Khama, strong-minded but principled old-fashioned democrats to their deepest cores, Lee during his prime ministership from 1965 to 1990 operated more and more as a Platonic autocrat with a democratic veneer.[64] All three ruled for and uplifted their peoples. They were consummate leaders, the first two operating largely by persuasion and the force of personal example to inculcate a democratic political culture capable of supporting sustainable institutions. Both Khama and Mandela were exceptions to the prevailing (bad) leadership norms of Africa, but they were also outstanding leaders across the global and developing world space. Both should be credited with uplifting and transforming their very different polities; Khama indeed created his nation and gave it stability, prosperity, and a sense of destiny that could not have been predicted in the 1960s.

Lee did more, employing rougher methods, to achieve unparalleled stability, prosperity, and a sense of destiny for the denizens of a swampy emporium who did not know, in 1965, that they could belong to one of the ten wealthiest (per capita) and most orderly places in the world. Without Lee, the counterfactual odds are that Singapore's fate would have been very different, probably as a small, corrupt, and disorderly part of a Malayan-dominated Malaysia.

Lee's leadership made the crucial difference. He had a clear, albeit evolving, vision. He had the skills with which to mobilize followers on behalf of that vision. He had the determination and the human wherewithal and talent to deliver positive practical results, thus enabling the selling of his vision to become progressively easier. By performance—by demonstrating his own integrity and by enforcing the integrity of his governmental colleagues—he held to his part of the Faustian bargain. If Singaporeans would accept limitations to their freedoms and natural liberties, he would provide order under law, rock-ribbed safety and security, and steady improvements in their real standards of living. Clear-sighted and effective as he emerged from the Malaysian merger debacle, he would also give Singaporeans a sense of larger purpose—a meaning to their lives as citizens. In 1965, most Chinese, Malay, and Tamil residents of the island did not know that they could be productive members of an important (if small) global nation. Lee worked toward that end and, as a responsible, prudent, devoted leader, succeeded. He offered "grandeur and glory to all those united with him as they [sought] virtue together. . . ."[65]

Lee was an architect and a master builder. He was disciplined. He was courageous. Except for enjoying power and enjoying being proved right, he was not merely buttressing his own ego. Lee was ruthless in overcoming the obstacles of human failings and inefficiency in achieving his goals for himself and for Singapore. He was also ruthless in hounding his opponents and his critics, captious or not. Yet, unlike the despots of the developing world, Lee was never corrupt, never content to give good results only to his family or his cronies. He did not, as so many of his contemporaries did, simply want to keep himself in office. Lee never fostered or indulged a cult of personality or even put his face on currency or postage stamps. His abiding motivation really was the betterment of Singapore—showing the world that a Third World backwater could become a First World oasis. Accomplishing that objective meant, admittedly, that Lee's life and leadership would be justified, and he would leave a heroic legacy behind. True enough. But in Lee there was a strong measure of built-in noblesse oblige. He knew what was best for his fellows. He began from the 1960s to demonstrate that his ideas and methods could triumph and deliver with surprising speed and effectiveness. Intellect was an advantage. He really believed in the importance of talent and the justification of merit, and thus in the guidance of the nation that he was creating, almost out of nothing, to reach its unheralded destiny.

Lee might well have done what he did with greater doses of democracy, and with greater respect for the individual rights of his subjects. He would argue that point strenuously, given what he learned in Britain and during the Japanese occupation. But it was also true that Lee, unlike Khama and Mandala, was impatient. More than those non-Asians (Lee's point of view), Lee would say that he lived in a harsher world and had to adapt to that difficult context by using "knuckle-dusters" freely. Lee would also argue that results are telling; what Singapore achieved during his prime ministership, and since, is more impressive, square kilometer by square kilometer, and person by person, than anywhere else in the modern world, or at any time. Given his undoubted self-mastery, and given his many other leadership qualities, it is incontestable that Lee's model provides important, bold lessons, not all of them positive, for the peoples and rulers of the developing world.

SIX

Kemal Ataturk: Uncompromising Modernizer

The Turkish Republic, created out of the veritable ashes of the Ottoman Empire, was officially established only in 1923. But, by 1919, Mustafa Kemal (later M. Kemal Ataturk) had emerged as the heroic defender of Turkish honor; as a victorious military entrepreneur against Britain, France, and Greece; as a new kind of secular political leader determined to unite the Turkish remnants of the empire; and as an energetic, visionary nation-builder. Neither the Ottoman Empire nor the war-ravaged wasteland that was Anatolia had ever known anything like the clear-sighted, intensely self-confident Kemal. Nor could Turks (or Europe and the United States) have anticipated how rapidly and consummately Kemal would unite the Turkish people or exactly where, and how far, Kemal's force of will would take them. Kemal's leadership was bold, resolute, astute, and transformative for Turkey and the Turkish people. As a leader, his skills and accomplishments were revolutionary, comparable to Lee's, albeit on a much larger scale and during a very different era.

The peace agreement of late 1918 between the defeated Turkish government and the Allies presaged a nation-state composed exclusively of the Turkish-speaking leftovers of the Ottoman Empire—essentially part of Thrace and all of Asia Minor and Anatolia. But, in order to accelerate the

Allied effort against the Germans and the Ottomans during World War I, Britain had also promised to carve up much of Asia Minor, giving territorial and trade concessions to Italy and France along Turkey's Mediterranean coastline. Together with France and Italy, Britain occupied Istanbul and controlled passage through the Bosphorus and the Dardanelles—the Straits. Britain also backed Greek claims to Asia Minor in line with President Wilson's self-determination enunciations and, fatefully, encouraged and abetted a Greek invasion of Izmir and western Anatolia in mid-1919.

"Victory Is Mine"

The potential dismembering of what was left of the Ottoman Empire, and the palpable threats to Turkish nationalism, enabled Kemal to mobilize and to take charge of the nascent indigenous forces of resistance in and after 1919. Earlier, in 1915, Lt. Colonel Kemal had emerged as the major Turkish hero of the defense of the Dardanelles. At the battle of Gallipoli Peninsula (on the western shores of the straits), Kemal had out-maneuvered attacking British forces, inflicting a major defeat on the invaders while holding important hills and critical military lines under conditions of great privation and distress. As British battleships pounded the Turkish redoubts in the major opening Allied assault on the Ottoman heartland, Kemal acted without specific orders and according to his own assessments of field strategy and tactics to repulse British attempts to land effective fighting forces. Kemal led his men in close quarter action, often in hand-to-hand combat with bayonets. He was in the right place at the right time, and for the right reasons. He managed almost single-handedly to arrest the British invasion and thus to prevent defeat at the Dardanelles, first in April and then in August 1915. He and his troops forestalled what would have been a long, unimpeded British march toward Istanbul. As a result of his courage and astute leadership at Gallipoli, Kemal became a popular hero amid an era of great distress for the German-commanded Ottoman army. He had exercised a "profound influence not only on the course of a battle, but . . . on the fate of a campaign and even the destiny of a nation."[1]

As Kemal later enunciated a critical military and leadership principle that guided his career and his modernization of Turkey: "Victory is won by the man who says 'Victory is mine,' success belongs to him who starts by saying 'I will be successful' and can then say 'I have succeeded.'"[2]

During the remainder of World War I, especially at its conclusion, Kemal, promoted to full colonel, remained one of the few successful Ottoman commanders, holding the line in the Caucasus and northern Syria and escaping capture on the Anatolian eastern front at a time when many other Ottoman generals were compelled to capitulate. He became known and revered as the only Ottoman military leader who had never suffered a defeat. Thus Kemal, with his European roots and affinities, and his practiced impatience with weak Ottoman authority, by 1919 had a patriotic stature and legitimacy that contributed to his aspirations as a modernizer and as a singular iconoclast.

Those aspirations had been nurtured for decades, initially in Salonika, where in 1880 or 1881 Mustafa Kemal was born and raised, the fourth child of a young, blonde, deeply religious bride and a former soldier, customs inspector, and timber merchant. Salonika was then a thriving commercial port controlled by Turks, heavily populated by Jews, and hosting a smaller community of Greeks.[3] Urbane, comparatively cultured, Salonika had been in Ottoman hands for centuries. It was a much more cosmopolitan and European city than other Turkish-speaking sectors of the empire. When Kemal was an older teenager, in military school, he often returned home to Salonika to enjoy its European quarter, with its unveiled women, its Greek bistros, and the easy availability of liquor.

Kemal's father, having made little success of his timber business and a subsequent investment in the salt trade, became a heavy drinker and then died of intestinal tuberculosis when Kemal was about seven. He was then raised by his young mother in circumstances that his psychobiographers say gave rise to "a precocious and vulnerable sense of autonomy . . . supported by fantasies of omnipotence."[4] Since the children who had preceded Kemal in the family had all died young, Kemal both embodied the hopes of his bereaved and now widowed mother and became the repository of her belief (like that of Lee's mother) that he was special and destined for greatness.

Equally important for Turkey's future, Salonika had Westernized secular schools, not just religious Muslim madrassas. The youthful Kemal was able to enroll at his father's behest in one of those secular institutions for his primary schooling. It was run by a controversial man with advanced ideas about learning and an affinity for discipline and the military calling. His father's death compelled Kemal and his family to interrupt this primary schooling and to leave Salonika for a few years to reside on a relative's farm. But Kemal, at least, returned to Salonika for instruction in a secular secondary school, taking up residence with an aunt. Kemal thus avoided the more usual training for young men in a religious establishment attached to a mosque. When he was about twelve, the self-motivated Kemal shifted from the secular stream of schooling to a military preparatory academy, apparently being attracted by the glamour of military dress, by some identification with his late father, and certainly by a feeling of rebellion against his religious mother.

It was at the military school in Salonika, where the young Mustapha excelled in mathematics and other subjects, that he received from a teacher the second name Kemal, meaning "perfection." In 1895, having successfully completed this first phase of his education by age fourteen, Kemal entered a military school in Monastir, now a predominantly Slavic city in the Republic of Macedonia and then on an outer edge of the Ottoman empire. His contemporaries knew him at this stage as a leader, and as someone who regarded himself as more important and more gifted than his peers. He began learning French outside of his regular studies.

In 1899, during a period of great turmoil within the Ottoman domain, Kemal completed his training at Monastir and entered the empire's main war college in Istanbul. There he performed well, ranking eighth of 459 students in his third year despite multiple and highly developed extracurricular relationships with women. Napoleon's exploits interested him, although he later praised Tamerlane more. In Istanbul, Kemal became more politically aroused than earlier, and more concerned about the authoritarian tendencies of Sultan Abdulhamid II.

Kemal was twenty-one when he was commissioned as a second lieutenant and promoted to the army staff college, also in Istanbul. In 1905, he graduated from the college, fifth in a class of fifty-seven. He became a captain and, with his military friends and housemates in Istanbul, continued to complain about the Sultan's rule. Kemal even created a handwritten newspaper to communicate the evils of the sultanate to other cadets.[5] After an informer was inserted into their milieu, Kemal and his close friends were arrested and imprisoned. But instead of being dismissed, they were all punished by being dispatched to remote outposts of the empire.

Kemal was banished to Damascus. He did not enjoy his Arab surroundings. Nor did he admire the pervasive corruption of the scruffy Ottoman army in the region. Indeed, his actual military duties were never heavy, leaving him ample time to form a subversive Society for the Fatherland and Freedom and to agitate quietly among his colleagues against the Sultan.

In 1907, such activities having gone undiscovered, Kemal was rehabilitated and sent home to Salonika to join the general staff of the army.

By this time, dissidents, some of whom were senior officers, permeated the Ottoman army. The Committee of Union and Progress (CUP) was the organization to which most of the Sultan's military opponents belonged, and Salonika was its central hotbed. The officers opposed to the Sultan's misrule railed against corruption and a lack of democracy within the army and the empire. They sought a restoration of the liberal Ottoman constitution of 1876. In Salonika, Kemal joined the local branch of the CUP on the eve of major battles in Macedonia between forces loyal to the Sultan and the CUP.[6] The Sultan capitulated in 1908, bringing back the parliament and constitution that he had dismissed in 1877. The Young Turks, as the "scientist" CUP conspirators were known, emerged as the leaders of the movement and, in effect, of the empire. At their head was the overbearing Enver Pasha, whom Kemal distrusted and who was to lead the empire into World War I on the side of Germany.

Kemal played a very minor role in these tumultuous events, partially because Enver, an ascetic, disliked Kemal's playboy manners and affectations. Other members of the CUP resented Kemal's critique of Enver as an indifferent and uncommitted reformer. In retaliation, the CUP sent Kemal into exile. He went to Libya as its representative. There the Sanusi dervish religious family was leading a revolt against Ottoman rule, and Kemal ostensibly was to report on the troubles. In Tripoli, Kemal managed by force of will first to assume control of the local Ottoman command and then to overcome indigenous religious disaffections by long, courageous discussions in the courtyard of a mosque.[7]

Returned in triumph to Salonika, Kemal soon served as chief of staff when the Third Army marched in 1909 on Istanbul as a strike force and deposed Abdulhamid II. The Sultan was replaced by his young brother Mehmed VI, and real power passed to the CUP, led by Enver. But Kemal took no leading role. He urged the army to stay out of politics and himself focused on his military career. He translated German army manuals into Ottoman Turkish, diligently trained army recruits, put down an uprising of Albanians, and attempted to hector and to nudge his superiors into improving their military techniques. None of these activities endeared him to those who could promote him, and Kemal remained a lowly captain despite his evident successes in Tripoli and Istanbul.

In 1913, as a result of the empire's major losses to Bulgaria and Greece in the first Balkan War, Enver led a brutal coup against the Sultan's government and managed to push back the invaders from the gates of Istanbul. Thence, Enver led the Ottomans in their reconquest of a slice of Thrace during the second Balkan War. Kemal had opposed the coup and remained publicly hostile to Enver. Thus, as Enver became a virtual dictator in 1914 and 1915, Kemal was exiled again as a military attaché in the Ottoman embassy in Sofia.

Only a Single Leader Would Do

In Sofia he enjoyed a constant social round, as befitted his position. He was surrounded by the onrush of Westernization that was engulfing the city as it emerged from its long thralldom to Istanbul and Ottoman suzerainty. Naturally, the Bulgarians were looking westward, and modernizing their city as rapidly as possible. Muslims, even Turkish speakers, were throwing off the veil. It was in Sofia, too, that Kemal adopted the Western hat in preference to the Ottoman kalpak. Kemal took part in all of this fervor but also kept a close watch on Enver and the CUP in Istanbul. He was alarmed by the alignment of what was left of the empire with the Germans, partially as a counter to Russian influence, and powerlessly opposed Enver's decision to put the Ottoman forces under the command of a German general. Kemal and many others knew that a wider war was coming; he was convinced that the Germans could not win the ensuing conflict. Allied to Germany, the Turkish enterprise would be destroyed. If not destroyed, it would be ruled by Germany. Kemal was despondent.

Often, Kemal was prescient, being a keen judge of shifting international challenges and opportunities. When World War I broke out, the Ottomans were not ready. Enver's fatal adventurism, first against the Russians in the Black Sea and then in Turkey's far east, brought a declaration of war by Russia against the Ottomans, and that in turn triggered a secret Ottoman-German alliance that Enver had earlier arranged. Kemal was finally recalled to Istanbul, and then sent on, fortunately, to take an obscure divisional command on the Gallipoli Peninsula under ostensible German command. The neglected, outspoken, irascible critic was now in a position, so Enver and the general staff may have thought, to be buried and forgotten in the onrush of battle. Instead, the opening of hostilities by the Allies against the Ottomans was to transform Kemal and Turkey for all time.

For Kemal, Gallipoli was an obvious triumph. Yet, for him, the war for Turkish independence began with the exodus of German commanding officers and the peace concessions to the Allies in 1918. He was incensed at the vague and demeaning terms of the Mudros Armistice. He feared Britain's "covetous designs" and opposed demobilization and any real or implied derogations of sovereignty.[8] He also railed at the weakness of Sultan Mehmed VI's dealings with the Allies and at the undermining of potential sources of Turkish political strength.

Kemal's scheming for Turkish independence began in earnest in early 1919, when he was immured in Istanbul as a retired general. Then local Ottoman Greeks and Turks began fighting in Samsun along the southern littoral of the Black Sea; there were fears that soldiers from Greece might try to intervene. A small number of British troops were present, but Sultan Mehmed's court dispatched Kemal, with far-ranging powers, to quell the disturbances and to keep the peace throughout much of northern Anatolia. Just before he was setting off for Samsun, the Greeks, seeking to recreate a lost empire of Byzantium, invaded Izmir, ostensibly heaping yet further humiliation on a Turkey supine. Kemal could glimpse the shape and the cause of his life's mission.

Kemal sought to be the embryonic Turkey's savior. "A single act of defiance" against the Sultan or the Allies by a prominent individual would establish a significant claim to "charismatic authority."[9] Kemal, more than most others, including the Sultan and the remaining politicians in Istanbul, knew that Turkey might soon cease to exist except as a memory. His problem was how to exert himself—how to project himself as Turkey's combined Simon Bolivar and George Washington—and how to arouse tired and war-weary Turks throughout Anatolia to resist (as a few Turkish martyrs did when the Greeks landed at Izmir). Initially, he had the imprimatur of an official appointment, and military stature, but within weeks of Kemal's arrival in Samsun and his swift withdrawal into the Anatolian hinterland, agitating all the while for a new national spirit, the Sultan set about dismissing him. Kemal believed it prudent to resign his military commission.

He was now a civilian without rational legitimacy, but the character of his noble cause and his traditional and folkloric heroic legitimacy, plus his steadfast determination to liberate a discarded and plundered Turkey, led Kemal rapidly to gain adherents from among the remaining commanding generals and their divisions in Anatolia and from among the mayors and other civic leaders in nonoccupied Anatolia. Building upon early expressions of fealty, he swiftly seized the mantle of revolutionary leadership and, as the newly elected head of a Defense of Rights congress in eastern Anatolia, in mid-1919 he helped issue a guiding document that became known as the National Pact. It called for the preservation of the borders of the Turkish provinces of the defunct Empire, the creation of a provisional national government, the revocation of privileges ("capitulations") previously secured by minorities and Europeans within the Empire, and self-determination for Turks in line with President Wilson's Fourteen Points. A few months later, at a "national" congress, the Pact was endorsed and Kemal's leadership ratified. It was at this conclave, in

Sivas, that Kemal made it perfectly clear to his closest supporters that he would not and could not share his leadership. No great enterprise succeeded under multiple leaders. If Turkey were to be freed from the foreigners, only a single leader would do.[10]

By the end of 1919, Kemal had begun consolidating his hold on leadership from his new, essentially permanent, headquarters in Ankara. Early in the next year, he began sending irregulars against the French-occupied enclaves in southern Turkey, soon harassing them into withdrawing. The Italians, angry at the Greek advance, began working with Kemal. Britain, however, soon officially occupied Istanbul and set about arresting nationalists; it declared martial law throughout the city. Fortunately for Kemal, the stepped-up British activity in Istanbul initiated a pell-mell exodus of parliamentarians and others to Ankara, and a swelling of the resistance. The arrival of so many influential refugees also enabled Kemal to legalize his position (and to regain for him official standing) by holding elections and convening a Grand National Assembly in Ankara, which elected Kemal its leader. It also authorized a commission to write a new constitution, enacted in 1921.

Controlling and marshaling the hectic and unruly Assembly (Kemal later called it a "zoo") was one of the critical early tests of Kemal's leadership talents. Able at first to count on unswerving support from only a minority of its "obstinate and querulous" members, many of whom were suspicious of Kemal's ambitions and personal hegemony, Kemal was compelled to persuade, to cajole, and to dominate his critics and opponents. Daily, reports Kinross, the youthful-looking Kemal would go into the Assembly. He would sit down and take notes, then fix the legislators with a "cold stare" and address them with a "frankness and clarity that took them aback." They would heckle him. But "with complete self-possession" and some brief words, "he would silence their murmurs." He would articulate his ideas and demands. "The charm [his emotional intelligence] would begin to work, their voices to acclaim him. . . ."[11]

A Turkish observer noted his "histrionic ability," his satanic shrewdness, and his "cheap street-corner heroics." Although there were men in the Assembly who surpassed Kemal in intellect, culture, and education, none "could possibly cope with his vitality" and his uncanny ability to "illumine some obscure problem with a flash of inspired [visionary] clarity." To this same companion, Kemal confessed, too, that he preferred to dominate. "I want everyone to do as I wish and command," he said.[12]

Bold, intuitive, and purposeful, Kemal, alone among the plausible new Turkish leadership cadre, was able to articulate a vision of independence and resurgence, and to mobilize generals and peasants alike. By early 1921, Britain's leading diplomat in Istanbul concluded that it was "useless to regard Mustapha Kemal any longer as a brigand chief. Angora government has a tight grip on the whole of Asia Minor. . . ."[13]

Unlike Mandela, Khama, and Lee, it was not his physical stature that gave Kemal a towering position, for he was of medium height. Unusual for a Turk, however, he had piercing blue eyes and blonde hair. He was always described as "handsome."[14] Rather than stature, it was his conviction, his austere competence, his proven integrity as a commander in the field, his immense self-confidence, and his unsurpassed ability to embolden and to uplift followers that vaulted Kemal from tentative to acclaimed leadership. The partnership with Ismet, three years younger and a compatriot from military staff training and from the battles in the Caucasus near the end of World War I, was also crucial. At a time of considerable peril and despondency, Kemal (backed by Ismet) provided a way forward for all of Turkey.

Britain and the other Allies were determined to humble Turkey further and to forestall any nationalistic upsurge. Britain wanted to settle "the eastern question." In mid-1920, Britain and the other allies dictated a punitive Treaty of Sèvres and compelled the Sultan to sign it. All of eastern Thrace, including symbolically important Edirne, was given to Greece. Eight Turkish islands in the Aegean Sea were to become Greek. Izmir was to be administered by the Greeks and then, after five years, to join Greece. Italy was assigned the Turkish coast from south of Izmir to Adana. The French, despite their loss of interior cities to Kemal, would be the acknowledged rulers from Adana to Sivas, north of Aleppo. An independent Armenia would be established under American protection. The Kurds would become autonomous. All of the Arab lands (from Aleppo to Mosul) would be placed under French and British mandates. The Straits would be controlled internationally, as would Turkish finances.

As part of Britain's pressure on the Sultan, the Greeks were authorized to cross an existing demarcation line between the Izmiri Greek salient and the Turkish hinterland. Bursa, east of the Sea of Marmara, fell quickly to the Greek army. Edirne was also captured easily. The Sultan, hapless and without countervailing forces, signed the treaty. Kemal, in control in central Anatolia, astutely resisted requests to attack the Greek forces. Instead he captured the distant eastern flanks of Turkey, reestablishing the older borders and forcing the Armenians to capitulate. In early 1921, he and troops under his close colleague Ismet pushed the Greeks back toward Bursa. Three months later, Ismet again defeated the Greeks on the

Bursa front. "[You] have reversed the unhappy fate of the nation," Kemal telegraphed to Ismet. "The eye can also discern the horizon of a future for our people. . . ."[15] But the Greeks, now led in person by King Constantine, were determined to avenge centuries of thralldom to the Turks. Pressing what they thought were strategic advantages, the Greeks moved north toward Ankara; Kemal decided on an important tactical retreat. Then he persuaded the Assembly to give him dictatorial powers for three months from August 1921. Kemal declared his "unshakeable faith" that success would shortly be theirs.[16]

It was a profound testimony to Kemal's leadership abilities that his unshakeable faith was capable of mobilizing the people of central Anatolia to procure and to prepare supplies for the coming battles, and of mobilizing them to become crude transporters of materiel to the front. Kemal personally took charge, ordering every inch of ground to be defended. His tactics and determination, together with arms procured from the Russians, proved decisive; the Greeks were humbled at the three-week long battle of Sakarya. The Assembly made Kemal marshal of the army and proclaimed him Ghazi, or victor over the infidels.

A year later, after the armies of the new Grand National Assembly had overcome dissidents in eastern Anatolia and along the Black Sea coast, after Kemal had obtained fresh supplies of arms from France, Italy, and Bolshevik Russians, and finally after Kemal had further strengthened his command of the resistance through political maneuvering and consensus building within the Assembly, he believed that a conclusive offensive to drive the Greeks from Izmir and all of western Anatolia was in order. The Greek and Turkish armies each comprised about 200,000 men; they faced each other from the Sea of Marmara to the Aegean Sea. In late August and early September, 1922, Kemal, overruling his generals and combining military vision with practical skills "in timing [and] anticipation of enemy movements and dissimulation," drove his men 250 miles from a victorious engagement at Dumlupinar (half way between Ankara and Izmir) due westward to the shores of the Mediterranean Sea.[17] The Greeks retreated hastily all along the front. The war of independence, as it became known, was over within six successful days. But the Greek forces pillaged and burned villages and towns as they retreated, and it took Kemal another three days to secure Izmir. But then his forces, and marauding Turkish civilians, attacked Greeks and Armenian Christian civilians in the city before many could be evacuated by Allied fleets. The Armenian quarter was set alight and much of Izmir destroyed. Kemal blamed the assaults and demagogy on his chief subordinate in charge of liberating Izmir.

The Forced March to Modernity

The Turkish victory was complete. All of Anatolia was now dominated by Kemal and his resistance followers, especially after the Turkish army moved north and west toward Istanbul from Izmir. Given his and the Assembly's clear dominance, it was relatively easy in succeeding months to persuade the Allies to end the Greek occupation of eastern Thrace and to begin to put Istanbul under Turkish, rather than British, French, and Italian, authority.[18] These arrangements were secured by the Treaty of Lausanne in 1923, which recognized Turkey as an independent polity, fixed its frontiers, and specifically applied to the new state "civilized" principles and standards. Although the Straits were demilitarized, and custom duties were limited, Kemal's Turkey gained everything that it wanted, bar control over Mosul and Mosul's oil.[19] (Kemal refused then and later to go to war against Britain over Mosul; in 1926, Turkey ceded all claims over the Kurdish region of northern Iraq to the British-mandated country.) Turkey also conceded western Thrace to Greece despite a large Turkish population resident there. Subsequently, more than 1 million Greeks in eastern Thrace were exchanged for 380,000 Turks in Macedonia and Crete, the new inhabitants of eastern Thrace.

Kemal had won the war and had demonstrated his unquestioned, but still often challenged, leadership abilities. He was the savior, as he had long wanted to be, of the Turkish people. But there was a national identity, a national consciousness, and a physical nation to be rebuilt. "Half of Anatolia had been reduced to ruins."[20] The re-conquered mass of Asian Turkey was largely devastated by war. Anatolians were desperately poor. The merchant class had been Greek and Armenian, and they were gone. Skilled tradesmen were rare; shoemaking, tailoring, carpentering, tanning, smithing, and farriering—all essential technologies for a nation seeking modernity—traditionally had been occupations reserved for non-Muslims. Moreover, the Kurdish east was still largely estranged from much of the new nation-state. Kemal had by resolute military and diplomatic effort, and by assiduous massing of personal power, transformed an Ottoman debacle into a potential Turkish protorenaissance. Now his task as leader was to uplift the battered Turkish people within a new national political dispensation of his own imagination. He sponsored a "forced march to modernity."[21]

Kemal told the people that the new Turkey was plagued by "general ignorance"—a "disease" that, together with Anatolia's isolation, was detrimental to Turkey's advancement. Turks had to acquire scientific knowledge: "We will acquire knowledge and science . . . and . . . will stuff them into the head of every individual in the country." He also promised a social revolution—ridding Turkey of "irrational, useless and harmful doctrines and provisions. . . ."[22] Many, if not all, of Kemal's envisaged reforms had been suggested in print and in conversation years before by prominent novelists and coffee-house intellectuals. In some sense, Kemal invented no single reform, but he articulated and enacted them in ways that were bold, transformative, and always beyond that which had earlier been mused about and explored.

Kemal, authorized by the Assembly, first abolished the Sultanate. Kemal needed no rival seat of authority within his realm. Sultan Mehmed VI soon escaped from Istanbul on a British warship, bound for Malta, Mecca, and eventual exile in San Remo. "The Ottoman dynasty appropriated by force," Kemal later said, "the government of the Turks, and reigned over them for six centuries. Now the Turkish nation," he continued, "takes back its sovereignty."[23] Kemal next declared the caliphate vacant, and the Assembly appointed the deposed Sultan's heir as the new caliph. Subsequently, Kemal also rescinded the Ottoman ban on human representation in the form of heroic statues and photographs. That teaching was no longer relevant, since new nations needed heroes. "A nation which does not make pictures, a nation which does not make statues, a nation which does not practice science, such a nation . . . has no place on the highroad of civilization." Indeed, Kemal told one influential gathering that a devotion to Islam only reinforced Turkey's fundamental backwardness. His young wife, at his request, adopted riding breeches, with high boots and spurs, and a bright silk handkerchief over her hair as one prominent costume. Kemal promised to jump-start the economy and to create a materialist, not a traditional, Muslim state so as to accelerate Turkey's drive away from backwardness. He advocated improved education generally, and—anticipating later social theory—better schooling for women than for men because they had to train the children of the new nation to embrace modernity.

Kemal was in command, but he still thought it wise in 1923 to build support directly throughout the countryside. He toured western Anatolia, made controversial speeches, and met with an endless succession of what in a much later era would be termed focus groups. In his speeches he repudiated Pan-Islamism and Pan-Turanianism. He demanded that clerics give their sermons in Turkish, not in Arabic. In Adana, he advised the audience that Turks should "learn what needs to be learnt." The nation had "fallen behind" its more progressive rivals and enemies. Reason and the public interest would prevail, particularly Kemal declared, because those principles always conformed to Islam.[24]

After the Peace of Lausanne was ratified, Turkey became a republic, with Ankara as its capital. Kemal also formed the People's Party so that he could control it and through it manipulate the deliberations of the Assembly. By November 1923, Kemal, 42, was president of the republic, with almost unlimited powers. The Party discussed and debated legislation in its caucus. When decisions were reached, they were carried forward into an Assembly where nearly every seat was held by a People's Party representative. Kemal, having labored for four years under nominally democratic conditions, with a need to consult and to bargain, now could reign supreme, often with Ismet as his implementer and prime minister. He could at last begin to mold the Turkish nation definitively in accord with his own expansive and ambitious vision, and to march relentlessly toward a civilized modernity.

A break with the "superstitions" and instruments of ignorance embodied in Islam was essential. Muslims everywhere were "subject to the will and contempt" of rulers because the limited education that they had received almost everywhere prevented them from breaking their chains. Thus, it was critical in the new Turkey to cease stuffing young minds with "rusty, numbing, fanciful superfluities."[25] For Kemal in 1924, and in fact for many years before, "religious knowledge was useless in the new age." Whether or not other Turkish nationalists and resistance fighters believed in the same bold analyses—and Kemal was very likely well advanced in his thinking, compared with his compatriots—there was no broad agreement that Islam was holding Turks and other Muslims back from becoming "civilized." Indeed, Indian Muslim leaders were among those in worldwide Islam who urged Kemal and others to strengthen the caliphate and to extend its influence throughout the vast global Muslim religious domain.

Instead, the massive social revolution that Kemal and Ismet imposed on the peoples of the new Republic, and which created the Turkish nation, began in early 1924 with the abolition of the caliphate by the Assembly, acting according to Kemal's expressed preferences and somewhat as a result of the caliph's attempt to rebuff Kemal's grand design and dominance. But before the deed was consummated, as was usual for Kemal, he made sure that the abolition would not be opposed by his key military supporters and by the army generally. And then he made sure that the Assembly did his bidding for him, so ending the caliphate (and simultaneously ending any Ottoman pretensions to continued authority in the new Turkey) without the need to use personal fiat. (Some opponents wanted these decisions to be put to a national referendum, but Kemal waved such objections away.)

The dispatching of the caliph to Europe also meant the closure of madrassas, the religious schools that had trained many of Turkey's young people and that had prepared the clergy who so annoyed and displeased Kemal. Those religious schools could now be replaced by secular, Turkish-language institutions; the transmission of Islam's religious and cultural heritage within Turkey, the holdover of Ottoman misrule, would cease. So would the teaching of Arabic, which had been the primary medium of the madrassas. The new schooling system would be dominated from Ankara by a unified ministry, and hence Kemal would oversee the education of Turkey's young.

There were additional consequences for Turkey. The new government, a secular one, would itself rule on faith and morals. The religious courts were shut, transferring all rulings on canon law and on inheritance, marriage, divorce, and so on to the state. The state, alone, would employ clergy, for Kemal was sufficiently cautious not to abolish Islam as a state religion. In preference, he subordinated religious practice to state control in the interest of strengthening what he always called civilization. By design and implication, Kemal converted the Islamic foundations and endowments, with their considerable wealth, into state entities. He also approved lifting the national ban on the consumption of alcohol, which had hitherto been honored by him and many others only in the breach. The rupture with Islamic traditions and norms could not have been made more complete, especially symbolically.

Some years later, Kemal's break with the strictures of Islam became even more defiant. To the horror of pious Muslims, he erected or allowed to be erected statues of himself all over Turkey, the first in 1926 and many in succeeding years. The strength of the new order was represented by those graven images of man. They were bronze representations of secularism, but to many Turks in Istanbul, if not in Anatolia, they also signified personal rule and denoted a compelling military hero and leader who had severe authoritarian tendencies. Financed by public subscription for the most part, and sculpted by foreigners attracted to Turkey for the commissions involved, they were the final word in a sycophancy that gathered more and more force so long as Kemal lived.[26]

Kemal's government abolished Muslim brotherhoods and shrines to Muslim saints. "I cannot accept the presence in Turkey's civilized community of people primitive enough to seek material and spiritual benefits in the guidance of sheikhs," Kemal pronounced. All dervish lodges were closed; turbans and robes were restricted to Islamic officials. After all, said Kemal, "the nation had taken the final decision to adopt in essence and in form the life and the resources which contemporary civilization grants to all nations." [27]

Off with the Fez

Later, shortly after peremptorily divorcing his wife, Kemal, who often wore Panama hats, decided that Turkish men should no longer wear the fez. With greater accuracy, what Kemal demanded of all Turks was "civilized dress" in the European manner. In his eyes, European dress and European style headgear would destroy the distinctions of status which, in recent Ottoman times, had been graded by turbans, fezzes, and other head coverings. The turbans had been restricted by the sultans to clergy, the fez to civil and military officials (and later to the middle class), and something akin to the chapeau (beret) to infidels—non-Muslims. (The first two had no rim, so foreheads could easily touch the ground in canonical prayer.) To Kemal these "Oriental" marks were signs of backwardness and exoticism, and had to go.[28] Doing so would theoretically make Turks more equal, and drive them toward modernity, but it would also put the emancipated citizenry more under Kemal's control and authority.

Wherever he spoke to sizable crowds, Kemal urged followers to abandon baggy trousers in favor of slimmer European suits and trousers, thus saving great amounts of cloth. He also defended the shift from fez to hat by declaring that the nation would save money by not paying foreigners to make fezzes and turbans. (But Italians produced nearly all of the new hats, because Turkey lacked suitable factories or experience.) Kemal also wanted men to don proper Western shoes and boots and shirts and ties, and generally to take on "civilized" raiment. When he glimpsed men in a crowd wearing traditional clothing, he derided them. "Would a civilized man wear . . . peculiar clothes and invite people's laughter?" he always asked. "In order to see the jewel shine," he added, "one must get rid of the mud."[29] Subsequently, after visiting many cities and towns and giving this same advice, Kemal made hats—traditionally the mark of the infidel—compulsory for civil servants, decreeing that tails and top hats should be worn by officials and others on ceremonial occasions. A law in 1925 declared that "the hat is the common headgear of the Turkish people," and forbade "habits to the contrary."[30] Prosecutions and martial law, over hats, followed. Those who fought against the new head covering rules were charged with rebellion, and hundreds were sentenced to death. One opponent was hanged for denouncing this attempt to imitate Europeans.

Kemal was less forceful about women's clothing, but he urged women to show their faces to the world. "After having inspired their sacred morality," Kemal declared, "explaining our national ethics to them, and furnishing their minds with enlightenment and purity, there will be no more need for selfishness. Let them show their faces to the world, and let them be able to view the world. . . ." He added: "Don't be afraid. Change is essential, so much so that, if need be, we are prepared to sacrifice lives for its sake."[31] That was a signal to throw off the veil, hitherto a middle-class custom, and to drop the use of long head-scarves, drawn across faces in the presence of non-family men. The government ultimately banned headscarves in official premises, including schools. Black pinafores became the compulsory dress of both boys and girls in Turkish schools.

Kemal was determined to use his revolutionary power to secularize Turkey according to a deeply nourished personal vision. At the end of 1925, Turkey adopted the international Christian era and the twenty-four hour clock. Banished were the Muslim solar calendar and a system of counting hours from sunset.

In the next year the Assembly finally dropped all Muslim pretensions and enacted a civil code based on Swiss law to regulate personal status. It gave women significant rights, ended divorce at the husband's discretion (despite Kemal's previous use of this provision), and afforded women equal inheritance rights rather than the half of a man's share that they had previously enjoyed. Women could now strive for emancipation, and many in the late 1920s became school teachers for the first time, entered medicine and the law, and even became civil servants. The new law no longer recognized polygamous marriages.

In 1925, Kemal also founded a law school in Ankara, the nucleus of the later Ankara University. His message was clear then, and throughout the burst of prolific modernization that he forcibly imposed on Turkey in the 1920s. "The civilized world is far ahead of us. We have no choice but to catch up . . . Uncivilized persons are doomed to be trodden under the feet of civilized people." [32] Much later, Kemal's appointee transformed the older and more established Istanbul University, attracting a number of prominent German Jewish academics fleeing from the Nazis. They helped to make that university a genuine center of learning, especially after its faculty of theology, critical and central under the Ottomans, was abolished.[33]

In order to protect his social revolution from criticism and potential undermining, Kemal authorized the government to establish its own newspapers in Ankara and Istanbul at the same time as he warned journalists, and the proprietors of other media outlets throughout the Republic, to focus on the project of nationhood, as directed by him, and not on critiques that would detract from his new civilizing enterprise. As United States Ambassador Joseph Grew commented in 1928, "free speech and an articulate opposition are nonexistent."[34] To some extent, marshaling the press and directing the media in such a manner meant that critiques of Kemal's drive against Islam could be muted and controlled. It also meant that alarm among his critics at the growing corruption in the new Turkey could be dampened, even if accusations about converting Greek and Armenian property illegally and otherwise taking unfair advantage of the new hegemonic dispensations were not necessarily directed at Kemal so much as at his followers. Indeed, flagrant cases of corruption were prosecuted, including at least one against a cabinet minister.[35]

The larger question in these early and succeeding months of the Republic concerned Kemal as an authoritarian. Since his party controlled the Assembly, and he controlled the Party, Turkey from 1923 functioned in practice as a one-party state. Yet, so educationally limited were the majority of the people of the country, and so complete was Kemal's influence nationally and within the Party and the Assembly, that his opponents were never able to mount a successful campaign against Kemal's usurpation of or side-stepping of democracy. "To be in the same city with him was to know ecstatic psychological intoxication."[36]

The leaders of the opposition came from within the resistance movement; nearly all were his former companions in arms, even previous prime ministers (but not Ismet) appointed by him. They resented being bypassed and overlooked. They resented that critical decisions were less and less debated and more and more imposed (even if ratified democratically by a captive legislature). In late 1924, they even formed an opposition political party that differed with Kemal not over secularization and religion, but primarily over the extent of his personal rule. But Kemal was astute in building support within the People's Party and among his closest legion of new supporters. He also ensured, by skillful attention to promotions and perquisites, that the chief officers of the army remained loyal. Indeed, Kemal managed over time to remove the army from the political arena. He also dissolved the opposition Progressive Republican Party, although its members remained as independents within the Assembly.

The Commanding Vision

Kemal's commanding vision was growing in ambition and aspiration. Others—mostly his former comrades in arms—might demand democracy, but Kemal was more determined than ever to rule Turkey alone, and without competition or loud objections. A political struggle was permissible only when Turkey became more civilized and its politicians more responsible. In other words, Kemal had become—at least in his own eyes—the embodiment of a responsible, benevolent, Platonic ruler. (For all his peremptory ways, and his fondness for tobacco, coffee, good food, and ample drink, Kemal lived on his modest presidential salary and paid for his comforts and staff out of that salary. He was not subsidized lavishly by the state.) No ordinary opponents could compete, nor could they effectively oppose a design which was bold, immense, far-reaching, transformational, and all encompassing. Indeed, as Mango remarks, the options for Kemal's opponents were stark: "participation in the Kemalist regime, withdrawal from politics or conspiracy."[37]

Some indeed became conspiratorial and ineptly plotted his assassination. Those few plotters were discovered and ultimately hanged. For Kemal, the discovery confirmed his immortality. But the fact of the conspiracy in 1926 created a vast web of fabricated guilt by association, purges of political opponents, and the continued employment until 1927 of so-called Independence Tribunals. These were nonjudicial bodies of a few close supporters of Kemal who had been empowered during the resistance movement years to try and summarily to convict and punish alleged miscreants and supposed traitors. There were no appeals from their ad hoc verdicts, most of which were arrived at by hearsay or tainted reports. Kemal considered the tribunals important to his cause of modernization and anointed rule, but they were hardly civilized, and many innocent persons were hanged or imprisoned by the several tribunals that roved across Turkey, especially after the assassination plot had been discovered.

Subsequently, after a short-lived Kurdish rebellion in southeastern Turkey had been repressed and its leaders hanged, Kemal decided to imprison journalists who had failed to be critical of Kurds. The newsmen were accused of attacking the government "unfairly and unnecessarily," and thus of contributing to the rebellion.[38] Kemal also steadfastly preferred absolute denial, refusing to accept or countenance the existence of a separate people called Kurds. He insisted throughout on a single Turkish nation embodying Turkish language and a reformed Turkish culture. Breaking profoundly with Ottoman notions of minority home rule and legal status, all residents of Kemal's Turkey were Turks, whatever their race and religion.[39] His government indeed refused to permit the use of the label Kurd (or Laz or Circassian) to denote minorities. Officially, the new Turkish nation had no minorities. It also enacted a draconian Maintenance of Order law, in effect to impose martial law on the Kurdish areas and to contain opponents elsewhere.

By the end of 1927, Kemal was in complete command of the Republic that he had created, and of its destiny. He choose all of the parliamentary candidates in the elections of that year; they were all elected, of course, and the Assembly was purged (appropriately from his point of view) of opponents. Having a legislature accustomed to rubber stamping Kemal's modernization edicts made it easy to complete a further rush of reforms—a completion of the modernization project that Kemal had envisaged even before World War I and had begun to develop in the early 1920s. In 1928, the Assembly removed all references to Islam from the country's constitution. Islam ceased to be the official religion. All oaths of office were secularized. Even the call to prayer shifted from Arabic to Turkish in the 1930s, and the Qur'an was "translated" (a heresy) into Turkish from Arabic so that ordinary Turks could read it. But the canonical language of prayer still remained Arabic.

As Kemal told a visiting British writer, "I have no religion, and at times I wish all religions at the bottom of the sea. He is a weak ruler who needs religion to uphold his government. . . . My people are going to learn the principles of democracy, the dictates of truth and the teachings of science. Superstition must go. . . ." He was pleased to permit Turks to worship as they would and to follow their own consciences, providing that doing so did not interfere with "sane reason" or the "liberty of his fellow-men."[40] But Friday as a day of national rest was replaced by Sunday, and the great basilica of St. Sophia, a mosque since 1453, became a secular museum in 1935.

Shortly after discarding Islam, Kemal shifted Turkey from the use of Arabic numerals to international ordinals. Next, the Arabic script for the writing of Turkish was abandoned, to be replaced by the Latin script, thus bringing the new Turkey even closer to the West. After a committee had provided recommendations and Kemal had altered several of them, Turkish phonetics were henceforth derived from the educated speech of Istanbul (which was close to Kemal's native Balkan version) and were translated into Latin script, with added and complicated diacritical marks to indicate sounds in Turkish that could not be represented by Latin letters. This reform was greatly resented by adult Turks, especially the Ottoman educated (most Turks were illiterate), but Kemal was right: henceforth Turks found it easier to learn the languages of the West, and, for the young, learning their own language was easier. The high Ottoman tongue, which Kemal himself used, gradually fell into disuse. National schools were subsequently opened throughout the nation to teach reading and writing and to provide diplomas of literacy as a compelling part of Kemal's grand national educational advance. Later, he advocated the Turkification of technical terms, replacing Arabic loan words. He and his closest associates spent hours coining new terms and later foisting them on an unsuspecting public. The Turkish Linguistic Society, created by Kemal, was given the task of simplifying and purifying the language by bringing the written form closer to spoken Turkish, and by removing archaic usages. He also sponsored a grand and ultimately unfulfilled project to write a new history of the world glorifying Turkish accomplishments from as far back as Akkadian and Hittite times. School histories were also produced under Kemal's personal aegis. In the process of these many changes, Turkish became more and more distant from its roots in Persian and Arabic, and ties to the Orient were lost—just as Kemal wanted.

Becoming Ataturk

Kemal subsequently demanded the writing of a civics manual to glorify the new nation and its many humanistic and linguistic accomplishments. The manual and other new works and declarations elevated Turkish religious practice over Islam, an Arab inspiration, and declared that Muslim notions of worship were manifestations of illicit Arab nationalism. Turkish nationalism should be more highly valued, hence his decision to repatriate religion to Turkey.

In the 1930s, Kemal insisted that all Turkish citizens, many of whom had used only one name for themselves, acquire surnames. Other traditional appellations and titles, such as Pasha, Bey, Effendi, and Hanim, were banned. Again, modernization and a sense of equalization were the excuses. So was practicality; the Turkish population was growing, and identifying individuals by their places of birth or their father's forename was inefficient. Kemal gave Ismet the surname Inonu, after his great victory. Kemal had to take a surname for himself, too, and chose Ataturk (father or progenitor of the Turks). This was fitting for the childless leader and for his aspirations, and capped his grand design for the Republic.

Kemal's social reforms were to continue for several more years. But he also was an earnest and far-seeing economic pioneer. As successfully as he had used the Ottoman-derived telegraph system to mobilize his forces against internal rebels and Greeks during the height of the resistance, so he and Ismet demanded new roads and railways to connect the Anatolian hinterland with its new central hub, and to permit the growth of commerce that would naturally follow. The dirt road network almost doubled from the 1920s to the late 1930s. A major new rail line connected Ankara to Sivas and Erzurum, begun in 1925 and completed in 1930. Other lines followed, using state funds. In addition to opening up commercial possibilities, the new rail lines to the east and southeast enabled the Turkish government to exert tighter control over the still fractious Kurds and other dissidents.

Building on his youthful experience in Macedonia, Kemal enthusiastically drained marshes, planted trees and crops, and started his own demonstration model farms to embolden others and to provide work and aspirations for the poor peasants of Anatolia. He frequently drove a tractor around one of his farms, always wearing a Panama hat. Kemal ordered the formation of agricultural credit cooperatives in order to edge out the grip of usurious middlemen on poor farmers and landholders. In order to provide additional developmental incentives, he avoiding conscripting or collectivizing the peasants. Indeed, Kemal ordered the abolition of the tithes that had traditionally burdened peasants under Ottoman rule. However, new taxes had to be imposed—on land and cattle, and for the construction of roads and bridges. So the peasants at the onset of the Great Depression were no better off.[41] Even so, urban consumers were in effect taxed more than before through purchases from the state monopolies, and rural dwellers benefited from this hidden taxation shift from the countryside to the city.

By the time that the worldwide depression reached Turkey, in 1930, the new Republic remained dependent on the export of a handful of primary products, predominantly tobacco and dried fruit, and could hardly pay its way. There was still no significant private economic sector. Nor was there an industrial base.[42] Because Turkey imported nearly all of its cloth, cement, iron, steel, and other manufactured items from the West, the Republic under Kemal consistently ran large trade deficits amounting to nearly a quarter of all external trade. Consequently, the immiseration of peasants and smallholders grew significantly as the Depression halved Turkey's earnings, and the Republic, a few years into the Depression, could no longer afford critical imports. Kemal blamed "the influence of superstitions" rather than his policies or the world economy for the nation's problems.[43]

Even so, Kemal was sufficiently astute politically to appreciate that the real economic insecurities of the new state and an increasing discontent among the bulk of the people of Turkey meant that he had to provide at least the appearance of greater participation and greater voice. So he gathered a number of loyal adherents, asked them to assemble an opposition political movement, himself chose the Free Republican Party name for it, and carefully selected members to be transferred to it from his own

Party's Assembly members. In the 1930 local elections, the Free Republicans were even permitted to win a handful of seats. More significantly, for the first time in Turkish elections, voters put marks directly beside the names of individual candidates, not members of electoral colleges. Women were also allowed to vote and to be candidates for the first time, as they also were in the 1935 parliamentary poll. Eighteen women were chosen (along with sixteen male independents). However much Kemal's democratic reforms were tame, and his emancipation of women tentative, these initiatives did commence major institutional modernizations for Turkey. They were completed, admittedly, only well after his death. Ambassador Grew also suggested that the new party "had become a clinical thermometer for taking the political temperature of the country and there could be no doubt of the fever which it registered."[44]

Yet, the Free Republican Party existed only briefly, and by 1931, Turkey was once again controlled by a single party, headed by Kemal. He called it a "wholly democratic" and populist institution, but simultaneously dissolved all competing independent societies, even the Freemasons. The Republican People's Party was now dedicated to republicanism, nationalism, populism, statism, secularism, and revolutionary reform—all as defined by Kemal's shifting and conceptualizing mind. At the same time that he refused to be declared "president for life," he saw the Party's objective as the transfer into Turkey of civilizing ideas, and not the running of a state that was still to be governed by bureaucrats. In other words, Kemal understood the importance for his young republic of the trappings and forms of democracy, providing that the country was disciplined (by him) and pragmatic (according to his notions of practicality.) He rejected, and was apparently untempted by, the authoritarian tendencies of Mussolini and Hitler's Europe during the same period.

Kemal's ideas on modernization extended to the legal field. Just as he Westernized domestic and civil law, so he introduced the German commercial code and Swiss-type laws on bankruptcy. Without a solid contractual system, he knew, Turkish entrepreneurs would continue to be insecure as they sought to displace the Christian merchants who had earlier provided credit and the commercial backbone of Ottoman business. The new penal code was modeled on an Italian design.

Kemal patronized Western music and the arts, installing Paul Hindemith as the dean of the state musical conservatory and national music composer, and favoring new Turkish operas combining Anatolian folk melodies with Western themes. He tried to impress the visiting shah of Iran with Turkey's first operatic production; more significantly, he personally involved himself in every aspect of its rehearsal and presentation.

Yet, for all his desire to force Turks to face outward, and to embrace Western ideas, languages, legal codes, dress, and pursuits, Kemal also felt that the humanistic and other arts had to serve the cause of national progress. They had to glorify his revolution and to advance the cause of Turkey, if in Western forms.[45]

Despite Turkey's intense poverty and its palpable bureaucratic and technological weaknesses, Kemal was an economic nationalizer who rejected open economic pursuits. He believed that the modernization of Turkey could best be managed by the state through a form of state capitalism later influenced strongly by Soviet planning modes. "The state must take charge of the national economy," he said.[46] At his prompting, the Turkish state thus assumed control over all foreign-owned utilities, and railway construction. The state created banks. It took over the formerly French-run tobacco monopoly, and set up a chain of mills to produce sugar for the Turkish population. But it never collectivized agriculture or interfered with small-scale private enterprise. Indeed, Kemal's state largely neglected and failed to motivate farmers; Turkey's agricultural production stagnated, and the social and economic problem of a landless peasantry, a holdover from Ottoman times, was never addressed.

The New Turkey

The new Turkey instead sponsored textile, silk, paper and cellulose, glass, chinaware, cement, and even steel factories, and encouraged local suppliers and contractors—the nucleus of an indigenous entrepreneurial class. Kemal protected their infant industries, and, in very difficult economic times, made recovery more difficult by trimming budgets and behaving with increasing degrees of autarchy. Foreign investors naturally fled, and injections of new foreign direct investment, desperately needed by Turkey, proved scarce. Additionally, new Turkish policies harassed the shipping trade in Istanbul, driving bunkering, chandlering, and other services to Greece, and depriving the new Turkey of sorely needed revenues.

The thorough modernization of Turkey was to take many decades. Nevertheless, Kemal provided the inspiration, the drive, and the foundations on which a truly progressive Turkey ultimately emerged, admittedly well after his death. Likewise, the political and legal institutions of the modern state only came later, but were stimulated and foreshadowed by Kemal in ways that guided and emboldened his successors. Throughout, he could not have made the gains for Turkey that he did, or presided so singularly over the country's destiny, without the astute partnership that he forged with Ismet, his understated but worthy and accomplished partner. It was to Ismet, a superb leadership choice, that Kemal delegated the details of implementing the grand vision. And it was to Ismet that Kemal transferred responsibility for ensuring that the grand civilizing design that Kemal pressed on Turks and Turkey actually worked and succeeded.

As his biographer writes, if Kemal were the designer and motivator of revolutionary change, Ismet was "the patient but disciplined builder and controller of the reforms." Furthermore, Ismet translated the Kemalist visions into reality and saw that they took root.[47] He was the man of detail, Kemal the man of drama. Ismet was deliberate, punctual, a family man, and always sober—the opposite of Kemal. Ismet imposed some order on Kemal's decisions, and opposed Kemal's less morally or politically acceptable shortcuts. Their differences were often stylistic: Ataturk saw the state as an instrument for massive and persistent social change, whereas Ismet preferred limited social engineering. He was much more cautious and thorough than Kemal, in some ways more Western and more sophisticated.

Kemal was aggressive inside Turkey, insistent always on uplifting the new country and its people by their bootstraps, whatever the potential resistance and political dislocations. But he was never ambitious internationally. He never chose to promote Kemalism abroad. He never sought to regain lost territories, particularly his birthplace in Macedonia, or any Arab or Kurdish lands—excepting the special case of Hatay—beyond the national borders. He was friendly and not at all vengeful to the Greeks, with whom Turkey signed a treaty of friendship in 1930. He sought peace in the Balkans, and concluded a major amity pact with Yugoslavia and Rumania in 1934. Three years later, Turkey concluded similar nonaggression pacts with Iraq, Iran, and Afghanistan. In foreign affairs more generally, largely guided by Ismet, Kemal was also content to pursue a lone, somewhat isolated trajectory for Turkey. He observed the accumulations of personal power in Italy, Germany, and the Soviet Union, but eschewed alliances. He preferred neutrality in foreign affairs, being determined primarily to maintain Turkey's integrity and independence. (Nevertheless, he detested Mussolini, thinking him but a caricature of a military leader, believed Hitler "mad," and detested communism.) His overriding ambition was to restore Turkey, not to gain international acclaim or global prominence for himself.

Unlike so many other dominant leaders and consummate nation builders, Kemal did not seek to create a personal dynasty. Kemal rejected the methods and pretensions, for example, of Reza Khan, usurping shah of neighboring Iran. Kemal had no real family, despite his many adopted daughters and sons, his wife, his several lovers, and so on. And he distributed no particular favors to them. Nor did he provide special sources of enrichment for his cronies, acolytes, and persons of sycophantic ilk. Turkey in his day was corrupt, but Kemal took little for himself and distributed patronage sparingly.

Moody, driven relentlessly by the grand design of the Turkish state and the Turkish renaissance, Kemal fluctuated between being (or appearing) gentle and shy and abrupt and aggressive. He was temperamental and emotional, pursuing objectives with "blind courage." Since he moved so swiftly, he hardly left time for his opponents to organize.[48] He ceaselessly devoted all of his energies to the realization of that one great burning ambition, "that the Turkish nation should with one blow be put ahead of all others."[49] In that quest, "I have succeeded," Kemal told a visiting journalist in 1936.[50] Comparing himself to Napoleon, Kemal told a European visitor that Napoleon "put ambition first," fighting for himself, not for "the cause." (He complained that Alexander also put himself ahead of his cause.) His European interlocutor commented favorably that "This power to drive right through a subject, to find the way out and take it, is one of the chief sources of his unique authority." She also said that "he never loses his head."[51] Kemal's pronounced narcissism (Volkan and Itzkowitz call it reparative narcissism rather than destructive narcissism) and increasing feelings of omnipotence never stood in the way of bettering, secularizing, and advancing the sense of self and emergence of Turks and the Turkish people.[52]

When Kemal (by then Ataturk) died young in 1938 from incessant chain-smoking and acute cirrhosis of the liver, his stature as an acclaimed leader, and the inspired manner in which he had led Turks to reclaim their national heritage, was evident. No one surpassed him as a visionary and as a transforming change agent. He articulated a grand design, mobilized all manner of Turks to follow him in pursuit of that overarching project, and employed reserves of legitimacy that came from his military exploits, the power of his new vision, and naked co-optive strength to transform the battered remnants of the Ottoman Empire into an effective and progressive Turkish state, eventually a nation.[53] He was ruthless and brave. Unlike other transformational nation-builders, however, Kemal was a successful organization man and bureaucrat. He was a careful tactician. Through Ismet, he ran a tightly controlled and reasonably efficient state. He painstakingly constructed a reliable political organization to support his reforms; he never moved far ahead of consensual backing in the Assembly and the army.[54] His emotional intelligence quotient was of high order; indeed, he used that gift to vault to power and to stay in power. Additionally and powerfully, he was a consummate communicator and publicist. From the aftermath of Gallipoli, when he used the press to trumpet his achievements, through the months of resistance when he bombarded Allied embassies and the sultanate with popular voices favoring his leadership and his vision of the new Turkey, Kemal used traditional and Western rhetoric and Western techniques to help gain his political objectives. As a British diplomat wrote to London during the Greek-Turkish war of 1921, Kemal's speeches "show considerable skill in handling people and situations. He is spectacular and domineering, but there is no reason to accuse him of lack of patriotism. . . ."[55] He used the Ottoman telegraph network to great effect, especially during the resistance war. He was endlessly resourceful, often commandeering the telegraph instruments himself and communicating feverishly with his commanders throughout Anatolia during critical moments of the war for independence. "I have never [seen] more efficient communications than I witnessed," an American correspondent wrote from Ankara.[56]

Kemal was a political realist. Yet his greatest gift to his people was the giving of pride and a sense of belonging to a great and worthy enterprise. If Kemal were less than formally democratic, and his actions shaped more by his military training and traditions than by any sense of obligation to take people's views into account, he also consulted and instructed and took his message to the Turkish hinterland on innumerable occasions. He behaved authoritatively without intending to be autocratic. "Few political transformations," Rustow concludes, "of such magnitude have been accomplished at such modest cost in lives [a few hundred]."[57] He had a strong sense of self and self-worth, was largely honest intellectually, and displayed integrity in public and with the public despite the frequent disarray and heavy drinking of his private life. He possessed abundant self-mastery and was surprisingly prudent.

Most of all, Turks could believe in Kemal. Turks did so because, like Lee and Khama, he delivered tangible results. Kemal did much more than talk about civilizing aspirations for Turkey. He demonstrated to intellectuals and peasants alike that he and they together would give birth to a new Turkey—that the decrepit Ottoman Empire would be succeeded at home by a powerful nation capable of taking its place honorably alongside the victorious nations of Europe. Vanquished the Ottomans may have been, but Kemal first persuaded his countrymen and then the rest of the world that no one could vanquish the spirit and determination of Turks in Turkey. As its self-anointed leader, Kemal the savior gave Turkey back to its people and his followers.

SEVEN

The Crisis of Contemporary Political Leadership

Across today's developing world there are too few leaders who can begin to match the attainments and achievements of Mandela, Khama, Lee, and Ataturk. Each was a consummate, dramatic, clear-sighted nation-builder. Each forged a new national identity, one by his dedication to inclusivity, two others by their systematic transformation of inherited cultures and religions, a fourth by plowing a distinctive political furrow that separated him and his countrymen from the poor choices of their neighbors. Each of the four gave his people a sense of pride and destiny—a profound sense of belonging to a transcending, exciting, worthy, all-consuming enterprise.

All four were supreme visionaries, with great abilities to articulate those transformational visions and to mobilize and embolden followers. They each had the organizational talents to produce positive results from their efforts at initiating good governance. They made a major difference during their periods of rule, and those differences today remain palpable and formative for and in their respective countries.

Three of these leaders stood squarely and firmly for integrity in every realm; two created beacons of noncorruption in the developing world. All of these four leaders, in their own individual ways, exhibited high orders of self-mastery and prudence, important navigating talents, and robust levels of analytical and emotional intelligence that enabled each of them, distinctively, to tap into and to enlarge the authentic needs of their followers. None was ostentatious. None abused authority for personal gain or to provide rents for cronies or followers. In President Kennedy's sense, all four were men of courage and integrity.

Khama and Mandela were thoroughly democratic in their ideals, their policies, and their actions. Both were intrinsically tolerant of opposition and dissent. They punctiliously observed the democratic norms, even within their ruling parties. Lee and Ataturk were more authoritarian in their actions and policies, but rarely in their overarching ideals and rhetoric. They certainly affirmed democracy and tolerance in the abstract, but in practice believed more in the rightness and appropriateness of their ends than they worried whether the means that they employed were just. Lee always argued, too, that the results that he and his policies delivered were the better test of democratic values than were quarrels about the kinds of instruments that he and his government employed. Ataturk, in an earlier age, believed simultaneously but confusingly in democratic pursuits and methods and in his role as the savior of the Turkish people. If the former blocked the latter, the latter always prevailed.

They each gained in legitimacy during the years of their respective reigns. One (Khama) came to power with a traditional legitimacy and converted that form of legitimacy into rational legitimacy and then into a sensitive all-encompassing "personal" legitimacy.[1] Another (Lee) built a special form of transformational appeal atop a rational legitimacy for which he fought hard. The other two were transformational leaders from the beginning; they had to strengthen their perceived legitimacy without losing their inspirational power. One did so by deepening his iconic and warming message of inclusivity, the other (Ataturk) by establishing order, decapitating the remnants of Ottoman religious and political authority, and building a successful, modernizing government. Along the way, each of these leaders fashioned and then strengthened the bonds of trust that were forged between themselves and their followers/citizens.

Each of our four exemplars was supremely self-confident, conscious that he carried the mantle of modernity for his people. Each was courageous when courage was required in battle, in prison, in exile, or in political combat against tightly arrayed and more powerful opponents. They were brave, too, in their iconoclastic choices, their decisions to undertake the unexpected—to behave independently of received or politically correct notions of how best to respond to challenges and crises.

In terms of tangible, material accomplishments, Lee and Khama transformed economically compromised embryonic colonies into prosperous, stable polities. They unquestionably delivered results. They performed for their peoples in ways that were unanticipated and that appropriately strengthened their ties of trust and bolstered their legitimacy among followers. Ataturk did so as well, but under much more straitened and complex circumstances. His great project of national renewal would have foundered on the shoals of secularism if he had not brought the promise of striking material progress and peace to a war-ravaged people scattered across a vast, scarred terrain. Mandela did not deliver material gains, only the promise of them. It was enough that he guided his people from the darkness of apartheid into the bright dawn of freedom—a freedom that he constructed without resort to vengeance.

The Founders and Their Successors

The probity of the founders is reflected in the continued reverence with which they and their accomplishments are held among the peoples of their countries and others. They continue to have followers, and debates on contemporary issues often refer back to principles enunciated or actions taken in formative times by the transformational quartet. But the transition from the founding leader to his successors has always been a fraught process, especially in new states where political institutions are nascent, political culture is in the process of being established, and a common vision is not always evident. Even where there is stability, newer leaders may pale by comparison, whether because of the transactional—seemingly mundane—nature of his or her responsibilities, or because of his or her own personal limitations.

Ataturk has had many successors. In today's very different Turkish Republic, political leaders are able to act independently of the Ataturkian model largely because the secular state, more powerful than before, was shaped and given confidence by the myriad ways in which Ataturk broke with the Ottoman legacy and offered Turkey a positive sense of itself. Modern political institutions gradually developed within the political culture that he and his close associates and engaged followers established, nurtured, and slowly matured. Perhaps paradoxically, the completion of Ataturk's model may have come in 2010, when the Turkish people ratified a new constitution that weakened military and judicial institutions, removed constraints on parliamentary supremacy, integrated minorities and minority languages, and—given a moderate Islamist hegemony—decoupled the state both from Ataturk and (paradoxically) from an Ataturkian brand of antagonism to fundamentalist versions of Islam.

Lee helped to guide Singapore through 2011, although Lee Hsien Loong, his son, held the official reins of power during much of the first decade of the twenty-first century.[2] Thus there has been no major deviation or shift from the Faustian model pioneered by Lee, only a tempering of its authoritarian qualities. Indeed, as a testament to extraordinary leadership, the political culture of the city-state, so methodically developed by Lee and his early compatriots, endures. Just as Ataturk gave Turkey an institutional basis for growth, so Lee and Khama fashioned their own national political cultures; those political cultures enabled institutions to emerge in positive ways that have hardly been duplicated in neighboring states or among their national peers. In Botswana, Khama's successors embraced and built upon his paradigm; in 2011, his eldest son carries on within that legacy, curtailed by well-functioning institutions and constrained by a unique Botswanan political ethos. In all of these situations, and in South Africa, good leaders consciously established effective, overtly democratic, political cultures. Those political cultural foundations enabled institutions to be constructed or, in South Africa's case, to be strengthened and modernized. Now those institutions can bear the full weight of modern competitive domestic politics, and actions of the leader matter much less.

Botswana arguably is the mainland African country where responsible leadership made an immense difference in terms of outcomes—in terms of the population's improved living standards, its citizens' sense of belonging to a larger and uplifting enterprise, and its population's general physical and psychological well-being. Seretse Khama set the direction and the tone, and also emphasized the importance of societal "tolerance" in a manner that has been equaled by only a very few other African and Asian leaders. He died young, before the political culture that he was shaping and the nation that he was creating were even fully formed. But his successor, Sir Ketumile Masire, had worked as closely with Khama as Ismet with Ataturk. Moreover, Masire could continue leading Botswana as Khama would have led it, and completed the task of nation-building as Khama would have wanted.

Masire was more than a carbon copy or a mere implementer of received notions. He conveyed a continuation of Khama's vision, as well as his own, and retained the leadership qualities of modesty, prudence, integrity, and self-mastery, and a focus on quality ends and good means, that were so integral to Khama's presidency. Masire was also strikingly nonostentatious and fiercely combative of corruption. Indeed, when Masire had become president and wealth from diamonds, tourism, and beef exports began to swell the national coffers, petty thievery escalated into a few major cases of serious peculation. Masire's answer was to demand powerful new legislation and to establish an anticorruption unit that tried to copy the methods and successes of the strong Hong Kong Colony example. He believed that the fact that his administration pursued serious allegations and hid nothing strengthened his presidency and matured the country.[3]

Masire recalls that as president he was often offered access to secret bank accounts in Switzerland. Locally, entrepreneurs tried to entangle him in various kinds of conflicts of interest by offering him shares in their businesses. But, as Masire says, "justice must not only be done but must be seen to be done."[4] Such pieties have often been uttered by African and Asian leaders. But in the case of the first, second, and third leaders of Botswana, and presumably the fourth, corruption was and is known to be harmful to successful leadership and to nation-building. Khama, Masire, and Festus Mogae, the third president, knew that if Botswana's leaders stayed clean, so would the country.

Mogae easily followed in his predecessors' path. By the time that he had become president in 1999, Botswana's democratic political culture had been solidly established. Its soaring economic growth trajectory had also become routine, thanks to the sensible management of diamond wealth. The political, economic, and social institutions that Khama had planted and Masire had nurtured were robust. Mogae could have undermined or dissipated the legacy that he had inherited, but he in fact extended the leadership attainments of the founder and of the second president by deepening the personification of the attributes that exemplify the best competencies of political leadership. The vision for Botswana had already been incorporated into the national political culture, and a nation (not just a state) had been created. But Mogae astutely was able to guide his country's responses to the new challenges—HIV/AIDS, South African independence, Zimbabwean weakness and collapse, and local economic diversification beyond beef, diamonds, and tourism—with skills similar to those earlier employed by Khama and Masire. After ten years of steady leadership, in 2009 he passed the still-unblemished mantle of national power to Ian Khama, Seretse Khama's eldest son. While being guided by his father and his country's established ethos, Ian Khama has since demonstrated his independence, internally by demanding heavy taxes on beer (a national and southern African staple) in order to curb alcoholism and by coping wisely with a massive strike by civil servants, and externally by branding Mugabe as the tyrant he is and by refusing to recognize Mugabe's usurpation of the Zimbabwean presidency. Few other new presidents, or older ones in office, have dared to be so politically incorrect or have been so willing to address heavy social issues within their countries. Botswana continues in 2011 to enjoy the unique African experience of gifted leadership for good, across four generations of presidents. None of Khama's African contemporaries left a legacy so vibrant, so firmly founded on the leadership competencies adumbrated at the beginning of this book.

South Africa's experience unfortunately stands in sharp contrast to what occurred in Turkey, Botswana, and Singapore. Thabo Mbeki and Jacob Zuma, Mandela's successors, quickly ignored the leadership lessons of his presidency and dissipated much of his legacy. For that reason, South Africa has increasingly come to exhibit the leadership insufficiencies of the rest of the continent. At their best, Mandela's successors, like most contemporary heads of state in the developing world, have demonstrated only a minimal vision of national renewal—one that little motivates their followers—so they by definition and by daily activity have behaved as transactional leaders only. They displayed little self-mastery, no particular prudence or proportionality and, along with many of their developing world contemporaries, seemed primarily preoccupied with preserving their own power and power bases. Zuma, as a model for other African heads of state, is tarred with allegations of corruption and promiscuity, is dependent on distributions of patronage, and is thus often focused on amassing party wealth and enabling close associates and their relatives to grow rich. As Archbishop Desmond Tutu told a university audience in 2011, discussing Zuma and his administration: "Our country with such tremendous potential is [being] dragged backwards and downwards by corruption, which in some instances, is quite blatant."[5]

No career illustrates that truth more than Mbeki's. Inheriting Mandela's position with the expectation that Mandela's favorable legacy would help him rule, he found his own presidency of South Africa soon overtaken by calamities, each of which betrayed counterfeit leadership and eroded trust, besmirched Mbeki's integrity and intellectual honesty, and quickly reduced his store of accumulated legitimacy.

Mbeki chose first to deny the importance of the HIV/AIDS epidemic, and then to attempt to deny that HIV/AIDS was a sexually transmitted disease. He followed hunches about other possible causes of the epidemic, and explored various alternative, mostly preposterous, remedies. Those actions severely delayed treatment possibilities for myriad sufferers. With regard to Zimbabwe, he tended to deny or to ignore the seriousness of Mugabe's crimes and the social and economic deterioration occurring in Zimbabwe and, partially, in his own country. Mbeki further condoned or overlooked mounting corruption scandals within his own party, even in the South African parliament.[6] He protected supporters and cronies, gave favorable treatment to backers, and attempted to centralize his control of the ruling party and the country in ways that eventually lost him the African National Congress Party's nomination for a renewed presidency. Beginning well, with Mandela's imprimatur, Mbeki's leadership deteriorated steadily. By the end of his tenure, in 2008, he could no longer claim many leadership competencies as his own.

Jacob Zuma, Mbeki's successor as South Africa's president, has focused far less on articulating a vision and more on making as few enemies as possible, on being thoroughly transactional, and on attempting as well as he can to redeem himself from his many personal missteps and failings. He has been content to create a competent cabinet of ministerial supporters, many of whom are relatively powerful, to cede remarkable levels of political prominence and authority to the ruling African National Congress party establishment and to its youth wing, and to attempt to tell every group, even disparate ones, what it wanted to hear. Hardly decisive, Zuma has not been uplifting, visionary, or transformational, but he has been blandly noncontroversial. Fortunately, South Africa has been a nation for a long time; Zuma does not have to engage in bootstrap nation-building. Nor does he need to perform as a navigator if he swims with sure strokes and stays afloat.

So far, so good. But South African political critics, and many foreign commentators, accuse Zuma of presiding over an "incapacitated" nation—a nation now without integrity, without vision, without a plan, and without any desire to retrieve and to build upon the Mandelan legacy.[7] Jobs are as scarce as ever. Nearly 40 percent of South Africans, and higher proportions of young people, remained out of work in 2011, with little hope of meaningful employment because the South African economy under Zuma is growing very slowly—at half the desired rate. Moreover, the wage gap between rich and poor blacks has widened considerably, exacerbated as it has been by rigid and constraining labor laws. Educational and medical outcomes have deteriorated, the country's economic competitiveness has plummeted, crime rates remain among the highest in the world, energy is short, foreign policy blunders are frequent, and Mandela's rainbow nation has become less coherent and less united than ever. Zuma is but another so-so developing world leader. His leadership competencies are few, especially as compared inevitably with those of Mandela.

Beyond South Africa, Botswana, Singapore, and modern Turkey, in much of Asia and Africa, there are many states with less than fully established institutions, incomplete political cultures, and an absence in large part of political leadership for good. Yet the quality of leadership still matters enormously, as it did when Mandela, Khama, Lee, and Ataturk emerged to build their nations. Indeed, echoing the theme of the opening chapters of this book, leadership actions condition the political cultures, democratic or not, that are developing in the states that are still to become nations. Only after today's leaders have helped to implant democratic political cultures can the institutions of democracy take root. Then the agency of leadership in the developing world will become less determinative, as it has in contemporary Botswana, Mauritius, and Singapore, in Turkey since the 1940s, and in Western Europe, the Americas, and the Caribbean.

The Crisis

That there are too few Mandelas, Khamas, and Lees today, and that only the successors to Seretse Khama build firmly upon his remarkable leadership legacy, is hardly unexpected. Not all of those who grasp the mantle of political leadership can be responsible and transformative. They come to power, after all, through mastering parliamentary parties, asserting themselves among fellow military officers, or being thrust forward by mass action and acclaim. But being complacent about such leadership deficits mistakenly ignores the difference that transformational leadership makes for human outcomes. The crisis of contemporary developing world leadership is the tragedy of low life expectancies, continued poverty, insufficient schooling, poor infrastructure, and stunted expectations.

Effective transformational leadership, if sustained as in Botswana and Singapore and if applied as in the few exceptional cases discussed below, makes a major difference to human happiness and to human spiritual as well as material attainments. The crisis persists, however. Too many of today's leaders in the developing world seek to uplift themselves, not their peoples. Moreover, the predominant transactional mode of leadership—that of Zuma and many others of his ilk—lacks vision and a concern for whole nations and thus condemns the peoples of the developing world to more limited and immiserated lives than they deserve. Even more tragically, a posse of remaining autocrats, presiding over countries from North Korea and Turkmenistan to Equatorial Guinea and Zimbabwe, do even less for their people, thus retarding the advancement of their citizen-helots. The despots' malign leadership deprives their peoples of freedom, yes, but also opportunity, health, schooling, and self-respect.

It is not that the developed world boasts no odious tyrants (Alexsandr G. Lukashenko still rules Belarus), but the crisis of leadership in the developing world is heightened by despotism being a prominent mode of leadership. Despots hold nations and peoples in thrall and perpetuate results for citizens that are more harmful than they would be under responsible, democratically run regimes. Despotisms are leadership experiments run amok.

Despots and Tyrants

In too many parts of the developing world, leadership has defaulted to Burns' "power wielders."[8] The peoples of a host of countries have rarely or never participated in governance as followers. They have instead been commanded by autocrats who prey on their own people and who use them as fodder for satisfying personal or coterie appetites for greed and power. The autocrats might hold mock elections and might even claim to speak on behalf of their disparate constituent components. But they regard followers as flock to be commanded, looted, and cheated.

In the failed and repressive near-failed states of the world—Afghanistan, Belarus, Burma, Cuba, Equatorial Guinea, Haiti, Iraq, Kazakhstan, Kyrgyzstan, North Korea, the (northern) Sudan, Syria, Tajikistan, Turkmenistan, Uzbekistan, Yemen, and Zimbabwe—leadership is "bad," irresponsible, corrupt, and so self-serving that whatever democratic political institutions once existed are decayed (if they ever flourished), and one man or a narrow elite rules despotically.[9] This mode of leadership is also called "counterfeit."[10]

There are many plausible examples of authoritarian, bad, irresponsible leadership—the antithesis of our ideal model—in the developing world. Four examples will have to suffice: Burma (Myanmar), Tunisia (until 2011), Uzbekistan, and Zimbabwe.

Burma has continued to wallow in a slough of self-serving, uncompromising autocracy and autarchy. Except for a very brief period in 1990, when Aung San Suu Kyi, leader of the forces of Burmese freedom, overwhelmingly won a popular election, since 1962 Burma has been ruled harshly by military officers. Ne Win, an unsmiling dictator, kept Burma under his rapacious thumb until 1988. Ever since, especially after the 1990 election, a shadowy group of officers have held Suu Kyi and her closest associates in prison or under house arrest, and the rest of the country in fear, hunger, and deepening poverty.

General Than Shwe has long been the big boss of the ruling junta. What we know of his methods—intimidation, assassination, imprisonment, collective punishment, arbitrary food scarcities, and an overall tight control of nearly everyone in Burma—suggests a leadership style and consequences for Burmese even more corrosive than life under Mugabe. A study of Than Shwe's Burma, confirmed by the United Nations special rapporteur's and many other investigations, documents "hundreds of extrajudicial killings . . . widespread and systematic use of rape and sexual violence . . . the forcible conscription of child soldiers, and the widespread use of forced labor." More than 2,000 political prisoners were inside the regime's jails in 2011. Torture was common. So was ethnic cleansing.[11] Than Shwe and his colleagues have tight links to China; the junta receives arms, funds, and moral support from the Chinese, who covet Burma's access to the warm waters of the Andaman Sea and the Bay of Bengal. China is building a port there, near the mouth of the Irrawaddy River, and constructing a pipeline to bring Middle Eastern oil swiftly to Yunnan and other parts of southwestern China. Certainly, the peoples of Burma chafe under the total loss of personal freedom, the economic penalties demanded by the regime, and all of the other exactions of the junta; they voted once for Suu Kyi and her party, and might again if ever given the chance.[12] They also protested violently in 2007, but were swiftly repressed.

Suu Kyi was an accidental leader after the failure of a 1988 student rebellion against military rule. But she led her supporters to victory at the polls in 1990, after which the junta returned Burma to the tight thralldom of 1962–1988. Nevertheless, even in the enforced shadows, Suu Kyi remained Burma's alternative leader. Maintaining the legitimacy of her leadership has not been without difficulty, however. Originally, and for many years, she possessed both rational legitimacy and a charismatic entitlement that came from three sources: her sudden and unexpected victory over the junta in 1990, the fact that she was the daughter of Burma's first postindependence military and civilian leader, and an inner radiance that gave her personal strength and confidence and that appeared transcendent and miraculous to her followers. In a Buddhist country, after decades of harsh military rule, she appeared to her people to possess the gift of grace, or divine favor. She herself believed that her inspirational instincts flowed directly from her followers: the love of her people, reciprocated by her, constituted charisma originally, and strengthened both her and her movement.[13] As one Western observer noted in the 1990s, watching Suu Kyi speak to a crowd of supporters outside her home, "She is open. She unlocks her heart for a thousand people. They unlock their hearts for her. Their faces shine as they listen, their eyes follow her, reverent and focused."[14]

Suu Kyi is or was a visionary, had a transformational message, and could inspire her people to believe in a worthy, redeeming, nation-remaking purpose. Suu Kyi possesses prudence, self-mastery, integrity, and well-tried patience. She is noncorrupt, moral, and dedicated to Burma's future and its freedom at some considerable cost to herself and her distant family. But in the years since 1990, her followers' trust in her has been buffeted by her inability to wreak change. She has not been able to work miracles for the Burmese or even to begin to moderate the vise-like control of the ruling junta. The junta has effectively dimmed the brightness of her leadership star.

Most Burmese can choose only between the long-deferred hopes of a Suu Kyi–engineered renaissance and the incessant reality of one of the world's most effectively repressive regimes. A controlled national election in late 2010 confirmed those choices and also confirmed Than Shwe and the junta's grip on power. Not only did officers from the junta (now mobilized as the Union Solidarity and Development Party) "win" nearly 77 percent of 330 parliamentary seats (in addition to the special seats, 25 percent of the total, reserved for other military), its hand-picked nominees for allied parties also triumphed easily, giving the ex-junta an overwhelming majority of 84 percent of the parliamentary representatives. But there was massive ballot-stuffing, fraudulent counting of the results, and a lack of transparency throughout. As the Shan Nationalities Democratic Party, victor in 57 constituencies, said afterwards, "We are well aware of the USDP's cheating, but we don't see any point in disputing the results of the election. If we sue them, we will have to pay one million kyat (US$1,150) for every constituency that they stole. We don't want to waste our time and money on this."[15] Some independents and a rump group from Suu Kyi's National League for Democracy were also permitted to win a sparse number of places, 16 in the case of the rump group; Suu Kyi had originally insisted that the main National League for Democracy should boycott the poll to protest how it was conducted and how its results would be manipulated and misused. She herself, 65, could not have contested a seat, anyway, because of a junta-enacted rule prohibiting Burmese married (or previously married) to foreigners from standing for parliament.

In 2011, Than Shwe and his designees continued to rule Burma with as much repression as before. Thein Sein, a leading recently retired officer, was Than Shwe's nominee for Myanmar's president, taking office in late March. Than Shwe also appointed all other government ministers and senior judges. He initiates the laws that the new parliament considers. Suu Kyi, receptive to a dialogue with Than Shwe and Thein Sein after being released from house arrest two days after the election, initially was regularly rebuffed by Than Shwe and Thein Sein, her overtures ignored and dismissed. Nevertheless, she professed to be content, and not anxious for regime change or to see the ruling generals prosecuted internationally. "I'm not very much concerned whether I personally come to power," she told an experienced visiting journalist, "but I am concerned about the power of the people." Real power was in their hands, she said.[16] Ignoring Suu Kyi, and having held and triumphantly "won" a long-prepared and carefully staged parliamentary poll, Burma's military rulers presumably believed that they could govern as before, but behind a fig leaf of electoral "success."

Farther west in Central Asia, there are three systematically repressive authoritarian regimes. Uzbekistan leads them all in rapacity and assaults on human rights. Islam A. Karimov, its maximum leader since 1991 and the end of the Cold War, controls everything in Uzbekistan through a strong-armed security service and a network of spies and informers. No human rights or civil liberties are respected. Free expression is banished. Islamists are hounded and imprisoned as threats to Karimov's total control. Torture, forced confessions, and trumped-up prosecutions for defaming the nation or Karimov are routine.[17] The judicial institution is a sham. In 2007, in the aftermath of the notorious Andijan atrocities, Uzbekistan was estimated to hold several thousand political prisoners. "Karimov is no more and no less than a straightforward authoritarian determined to maintain a firm grip on power and on the corrupt distribution of wealth within his cotton-growing country."[18]

In 2007, when Karimov's Uzbekistan was rated the eighth-most odious nation-state in the world, it suffered from low international ratings for human development (113 of 177); from low per capita gross national income ($500); from poor health indicators, such as infant mortality, maternal mortality, and life expectancy; from corruption (151 of 177); and from little economic freedom (132 of 177). All of these unfortunate outcomes testified to severe leadership failures and severe neglect and incompetence.[19] Clearly, Karimov's vision of Uzbekistan was narrow, focused on maintaining a personal and family hegemony over its 30 million inhabitants.

Tunisia, the tenth-worst nation-state before 2011, is much wealthier and more literate, with (in 2010) half the estimated level of corruption in Uzbekistan, but with an equally repressive leadership. In 2007, twenty years after a coup that brought Zine El Abidene Ben Ali to power, Tunisia held hundreds of political prisoners, the use of torture and assassination was routine, and the U.S. Department of State reported every manner of human rights violation. Tunisia was "intolerant of public criticism and used physical abuse, criminal investigations, [a military] court system, arbitrary arrests, residential restrictions, and travel controls . . . to discourage criticism. . . ."[20] The government also restricted freedom of assembly and association. The media were "asphyxiated," with self-censorship prevalent. Police numbers per capita were higher than those for Britain, France, and Germany. There were no independent judicial or legal institutions. Elections were always manipulated and essentially cosmetic. The state, in other words, existed to serve Ben Ali and his family, and to enrich them, as the student and worker riots of 2011 revealed. Tunisia, despite its relatively outdated benign reputation, its comparatively high per capita incomes, its proximity to and affinity with France, and its cosmopolitan outlook, was but another example of a leadership that preyed upon rather than ennobled and uplifted.[21]

When Ben Ali fled Tunisia in early 2011, he responded to escalating attacks on his family for its accumulation of wealth and its nepotism, mounting opposition to a palpable lack of free expression and free assembly, and the sense that he had lost the support of leading military officers. His legitimacy vanished in a flash. Although his leadership acumen had earlier helped to modernize Tunisia and to attract foreign investment and foreign tourists, the rise to prominence of a greedy second wife and her relatives, and the spreading sense throughout the nation that most Tunisians were being cheated as well as being oppressed, led Ben Ali's leadership in 2011 to be viewed as counterfeit. His presidency tipped from being tolerable to being illegitimate, integrity having long been lost and his initial strong vision dissipated.

The consequences of similar reprehensible, personalistic leadership in contemporary Africa are epitomized by a close examination of the impact of Robert Mugabe's thirty-one presidential years on outcomes in Zimbabwe. He inherited a rich African country in 1980. It had the most balanced economy in Africa, with a healthy dependence on both mineral and agricultural exports. Its infrastructure was modern, its medical facilities advanced, and its schools competent. Indeed, at independence in 1980, Zimbabwe boasted the best-educated indigenous population per capita in Africa, a situation which prevailed until 2005 or 2006.

Mugabe's government initially built upon those colonial foundations, strengthening the educational and health sectors, improving agricultural productivity, and providing reasonable security and opportunity for its mining sector. He presided over a period of solid economic growth, even encouraging white farmers and white-owned businesses to invest and to flourish.

At the same time, throughout the first decade of independence, Mugabe tolerated little dissent within his ruling party, or in the country at large. He even sponsored an early ethnic cleansing episode that killed 20,000 to 30,000 members of the minority Sindebele-speaking group.[22] But this ruthlessness and breach of democratic norms was overlooked and excused by much of the majority Shona-speaking group, and by the white minority. Foreign observers also gave Mugabe a certain degree of leadership space because, overall, Zimbabwe continued to perform well economically and socially. By 1990 or even 1995, a political culture existed that supported Mugabe's personal rule, but within a nominally democratic frame. Some political institutions inherited from the colonial regime continued to function, but more and more under the shadow of an increasingly harsh, intolerant, and paranoid regime.

By the beginning or the middle of the 1990s, Mugabe was condoning or sponsoring a spasm of accelerated looting from the state. Corruption, always present in Zimbabwe, now became a rampant phenomenon.[23] Much of the proceeds from these illicit, large, venal transactions were gathered by Mugabe's relatives and family; he and his second wife developed a penchant for lavish new accommodations in Zimbabwe and in Britain and Hong Kong. His second wife began using Zimbabwe's national airline as her personal transport service and, with Mugabe, went on shopping sprees in Asia and Europe.

Greed begat more greed, and corruption more corruption. Among the motives for Mugabe's decision to send 13,000 Zimbabwean soldiers to bolster support for Laurent Kabila's decaying Congolese regime in 1998 was the opportunity to loot the cobalt, cadmium, copper, and diamond mines of Katanga. The Zimbabwean taxpayer supported the military invasion of the Congo while Mugabe's family, the generals and other commanders of the Zimbabwean security forces, and several highly placed party officials profited from this beneficiation of Congo's resource wealth.

By 1999, if not before, Zimbabwe was nearly bankrupt, the invasion of the Congo and special payments to so-called war veterans having exhausted the national exchequer and having depleted Zimbabwe of foreign exchange. As a result of this unexpected privation and an increasing internal awareness of corrupt dealings and governmental arbitrariness, Zimbabwe's national trade union and some of the hitherto loyal members of the ruling party began to criticize Mugabe and his "bleeding" of Zimbabwe. Judges were increasingly harassed, some even deposed, when their rulings offended Mugabe. Early in that same year, he defended the torturing of two journalists employed by the nation's only opposition daily newspaper, declaring loudly and openly that no judge could order the men freed.

Such judges were impudent and "impertinent." The constitution, he declared, was what he the president said it was, and he was boss.[24]

Zimbabwe entered a long period of political siege. An opposition party was formed to contest first a constitutional referendum in early 2000 and, a few months later, a parliamentary election. Mugabe's proposed new constitution was defeated in the referendum, to everyone's surprise and to his consternation. But he managed to rig the results of the subsequent parliamentary election effectively enough to maintain his party's dominance. Mugabe and his followers later manipulated the results of the 2002 presidential poll, the 2005 parliamentary contest, and the delayed 2008 presidential election, denying a series of victories to the opposition Movement of Democratic Change (MDC) and to Morgan Tsvangirai, its leader. (The first balloting in 2008 was won by the opposition but never declared so by the official electoral commission; the second poll in 2008 was boycotted by the opposition because of a wave of intimidation and killings arranged by the ruling party.)

Motivated in part by his personal anger at losing the 2000 referendum and at being opposed for the first time by a serious political movement, Mugabe decided to employ a political tool that had in previous years gained him widespread black support. He blamed the MDC's near successes and the referendum defeat on the support that the MDC was supposedly receiving from white farmers. He sent so-called war veterans forcibly to occupy several thousand farms, to oust their white owners, to destroy their equipment, and to turn 400,000 or so indigenous farm laborers out of their jobs and onto the unemployment rolls. The war veterans or well-placed political and military cronies gained control of the farms despite legal impediments and court judgments. This wave of theft and destruction continued throughout the rest of the decade, accompanied by unspeakable atrocities and human rights violations against farmers of whatever ethnicity or background. In 2005, Mugabe ordered the cleansing of urban areas of MDC supporters, dislocating many thousands.[25] He ignored a cholera epidemic, deprived schools and hospitals of funding and critical supplies, and generally ran down his country and his people. He used hunger and food scarcity to get his way in the middle years of the new decade. In 2008, 2009, and 2010, too, Mugabe and his associates commandeered newly discovered diamond finds and appropriated them for their personal caches, again accompanied by large-scale violence.

As a result of all of this mayhem—consciously created by the leadership—Zimbabwe plunged economically into the depths of depression; the commercial farming sector had previously accounted for upwards of 70 percent of Zimbabwe's foreign exchange earnings and 20 percent of its GDP. That was largely gone by 2004 or 2005. Inflation set in as the government printed money to pay its way and reward the security forces. By 2007 and 2008, the Zimbabwe dollar reached absurd levels of inflation—at its apogee about 3 million percent inflation a year. At no time did Mugabe or his officials seem to care. They continued to travel and to loot while national unemployment rates rose to 90 percent and a quarter or so of the country's population—a full 3 million—fled to Botswana, Mozambique, and South Africa.[26]

Mugabe's assault on his people reminds us of the equally pernicious reigns of such African tyrants as Idi Amin, Gnassingbe Eyadema, Macias Nguema (and his nephew, Teodoro Obiang Nguema, still in power), Mobutu Sese Seko, Jean-Bedel Bokassa, Siaka Stevens, and Charles Taylor, and such Asian despots as Pol Pot and Ne Win.[27] In all cases, as in his, human agency was critical to the impoverishment and victimization of innocent civilians. In no case did the immiseration of peoples occur in fits of absence of mind. Each feature of Zimbabwe's downward spiral was orchestrated by Mugabe and his team; each maneuver was meant somehow to strengthen his power and his grip on the nation's available wealth.

Whereas in 1980 Mugabe might have been said to have had a national vision, that leadership competence was gone by the end of his first decade in office. Throughout the 1980s some might have asserted that Mugabe had provided his people with a sense of belonging to a larger, uplifting whole, but, by the 1990s, most of his followers had become jaundiced and skeptical. He enjoyed rational/traditional forms of legitimacy possibly as late as 1999, but never afterwards. Nor could he have claimed, before or after 1999, any of the other attributes of good leadership. Absolute power certainly corrupted Mugabe absolutely, and does so still.

Despite clear evidence of Mugabe's pernicious despotism, Tsvangirai in 2009 agreed to enter a government of national unity, trusting assurances from Mugabe that he would honor the agreement establishing that unity arrangement. Mugabe would remain president with supposedly curtailed powers and Tsvangirai would run the country as prime minister. By 2010, if not before, it was obvious to the world that Mugabe remained a bully, giving Tsvangirai no governing space and thumbing his nose at the unity arrangement. As Tsvangirai finally admitted in late 2010, "Mugabe believes that the offices of the Government of Zimbabwe are there to serve him, not the people, which is what the Constitution seeks to ensure. We are all well aware of the other breaches which occur all too regularly. Every extrajudicial arrest of citizens is a clear breach of the Constitution.

Every act of intimidation or violence by state or ZANU PF [Zimbabwe African National Union–Patriotic Front] actors is a clear breach of the Constitution. . . . Every act of censoring or curtailing individuals' or journalists' freedom of speech is a clear breach of the Constitution." Tsvangirai continued: "Zimbabweans will know that I have desperately tried to avoid a Constitutional crisis in Zimbabwe. I have worked tirelessly to try to make this transitional Government work, in the interest of all Zimbabweans. I have worked and spoken in support of this Government. But neither I, nor the MDC, can stand back any longer and just allow . . . Mugabe and ZANU PF to defy the law, to flaunt the Constitution, and to act as if they own this country."[28] But Mugabe continued to do what he pleased, driving Zimbabwe downward well into 2011.

Transactional Leadership

Despots and tyrants fortunately remain a minority in today's developing world. They are anachronisms, but powerful reminders that another leadership model often prevails when democratic political cultures are weak or nonexistent, when democratic institutions are nurtured only in the breach, and when autocrats manage to ignore or subvert constitutional or political cultural safeguards.

Transactional leaders constitute the majority of heads of state and heads of government in the developing world. Often closet autocrats, transactionalists are the men and women who find it hard enough to preside, much less to lead with vision and integrity. They have come up through party ranks, or through military coups, and their limitations as leaders are unremarkable. After all, it is only the exceptional leader who makes a difference, who transforms his country and his people. Most of the leaders in the developing (and developed) world are much more pedestrian in their aspirations and their abilities, however cleverly or mendaciously they have risen to power. But their limitations deprive their peoples of opportunities, skills, stability, and prosperity. Each transactionalist could do so much more for his state and his citizens.

Although their societies may cry out for and may need transformation, in so many cases the relevant leaders, even if elected and nominally democratic, are still stuck in a determinedly transactional trajectory. That business-as-usual mode often includes a reliance on patronage and corruption, an intolerance of opposition and dissent, a mistrust of open media, and a partiality to one or more privileged ethnic groups and elites.

Such embryonic political institutions as may exist are abused or devalued, even within a democratic framework. The executive is in control, sometimes tensely sharing power with legislatures or the military, sometimes not.

These are the patterns of everyday transactional leaders—the ones who predominate in the developing world—governing sometimes well, sometimes indifferently. They include persons such as the presidents or prime ministers of Bangladesh, Benin, the Central African Republic, Chad, Ecuador, Fiji, Guyana, Jamaica, Kenya, Malawi, Namibia, Papua New Guinea, the Solomon Islands, South Sudan, Tajikistan, Tanzania, Thailand (until mid-2011), Turkmenistan, Uganda, and Zambia. Few have fully articulated visions or, at best, their visions are limited to the worthy objectives of touting new prospects and routes to economic growth, talking about alleviating poverty, promoting literacy or other commendable social attainments, planning medical advances, and designing infrastructural objectives. They are focused more on managing followers rather than leading them or on attempting to uplift and to embolden them. Foremost, they worry about reelection, not necessarily about strengthening governance and performing new services for their far-flung, usually impoverished, constituents.

Some of these leaders may be genuinely popular and others may be regarded as fairly dour. They approach their leadership challenges tactically, rarely strategically, and rise or fall in public esteem based in large part on the vagaries of the global and regional context (the price of imported petroleum, say, returns on national commodity exports, unanticipated natural disasters and health challenges, or the episodic impulses of donors). They preside more than they lead, in other words, and sweep across their countries from one ceremonial event to another in vast motorcades. Their followers—their citizens—are fully in an exchange mode with these common varieties of leaders. The followers are looking for employment opportunities, agricultural subsidies or good farming returns, schools, clinics, and roads—components of governance. The followers seek honest dealings, fairness, and transparency, often in vain. They may also thirst for hope and for transformational, inspirational encouragement from their putative leaders. But that is almost never their lot. When elections, free or not, periodically come around, followers dutifully go to the polls to vote their ethnic, economic, and social interests, and to reanoint serving leaders or to choose replacements.

These are the situations prevalent in the nominally democratic parts of the developing world. Political cultures remain embryonic because vision-lacking leaders are less change agents than treaders in executive place. Institutions derived from long-ousted colonial mandates or from successive postindependence constitutions, as in Sri Lanka, Timor Leste, Côte d'Ivoire, Kenya, and Nigeria, work fitfully but, in times of stress, are easily discarded or ignored. In nearly all of these cases, nations are still not fully built or being built. Too much attention is being paid by successive governing elites to enjoying the perquisites of office and correspondingly too little to embracing and uplifting all peoples in the pursuit of a common good. That supreme task of leadership is much too often ignored.

One example of reasonable, but purely transactional, leadership of this kind in Africa is Bingu wa Mutharika's presidency in Malawi. Desperately poor Malawi has been looking for a responsible, transformational leader ever since donors and the Malawian electorate forcibly retired Hastings K. Banda, its first self-styled president for life.[29] He ruled Malawi despotically, erratically, and idiosyncratically from 1964 to 1993. The elections of that last year restarted and reenergized Malawi's search for democracy, observance of the rule of law, and attention to economic growth and human development. The United Democratic Front won a clear victory, and Bakili Muluzi, its head, succeeded Banda as president. (Muluzi and other members of his winning entourage had all served in Banda's government.)

Muluzi's ten-year, two-term period as national leader began with great promise but soon defaulted into the usual pattern of African disappointment. Economic plans were made but little sustainable growth was accomplished. National incomes fluctuated according to the strength and distribution of the annual rains and the price of tobacco, Malawi's main export. Smallholder farmers suffered while well-connected businessmen and politicians profited from connections to Muluzi and his close associates. The president and those cronies also grew wealthy from various food and transport monopolies and from the spread of corruption. Some cabinet ministers arranged lavish textbook contracts, with kickbacks, or used government x-ray machines in their private medical practices. Civil servants and policemen noticed and joined the stampede into rent seeking. Soon citizens and voters appreciated that their great hopes of enlightened and uplifting leadership after Banda were misplaced. Muluzi's government forfeited its post-Banda legitimacy and became excessively transactional. Whereas Malawians wanted to replace the dark days of Banda's rule with a new dawn of probity and productivity, all they received was a muddled version of the old dispensation.

After Malawi's parliament refused to permit Muluzi to overthrow a constitutional provision against a third presidential term, the voters elected as his personally anointed successor Mutharika, an economist. As has happened elsewhere, the successor in Malawi soon turned on his predecessor, accusing him of corruption. Mutharika also alienated large numbers of his original supporters, especially those sitting in parliament. But otherwise he did very little to nurture the democratic political culture and institutions that Malawi had embraced only nominally.

Mutharika overwhelmingly was reelected president in 2009 because of his administration's ability to improve national food security and because of widespread attention to (Chinese-assisted) road construction and repair. Under Mutharika, Malawi shifted from being an importer of maize (corn), the national staple, to being an exporter. Although his detractors accused Mutharika of devoting himself too thoroughly to amassing and keeping power, and to attacking corruption without much perceived success, Mutharika at the beginning of his second presidency was much more popular than any of his predecessors.[30] That is, he was credited with performing as president better than Muluzi, a low threshold, and with being concerned somewhat more with solving national problems than with working only for himself and his loyal supporters.

Despite Malawi's advance under Mutharika economically, and its remarkably high placement in the Index of African Governance as the fourteenth-best governed country in Africa (ahead of Senegal, Egypt, Tanzania, and Zambia), Mutharika has lacked more than a stunted vision of Malawi's future.[31] Mutharika is stuck predominantly in the transactional mode, behaving essentially only a little better than the common run of recent African leaders. He provides no uplifting vision and does not attempt to engage the spirits or the aspirations of his people. Like most contemporary leaders in Africa, too, he permits corrupt practices to continue despite abundant anticorruption rhetoric, the forward-looking report of a thoughtful anticorruption commission, and prosecutions of high-level miscreants. Lashing out at Malawi's free press, he also backed legislation that permits the minister of information to ban publications deemed to be contrary to the "public interest."[32] The British High Commissioner suggested in 2011 that governance was deteriorating, media freedom and free speech eroding severely, and minority rights suffering. The High Commissioner, representing Malawi's largest donor, described "this combative president" as "ever more autocratic and intolerant of criticism."[33] Under Mutharika, nation-building and the implanting of a democratic political culture that could strengthen political institutions remains a slow-motion work in progress, with little inspiration from the chief executive.

Two other very dissimilar African cases illustrate this category of contemporary transactional leadership. One is Uganda, the other neighboring Kenya.

President Yoweri Museveni came to power in Uganda in 1986 after leading an insurrection that theoretically reclaimed the country for democracy, after years of abuse by his predecessors Idi Amin and A. Milton Obote. But as much as Museveni might have wanted to assert that his movement was a popular, fully national one, in fact it returned power in Uganda largely or exclusively to southerners, especially southwesterners, after that power had been usurped for years by northerners. The south-north struggle also encapsulated a struggle between Bantu speakers and non–Bantu speakers and between the peoples of the kingdoms in the south and the very differently organized and aggregated peoples of the north. Museveni failed to demonstrate a Mandela-like inclusivity, or to do much during his first three terms in office to build a nation. " . . . Our own politicians just care about their own stomachs," a disenchanted voter said in 2011. Although he has long asserted democratic values, and has won carefully controlled and limited elections, Museveni's earlier conflict-derived legitimacy has been dissipated by persistent authoritarianism. He has been a leader, and a decisive one, who is widely seen to have favored his own kin of the kingdoms of the southwest, both politically and militarily.[34]

Thus, no matter how effective Museveni has been in increasing national security (by finally overcoming the Lord's Resistance Army and a minor militancy in Ruwenzori) and in propelling Uganda back along the road to economic development, his once national vision, widely embraced and highly regarded in the region, has since become a much more limited gaze—a gaze that has been viewed by at least a plurality of Ugandans as partial. Museveni has rarely been prudent in intensifying his vise-like grip on Uganda, in marginalizing opponents, or in limiting political participation severely. Even the African Peer Review Mechanism report on Uganda criticized Museveni's lifting of two-term presidential limits. It said that the overbearing influence of the executive had progressively reduced democratic gains.[35]

"Some people say Museveni has overstayed his power," the president told journalists and others in Mbale in early 2009. But "I have been here for long to solve your problems, not to cultivate in my garden. The problems are so many that I have to keep around." Museveni has always believed in his indispensability. "Poor leadership," he averred, "is partly due to ignorance."[36] Museveni is strong willed, but no tyrant. He, along with so many of his African contemporaries, has simply not yet made the transition from conquest to responsible national leadership. His broad and uplifting original vision later became, through acts of both commission and omission, a narrow agenda tailored for Museveni, his cronies, and their military colleagues. Nevertheless, his political and electoral durability derives from the realistic trade-off that most Ugandans (like so many Rwandans and Singaporeans) have been prepared to make between "peace and plurality."[37]

Uganda's 2011 election gave Museveni an unprecedented fourth five-year presidential term. He was easily reelected with 68 percent of the vote against one serious and four other contenders. His opponents cried foul, complaining of various electoral infractions including abuse of the state election machinery, the use of state resources for his campaign, and favorable votes obtained by outright payoffs. "In previous elections," Museveni bought individuals. "In this election he is buying constituencies and groups," and with government funds.[38]

Neighboring Kenyans, despite or because of their relative prosperity and sophistication compared to their neighbors, have similarly experienced leadership lacking competence and a national focus. President Jomo Kenyatta was Kenya's first leader; he could wield power with comparative ease, and over an entire embryonic nation, because of the traditional/rational/charismatic legitimacy that he enjoyed after a decade in detention. He also was an early nationalist from pre-World War II days, and was therefore able in the 1960s and 1970s to transcend his relatively narrow ethnic base to preside over all of Kenya.[39]

Unfortunately, Kenyatta neglected to complete the nation-building project. Partially because of rent seeking, partially because he lacked a broad vision for the new Kenya, Kenyatta never tried to create a nation with a fully democratic political culture and vibrant institutions. As a result, his immediate successor, Daniel arap Moi, was easily able to take Kenya backwards into wanton brutality, corruption, and extreme ethnic particularity. The election of Mwai Kibaki, Kenya's third president, in 2002, was supposed to usher in an era of consultative leadership capable of moving Kenya along the path of modernity, tolerance, and nation-building. But Kenya instead descended into a paroxysm of renewed corruption and ethnic preferentiality. The supposed alliance between the Kikuyu and the Luo, Kenya's dominant ethnic groups, turned first antagonistic, then violent after Kibaki and his cronies rigged the 2007 parliamentary and presidential elections.[40] Even the popular approval of a new constitution in 2010 that curtailed presidential powers and devolved significant authority to new decentralized counties need not provide a foundation for strong institutions and a fully formed democratic political culture. Only leaders can breathe life into paper promises and plans.

Leaders Making a Difference

In great contrast to the modal pattern of the transactionalists, a limited number of contemporary or very recent developing world leaders have attempted in one or more ways to emulate the signal leadership achievements of Mandela, Khama, and Lee. They have demonstrated what is possible with committed and collectively focused leadership. In pursuit, initially at least, of genuinely collective goods, they have begun to establish political cultures, institutions, and nations in the manner of Khama and Lee, and with the all-embracing approach of a Mandela. Several, too, have implicitly modeled themselves on Ataturk. All have espoused visions for their countries. All have mobilized followers behind their national objectives, albeit sometimes relying on coercion more than on persuasion. Each has had to project power, to establish and to maintain legitimacy, and to make minor or major compromises with democratic values. Several have indeed decided that the ends of transformational nation-building justified means that were decidedly autocratic.

Context matters, too, since leadership germinates in distinctly different resource, geographical, material, and historical surroundings. Mandela battled apartheid and white power, Lee coped with a swamp of pirates and Malaysian dominance, Khama was surrounded by apartheid-ridden South Africa and Afro-Socialist black Africa, and Ataturk had to fend off both invaders and would-be colonizers. Contemporary leaders govern after failed governance experiments, civil wars, genocides, and predecessors who were, at best, self-aggrandizers and, at worst, wanton killers. Nevertheless, some show that transitions to good governance are possible.

Indonesia's first leaders, Sukarno (1950–1966) and Suharto (1966–1998), were both autocrats who cared more for the perquisites and rewards of office than they did for the welfare of their many peoples. Sukarno was a liberator, but hardly a nation-builder. He purged Chinese merchants and Communists, persecuted minorities, and destroyed a thriving economy. He eviscerated Indonesia's existing rule of law and the judiciary as an institution. Suharto revived the economy but empowered the military and repressed dissent, opposition, and minorities. Neither leader was transformative, although Sukarno professed to be. Both were wildly corrupt, and Suharto famously enabled his family to grow wealthy and the country's generals and Javanese and Sumatran oligarchs to enrich themselves fabulously.[41]

One of those military leaders was Susilo Bambang Yudhoyono. A top graduate of Indonesia's military academy with a doctorate in agricultural economics, he served successfully under Suharto, and then under Bacharuddin Jusuf Habibie, Abdurrahman Wahid, and Megawati Sukarnoputri, the lackluster presidents who succeeded Suharto. Yet, despite those unpromising leadership legacies, Yudhoyono as president has demonstrated uncommon leadership skills and an ability to move decisively away from the prevalent ruling model and the political culture of criminalized democracy that he inherited from his predecessors. From his election as president in 2004 (he was overwhelmingly reelected in 2009), Yudhoyono has rescued the Indonesian presidency from its accustomed partiality and lack of integrity. He has also managed, because of his astute handling and settlement of the Aceh insurgency (especially in the wake of the 2004 tsunami that devastated northwestern Sumatra), to make progress on the very difficult task of creating a real nation out of the 240 million very disjointed and disaffected peoples who scatter themselves across the vast Indonesian archipelago.

Yudhoyono after 2004 projected a steady, subtle vision of a united Indonesia, articulated that vision, and began the difficult and prolonged process of mobilizing his various peoples on behalf of the new national enterprise. One of the secrets of Yudhoyono's success has been his seeming break with the corrupt and partial leadership postures of his predecessors. Yet, money still rules. The oligarchs remain powerful, especially at the district level. They continue to defend their perquisites and to influence governmental actions at all levels. Yudhoyono has not contemplated much economic redistribution or social equalization. But, whereas Yudhoyono has been timid in these spheres, he has demonstrated a Mandela-like inclusivity in a very difficult environment. He has brought the outer islands, some with minorities, into the wider nation. He has managed to remain a modest Muslim, and not an Islamist, despite electoral pressures in that latter direction. Yudhoyono acts cautiously, prudently, and he carefully constructs consensus before moving forward. Sometimes his deliberateness has been irksome to his compatriots, but given the excesses of his predecessors, he has won support throughout Indonesia by his insistence on policies that have a consensual basis. He has also done what the best leaders do well—given his countrymen a sense for the first time of belonging to an enlarged and enlarging project of national revival and nation-building. His skills are those of a legitimate, steady leader.

Foreign investment in Indonesia grew 52 percent in 2010. The country's credit rating improved. GDP per capita rose more than 6 percent. All of these and many other betterments in Indonesia's economic outlook were likely the results of Yudhoyono's sober fiscal management and good governance. This is not to say that Indonesia has overcome its lamentable infrastructure, its inefficient bureaucracy, and its embedded corrupt practices. But Yudhoyono's enlightened approach to the challenges of governing such a vast, rambling, disjunctive nation as Indonesia has brought positive results.

Yudhoyono could have remained a transactionalist, in the manner of his immediate predecessors. But, possibly because of his military experience, possibly because of his analytical skills, Yudhoyono understood that Indonesia when he assumed office remained a series of disconnected islands and political fiefs. The largest Muslim country in the world was neither united nor pursuing national goals. He gradually unveiled a vision of an Indonesian nation and thereafter set about ending rebellions and separatism (everywhere but Papua), extending services to the entire archipelago, not just Java, and showing material progress. Admittedly, many of those who profited during the Suharto dictatorship remained prominent and powerful, and the bureaucracy remained inefficient and mostly still corrupt. But Yudhoyono demonstrated a sense of integrity and purpose that was novel for Indonesia. It strengthened Yudhoyono's message and enabled him to distribute power and resources away from central Java.

Yudhoyono may not have personally or politically embraced the challenge of transformational leadership in an explicit manner. But Ellen Johnson-Sirleaf, in Liberia, hardly had the luxury of choice. On entering office in 2006, she had to engage herself and her followers in nation-building as a first-order priority. War-torn Liberia was a looted shell of its former self. More than 250,000 people had been killed in two civil wars. Monrovia, the capital, had not enjoyed running water or electricity since 1992. The up-country peoples, less literate and less prosperous, were alienated with reason from those who lived along the coast. The elected legislature included many of Johnson-Sirleaf's sworn enemies, all of whom were hostile to serious political and social reform.

In order to govern and to survive, she had to offer a vision of a new Liberia, reconstructed and revitalized. She promised to transform the way Liberians viewed themselves and their mission. She pledged to integrate and to unify her small but historically divided and fractured state. To succeed, she had to demonstrate unquestioned personal and political integrity as compared with Taylor and others such as Prince Johnson. Then she had to sell her vision to Liberians skeptical of promises and cynical about leaders and their designs.[42] Gradually, by Mandela-like acts of inclusion and mediation, she showed her people and the world that she possessed the competencies necessary to oversee and to invigorate a major overhaul of her tiny country. She was also forced to try to deliver basic goods and services, such as electrical power and refurbished roads, in order to buttress the legitimacy with which she entered the presidency. She reopened mines and plantations, fought off international drug traffickers, and extended schooling and medical care to remote regions. But her most telling accomplishment was an Ataturkian-like determination to trump ethnic sentiments and preferences with a burgeoning sense of Liberian national identity.

Security is one of the key political goods supplied by effective leadership, and Johnson-Sirleaf's administration fortunately was backed for a number of years by 13,000 United Nations peacekeepers. A new army and police force were trained by an American firm. Another political good—transparency—was also pursued rigorously by Johnson-Sirleaf; she discharged senior and allegedly corrupt civil servants from key ministries. Despite serious foot-dragging by the Liberian legislature, an Anti-Corruption Commission began to function in late 2009. The legislature also passed a Code of Conduct bill regulating behavior and reducing the temptation of corruption throughout the government.

Nevertheless, despite her best efforts, all kinds of corruption continued well into 2011. A project of the Fund for Peace collected numerous credible reports of rural infractions–ghost workers in Grand Kru, finance ministry officials soliciting bribes in Nimba, judges and jurors accepting payments in Bomi, embezzlement in Grand Gedeh, and the usual solicitation of gifts from motorists almost everywhere. Fortunately, and in a departure from the usual practice in developing countries, the scourge of continuing corruption is noticed transparently and combated. In Liberia, journalists report freely on what Johnson-Sirleaf has labeled Liberia's "debilitating cancer" of corruption and on what Liberia's own General Auditing Commission has called Liberia's "speedy torpedo–like" rampant public thefts.[43] Prosecutors prosecute and courts convict, if slowly.

If anything testifies to the success of Johnson-Sirleaf's leadership, however, it is gains on the economic rejuvenation front. By the time that she had taken office, in 2006, Liberia's GDP per capita had fallen to about $100. Years before, Liberia had been much more prosperous. Johnson-Sirleaf has encouraged the resumption of iron ore mining, has brought moribund rubber plantation activities back to life, and has been seeking to create a well-regulated forestry industry. China is helping slowly to improve the country's lamentable infrastructure, too. All-important roads are gradually being paved and rail-links laid, and attention is being paid by other donors to critical water needs. Johnson-Sirleaf rightfully can take credit for these improvements and for a massive reduction in official public debt. She has also presided over a 40 percent improvement in primary school enrollment.[44] By late 2010, GDP per capita had at least doubled since 2006. Absent her vision and ability to mobilize followers, Liberia might well have stagnated as neighboring Sierra Leone, lacking post–civil war dynamic leadership, has done.[45]

The challenges faced by Paul Kagame of Rwanda arguably were more severe than even those faced by Johnson-Sirleaf. A major source of his legitimacy came from his leadership of the victorious Tutsi-led postgenocidal military force that freed Rwanda from the consequence of Hutu-directed mass atrocities. Kagame has since developed a consummate vision for his small, populous, land-locked country. He still needs to create a complete nation from a country divided by ethnic rivalries, traumatized by atrocities, and facing external challenges, but is intent on doing so. He has abundant self-confidence and self-mastery. His people, like Lee's followers, chafe at the need to conform and to obey, but also welcome the peace, order, and security that come from being tightly controlled. Kagame is attempting to create a noncorrupt society by emphasizing his own integrity and making examples of any high or low officials who flout his relatively newly enforced determination to stamp out corrupt practices. "Corruption," Kagame has declared, " . . . is clearly, very largely, behind the problems [that] African countries face. It is very bad in African or Third World countries. . . ." Corruption is hard to eliminate, Kagame also has said, because it "has become a way of life in some places." Moreover, he believes that "you can't fight corruption from the bottom. You have to fight it from the top." Kagame has prohibited his government from employing any of his own relatives or relatives of cabinet ministers. He has shamed and prosecuted cabinet ministers who have slipped off the high road of integrity. "Nor," reports Kagame's biographer, "are the guilty quietly rehabilitated . . . as happens [elsewhere]. They can never return to public life, because they are considered guilty of something even worse than dishonesty."[46]

There are billboards all over Kigali, Rwanda's capital, exhorting citizens to behave noncorruptly and to cease giving bribes. "He Who Practices Corruption Destroys His Country." All public officials—more than 4,000—are required to file annual statements of their net worth, copying one of Lee's methods. According to the *Economist,* the police are professional, enforcing laws in Kigali in a manner that makes Rwanda the "cleanest country" in Africa.[47] Transparency International in 2010 rated Rwanda as the seventh-least corrupt country in sub-Saharan Africa, an improvement from its ranking as the sixteenth-least corrupt of forty-eight such countries in 2008. Rwanda also rated twenty-sixth on the governance rankings table for Africa published in the Index of African Governance in 2009.[48] These attainments were reached by tough, uncompromising leadership, not by preexisting strong institutions. Kagame, in other words, has begun by force of leadership and by example to transform Rwanda from dirty to clean and from somewhat disorganized to remarkably efficient, along the way creating a new quasi-democratic political culture and giving structure to emergent institutions.

There is a cost, however, for Rwandans, just as Lee's methods were costly for Singaporeans. In Rwanda, Kagame's followers have had to learn to forfeit voice for conformity, to reduce the extent to which their political participation might be fully free, and to adapt to, if not to internalize, a strong leader's approach to many if not all aspects of contemporary Rwandan life. It is not so much that Kagame is heavy handed; more important is that (like Lee and Ataturk) he accepts no competing visions and demands a level of obedience from the citizenry that is rare in contemporary Africa. Khama and Mandela never required obedience. They led by force of example and persuasion. Kagame believes that the postgenocidal fears and weaknesses in Rwanda have compelled him to be more authoritarian, trading citizen autonomy for stability, peace, and an opportunity to prosper. Kagame very much wants Rwanda to be the Singapore of Africa.

Kagame and his ruling party were easily reelected in 2010, but not without widespread criticism of the bitter way in which opponents were prevented from campaigning, in some instances assassinated and exiled, and in which freedom of the media was abridged. Vibrant dissent is hardly tolerated, nor are majority Hutu permitted too much political space. Nevertheless, Kagame is an able and skilled visionary. He is the brainiest of Africa's presidents in terms of analytical intelligence. He also performs well for his poor people in the economic sphere, even though he will be unable in this era to produce the kinds of rapid social, educational, and health results that Lee achieved in Singapore in the late 1960s and early 1970s; Rwandans are too poorly educated, too ill, too numerous and overcrowded, and too isolated geographically and economically for positive results to come easily. Nevertheless, Rwanda grows stronger, more proud, and arguably better governed by the day—all a tribute to Kagame's transformative skills, his Machievellian willingness to compel, and his integrity.

Strengthening Leadership in the Developing World

Across Africa, Asia, the Caribbean, Oceania, and Latin America, there are many more Mugabes and Mugabe-wannabes than there are Yudhoyonos and Kagames. Leaders and nation-builders in the mold of Lee, Khama, and Mandela are equally rare. Occasionally, the meteor of a Muhammad Mahathir of Malaysia or an Abdoulaye Wade of Senegal shoots across the sky only to fall to earth in flames. Infrequently, too, there are well-meaning, appealing heads of state and government who lead in the hopeful manner of Kenneth Kaunda, president of Zambia from 1964 to 1991. Like Kaunda, they ultimately know little of the arts of modern leadership and are prey to persuasive panaceas or formulistic recipes that turn out to accomplish little in terms of advancing their citizens socially, politically, or economically.

That is the central issue for leaders in today's developing world: How can they most effectively and most sensibly lift up their peoples in the manner pioneered in Botswana, Mauritius, Singapore, and—much earlier—Turkey? For example, if Africa, which was far ahead of Asia in the 1960s, is ever to catch up to Singapore, Taiwan, Malaysia, and Indonesia in this century in terms of personal incomes and social and political outcomes, then responsible leadership will lead the way as it has already done spectacularly only in Botswana, Cape Verde, Ghana, Mauritius, and Rwanda. If the intrastate wars of the world are to end and its preyed-upon peoples are to be spared further killings such as those in Colombia, the Democratic Republic of the Congo, East Timor, Guatemala, the Sudan, and Thailand, then enlightened leadership will help to achieve such results.[49] If life expectancies are to grow and maternal and child mortality rates to fall, farsighted leaders will help to make such results possible. In the fragile polities of the developing world, leaders—guiding and lifting up followers and building new political cultures and then institutions—have the ability to make that profound difference.

This is what the new burgeoning middle class of the developing world craves. First in Asia and Latin America, and now in Africa and the Middle East, the younger generations who have populated the cities and some rural areas of the developing world seek better leadership and stronger governance than their fathers and mothers experienced. They seek stronger rules of law, more transparency and less corruption, more opportunity for educational resources and personal advancement, and attention to the social and institutional deficits within their countries. They want positive change and recognize that improved, reformed leadership is at least one route to such shifts in their national terrains.

For them, autocracy has little utility. They also are beginning to understand, with Lee, that leadership by routine transactionalists—the common situation—is insufficient, failing as it so often does to address contemporary social and economic complaints in a serious manner. The middle classes appreciate that the lackluster democratically elected cohort of African, Asian, Caribbean, and Latin American leaders still offer limited visions. Only a few demonstrate integrity and work conscientiously to reduce corruption, striving simultaneously to deliver reasonable qualities and quantities of good governance. Few are courageous. Few—a major issue—put the common good ahead of personal or group gains.

Indeed, too few leaders in the modern developing world are transformational in a positive sense. Only a handful over the past seventy years have understood the nation-building project, despite many if not most coming to power as populists and nationalists. Few have projected national visions instead of parochial ones. Nearly all have been exclusionists, content to favor particular families, lineages, and ethnic groups. Only Mandela, Khama, Lee, Ramgoolam, Yudhoyono, and Johnson-Sirleaf have been true inclusionists. Others have favored one group or one region over another; neglected ethnic, religious, or linguistic categories of citizen; or attempted after the fact to claim that opponents were foreign aliens, or that their mothers were (notably in war-torn Côte d'Ivoire and sections of Nigeria).[50]

With key exceptions, the leaders of the developing world have paid and pay lip service to democracy and participation without necessarily understanding what those words meant or mean or how critical and important those concepts, if realized in practice, were and are to the strengthening of fragile, embryonic nation states. Their middle classes know better. Likewise, legitimate rulers have almost always and almost everywhere, to the present day, lost their legitimacy during a first or second presidential term by pandering to particular ethnic groups and excluding others, by succumbing to greed, or by breaching constitutional prohibitions without proper authority. Some, too, have lost legitimacy by failing critical tests—by responding inadequately to national disasters like a typhoon or epidemics of HIV/AIDS or dengue fever—by criminalizing their own states, by enabling drug smugglers, or by focusing on themselves more than the needs of their people.[51]

The results of these largely human failings are palpable: Only a few African and a few more Asian states have thus far gone from statehood to full nationhood. Most are struggling to incorporate all of their disparate nationalities into a single, moral, persuasive nation. Most have instead succumbed to the vanities and aggrandizements of manipulative, willful, dangerous leaders. By contrast, in those developing world nations where positive human agency has led to good governance and a democratic political culture, institutions have grown and now rein in and check leaders, as in Botswana, Brazil, Chile, Colombia, Costa Rica, Mauritius, Singapore, South Africa, and Taiwan.

Fortunately, the tide of accomplishment may recently have turned. Joining the obvious Asian and Latin American examples, Africa and the Middle East now insist on being well led. There is a pent-up demand, especially in North Africa and the poorer parts of sub-Saharan Africa, for what the citizens of Botswana, Mauritius, and Singapore have achieved and for what they have gained materially because of responsible, committed leadership. Democratic values are enshrined everywhere, even (or particularly) within the despotisms. Good governance and democratic attainments, plus stability and peace, are among the driving aspirations of most peoples scattered across the developing world. The next task is to nurture leaders who can respond appropriately and effectively to these new popular sentiments.

Building capacity for accomplished political leadership among upcoming leaders—the contemporary cadre of parliamentarians and deputy ministers—may spare Africa and Asia, the Caribbean, Latin America, and the Middle East from additional destructive and counterfeit models. Rigorous exposure to positive examples, and some unabashed competency training, may be required to strengthen the ability of upcoming leaders to learn how and when to do the right thing—to enunciate and to embody national visions over narrowly secular ones, and to rebuff those who would tempt base instincts. Lee says that leaders are born, not made—"[it] is either in you or it is not"—but leadership competencies can be inspired and refined, and talents honed.[52] Broad horizons can be substituted for limited ones, and at least a modicum of discipline, prudence, and self-mastery can be transferred from leadership masters to those ready and anxious to take their places. That is the urgent task of this decade.

Acknowledgments

Much of my own research experience has occurred over several decades in Africa, Asia, and the Caribbean. I have been a student of leadership and leadership performance especially and intensively in East Africa, West Africa, Southern Africa, Southeast Asia, and the island-states of the anglophone and francophone Caribbean. I know Central Asia, Latin America, and Oceania, but less directly. This book reflects the vicissitudes and challenges of all of those regions—today's developing world. Many examples in this book draw on Africa's richness, the continent with the greatest number of countries—fifty-four. Other continents or subcontinents contain many fewer nation-states, less poverty, and stronger institutions.

The case studies in this book are largely but not exclusively synthetic, drawing on a large body of existing research in order to demonstrate how four effective political leaders in the developing world perform and offer effective leadership for good. The case studies also draw on the author's personal knowledge of and interaction (and interviews) with Mandela, Khama, and Lee. I am grateful, especially, for Lee's willingness in 2006 to respond at length to questions and then to summon me back for further dialogue on succeeding days. My interviews with Khama and Mandela were less formal, occurring in meetings in the 1970s and early 1990s that, although one-on-one, were not arranged with this book in mind. Many of the modern political leaders examined in the final chapter are persons whom I knew and with whom I had extensive conversations over many years, but, again, without this book having been conceived at that time. The conversations with Jomo Kenyatta of Kenya, Kenneth Kaunda of Zambia, Thabo Mbeki of South Africa, Robert Mugabe of Zimbabwe, and Julius Nyerere of Tanzania, for example, took place at various times and in different places across the decades from the 1950s to the 1990s and then well into this century. Those with President Kaunda began in the late 1950s, for example, and continued throughout the 1960s, 1970s, 1980s, and 1990s, and after 2000. Other talks were less frequent or ended early with persons such as President Kenyatta. But discussions with some of the additional leaders mentioned in the final chapter continued episodically almost up to the date of this book's publication. Discussions with Sir Ketumile Masire and Festus Mogae of Botswana date from this century, but have been extensive and ongoing. President Masire chaired the African Leadership Council from 2004, when a number of African leaders and I established it. I also spoke about leadership concerns at length with Oscar Arias of Costa Rica, Mohammed Mahathir of Malaysia, Tommy Koh of Singapore, and Jacob Zuma of South Africa on several occasions in recent years. All of these stimulating formal and informal engagements, plus many more that were less intensive, provided grist for this book.

The impetus to write this book was stimulated by engaging multidisciplinary and cross-faculty seminars on leadership organized by the Center for Public Leadership in the Harvard Kennedy School, beginning in 2002 and led at different times until 2008 by Barbara J. Kellerman, Richard J. Hackman, and Joseph S. Nye. Indeed, the nucleus of this book was presented and critiqued several times in those Leadership Theory Prospecting Group meetings as well as over many years in my graduate courses on leadership and the politics of the developing world at the Kennedy School. The participants in the seminars and the students in what were invariably lively classes always offered excellent feedback on the leadership model presented to them, the sense of which has found its way into and has measurably improved the arguments presented in the body of this book.

Rosabeth Moss Kanter, Vamik Volkan, Barbara Kellerman, and anonymous readers for the University of Chicago Press provided telling and extremely helpful critiques of early versions of this book. David Pervin of the Chicago Press skillfully added important editorial suggestions. I owe all of them, the persons interviewed, my fellow seminar participants and students, and Kellerman, Ronnie Heifetz, and Dean Williams, friends and instructive colleagues, an enormous debt of gratitude for their willingness to offer guidance and to share wisdom. Dean Kishore Mahbubani of the Lee Kuan Yew School of Public Policy in Singapore kindly did much, and most hospitably, to facilitate my meetings with the then–Minister

Mentor Lee, and I remain grateful for his efforts and his friendship. Emily Wood, amid difficult and busy months, helped to organize an earlier version of this book and to provide research assistance, as did Julia Mensah. I am indebted to them and their uplifting companionship. The Center for Public Leadership kindly provided a very early travel grant, which helped to jump-start research on this book; so did John Thomas and the Kennedy School's Singapore Program. Both components of the School thus helped appreciably to make this book possible.

The original title for this book was *The Vision Thing*. After convening a series of very informal "focus" groups in Geneva and Oxford, and after discussions with Pervin and others at the University of Chicago Press, new titles emerged. This book's final title thus benefited from the collective and generously offered wisdom of Thomas and Nancy Biersteker, Caty Clément, Sir Ivor Crewe, and Donald C. Markwell (and others at a seminar at Rhodes House, Oxford). Finally, Cornelia C. Johnson came up with a winning formula, endorsed by the Press. I am significantly in the debt of all of those who contributed so tellingly to constructing the winning title.

—R. I. R.
July 14, 2011

Notes

INTRODUCTION

1. "Zuma's Two Bad Calls," *Economist,* September 4, 2010.
2. For a very telling critique of this leadership literature, see Nitin Nohria and Rakesh Khurana, "Advancing Leadership Theory and Practice," in Nohria and Khurana (eds.), *Handbook of Leadership Theory and Practice* (Boston, 2010), 5, 6–25. Of the comprehensive *Handbook's* twenty-six chapters, only three allude to political leadership and only one, obliquely, touches on leadership in the developing world.
3. Rosabeth Moss Kanter, "Leadership in a Globalizing World," in ibid., 573.
4. For examples and the literature, see Jerrold M. Post, *Leaders and Their Followers in a Dangerous World: The Psychology of Political Behavior* (Ithaca, 2004).
5. "Crisis" consciously echoes the motivated opening pages of James MacGregor Burns, *Leadership* (New York, 1978), where he wrote much more sharply about the "mediocrity or irresponsibility of so many of the men and women in power."

CHAPTER ONE

1. Stanley Lieberson and James F. O'Connor, "Leadership and Organizational Performance: A Study of Large Corporations," *American Sociological Review* 37 (1972), 117–130. Equally telling is Michael D. Cohen and James G. March, *Leadership and Ambiguity: The American College President* (New York, 1974), which shows that presidential leadership did not alter institutional results.
2. Joel M. Podolny, Rakesh Khurana, and Marya L. Besharov, "Revisiting the Meaning of Leadership," in Nohria and

Khurana (eds.), *Handbook*, 73, 93, 95; Jennifer A. Chatman and Jessica A. Kennedy, "Psychological Perspectives on Leadership," in ibid., 159–160, 173; Manfred Kets de Vries and Elisabet Engellau, "A Clinical Approach to the Dynamics of Leadership and Executive Transformation," in ibid., 192–193. But see Richard J. Hackman, "What Is This Thing Called Leadership?" in ibid., 113.

3. Margaret G. Hermann and Joe D. Hagan, "International Decision Making: Leadership Matters," *Foreign Policy* 110 (1998), 124, 135, and the studies cited therein on 125, 129, 135–137.
4. "One standard deviation change in leader quality leads to a growth change [upward] of 1.5 percentage points a year," especially where institutions are weak. Benjamin F. Jones and Benjamin A. Olken, "Do Leaders Matter? National Leadership and Growth since World War II," *Quarterly Journal of Economics* 120 (2005), 835–864. Many of the leaders in Jones and Olken's sample of presidents who died or who had been replaced randomly were from the developing world.
5. For the argument on state failure and how it occurs, see Robert I. Rotberg, "The Failure and Collapse of Nation-States: Breakdown, Prevention, and Repair," in Rotberg (ed.), *When States Fail: Causes and Consequences* (Princeton, 2004), 1–45. For a comprehensive, cogent, recent analysis of the earlier theories of the significance of structure and of subsequent social-science discussions of the salience of human agency in democratization and nation-building, see Renske Doorenspleet, *The Fourth Wave of Democratization: Identification and Explanation* (Leiden, 2001), 82–100. She concludes that structuralist (the world system, economic dependency, class structure, etc.) and actor-oriented approaches complement each other more than they compete (94). See also Michael Bratton and Nicolas van de Walle, *Democratic Experiments in Africa: Regime Transitions in Comparative Perspective* (New York, 1997), 19–48.
6. Scott Shane, *Born Entrepreneurs, Born Leaders: How Your Genes Affect Your Work Life* (New York, 2010), 123–124. Shane cites, among others, A. Johnson, P. Vernon, J. McCarthy, et al., "Nature vs. Nurture: Are Leaders Born or Made? A Behavior Genetic Investigation of Leadership Style," *Twin Research* 1 (1998), 216–223; Johnson, Vernon, J. Harris, and K. Jang, "A Behavior Genetic Investigation of the Relationship between Leadership and Personality," *Behavior Genetics* 7 (2004), 27–32.

   Warren G. Bennis and Burt Nanus, *Leaders: Strategies for Taking Charge* (New York, 1997), 207, disagree (and also with Lee, below), saying that "major capacities and competencies of leadership can be learned. . . ."
7. At the city level, mayors with set ideas also make a profound difference. Moscow Mayor Yuri Luzhkov refused to extend the city's subway or to revive trams. He built new roads instead, each new ring wider than the previous one. As a result of his twenty-year-long preference for roads over

public transport, traffic in Moscow lurched from one massive jam to the next. Keith Gessen, "Stuck: The Meaning of the City's Traffic Nightmare," *New Yorker,* August 2, 2010, 26. Mayor Luzhkov was sacked a month after this article appeared but for very different reasons.

8. Atul Kohli, "On Sources of Social and Political Conflicts in Follower Democracies," in Axel Hadenius (ed.), *Democracy's Victory and Crisis* (New York, 1997), 74, never mentions leadership in the Indian case, believing that India's democratic emergence depended upon the strength of a nationalist movement that generated a unifying ideology and a hegemonic party.
9. Samuel P. Huntington, *The Third Wave: Democratization in the Late Twentieth Century* (Norman, 1991), 316.
10. See Robert I. Rotberg, "Peripheral Successor States and the Legacy of Empire: Succeeding the British and French Empires in Africa," in Karen Dawisha and Bruce Parrott (eds.), *The End of Empire? The Transformation of the USSR in Comparative Perspective* (Armonk, N.Y., 1997), 198–217.
11. Gayle C. Avery, *Understanding Leadership: Paradigms and Cases* (London, 2004), 8, 119; Gillian Peele, "Leadership and Politics: A Case for a Closer Relationship?" *Leadership* 1 (2005), 192.
12. Max Weber, "Politics as a Vocation," in H. H. Gerth and C. Wright Mills (eds.), *From Max Weber: Essays in Sociology* (New York, 1958), 77–78; Charles E. Merriam, *Four American Party Leaders* (New York, 1926; reprint, Freeport, 1967), 100–101; Jasper B. Shannon, "The Study of Political Leadership," in Shannon, *The Study of Comparative Government* (New York, 1949); Lester G. Seligman, "The Study of Political Leadership," *American Political Science Review* 44 (1950), 904–915; David A. Easton, *A Systems Analysis of Political Life* (New York, 1965), 212–216, 302–307; Lucian W. Pye, *Politics, Personality, and Nation Building* (New Haven, 1967), 43; Dankwart A. Rustow (ed.), *Philosophers and Kings: Studies in Leadership* (New York, 1970), 687; Glenn D. Paige, *The Scientific Study of Political Leadership* (New York, 1977), 1, 3, 6; Howard Elcock, *Political Leadership* (Cheltenham, 2001), 43–44. See also, on political leadership, Barbara Kellerman, "Leadership as a Political Act," in Kellerman (ed.), *Leadership: Multidisciplinary Perspectives* (Englewood Cliffs, 1984), 71–73. For Nannerl O. Keohane's experienced view of this question and the "great man" issue, see her *Thinking about Leadership* (Princeton, 2011), 13.
13. Burns, *Leadership,* 18, 439. But see Jean Blondel, *Political Leadership: Towards a General Analysis* (London, 1987), 3–4, on political leaders' determination to coerce. Barbara Kellerman implies that Burns' attempt to exclude bad leaders from the study of leadership, which others have echoed, does disservice to the field of leadership and is confusing and misleading. Kellerman, *Bad Leadership: What It Is, How It Happens, Why It Matters* (Boston, 2004), 11–14. On the distinction between how "bad" leaders come to power using soft power and how they then coerce and employ hard power,

see the discussion in Joseph S. Nye Jr., "Power and Leadership," in Noria and Khurana, *Handbook*, 310, 317.

14. Adapted from Richard E. Neustadt, *Presidential Power and the Modern Presidents: The Politics of Leadership from Roosevelt to Reagan* (New York, 1990), 11.
15. Barbara Kellerman, *Followership: How Followers Are Creating Change and Changing Leaders* (Boston, 2008), 23, 73, 85–93, 239, 243, 258. Keohane has a thoughtful chapter on followership in her *Thinking*, 48–82. The present book avoids discussion of leadership types, believing "types" less instructive than an analysis of core competencies. For a summary of the (misleading) research on "types," see Bernard M. Bass, *Handbook of Leadership: Theory, Research, and Managerial Applications* (New York, 2008, 4th ed.), 33. For Africa and an attempt to typecast, see Robert H. Jackson and Carl G. Rosberg, *Personal Rule in Black Africa: Prince, Autocrat, Prophet, Tyrant* (Berkeley, 1982). They classify Jomo Kenyatta, Haile Selassie, Gaafar Numeiri, and others as princes; Omar Bongo and Felix Houphouet-Boigny, Hastings K. Banda, and Mobutu Sese Seko as autocrats; Kwame Nkrumah and Julius Nyerere as prophets; and Idi Amin and Macias Nguema as tyrants. But typing them does not tell us how they led. Shane says that leadership "types" and styles are influenced by genes. Shane, *Born*, 129.
16. Blondel, *Political Leadership*, 74, insouciantly states that the strategy of "ignoring social and economic policy-making" is no longer available to contemporary [1987] rulers. But Mugabe and so many other 2011 despots blithely do what they want, with impunity.
17. President Obama, quoted in *Economist*, July 18, 2009.
18. See the discussion in Ann Ruth Willner, *The Spellbinders: Charismatic Political Leadership* (New Haven, 1984), 46–47.
19. See Robert I. Rotberg, "Improving Governance in the Developing World: Creating a Measuring and Ranking System," in Robert I. Rotberg and Deborah West, *The Good Governance Problem: Doing Something about It* (Cambridge, Mass., 2004), 5–6.
20. Fred E. Fielder, *A Theory of Leadership Effectiveness* (New York, 1967), 8, 261. Interestingly, Fiedler found no correlation in most situations between tested intelligence and leadership effectiveness. But, as one would expect, successful leaders at the group level (in military or corporate settings) exhibited a high order of interpersonal relationship skills (46). Burns believes that "contribution to change" is a good measure of leadership function, *Leadership*, 427. See also Avery, *Understanding Leadership*, 11–13. Conger and Kanungo, from their analysis of corporate leadership behavior, do not accept that end results are appropriate measures of a leader's effectiveness; such results depend on external contingencies and constraints over which leaders have no control. The instrumental behavior of followers is also important. But the political realm may operate differently. Jay A. Conger and Rabindra N. Kanungo, *Charismatic Leadership in Organizations* (Thousand Oaks, 1998), 40. For a recent survey of the field, see Sean T. Hannah, Bruce

J. Avolio, Fred Luthans, and P. D. Harms, "Leadership Efficacy: Review and Future Directions," *Leadership Quarterly* 19 (2008), 669-692, doi:10.1016/j.leaqua.2008.09.007.

21. Burns, *Leadership,* 106. See also ibid, 425, 430, 434. John Locke, *Second Treatise on Government* (1690), 9:131, in Peter Laslett (ed.), *John Locke: Two Treatises of Government* (1960; reprint, Cambridge, 2002), 353.
22. President Kennedy, addressing the Great and General Court of Massachusetts, January 9, 1961, speech reprinted in *Boston Globe,* January 9, 2011. Desiderius Erasmus expressed similar sentiments in the early sixteenth century. See Keohane, *Thinking,* 41, 242.
23. Robert I. Rotberg and Rachel M. Gisselquist, *Strengthening African Governance: The 2009 Index of African Governance* (Cambridge, Mass., 2009).
24. Gabriel A. Almond and G. Bingham Powell, *Comparative Politics: A Developmental Approach* (Boston, 1966), 50, define political culture a little more strictly as "the pattern of individual attitudes and orientations toward politics among the members of a political system." They discuss the importance of "individual action" but not exactly in the manner here advanced. See also Almond and Sidney Verba, *The Civic Culture* (Princeton, 1963), where some of these concepts were first advanced.
25. See also Morton Grodzins, "Political Parties and the Crisis of Succession in the United States: The Case of 1800," in Joseph LaPalombara and Myron Weiner (eds.), *Political Parties and Political Development* (Princeton, 1966), 323–325, for observations that extend these conclusions.
26. Robert Mugabe, quoted in Michael Hartnack, "Mugabe Rails at Judges," *Business Day,* February 9, 1999; Kassoum Denon, head of the Office du Niger, quoted in *New York Times,* December 22, 2010. Keohane, *Thinking,* contains some very interesting reflections on power wielders, 41–43, 194–201.

CHAPTER TWO

1. These numbers are from the World Bank, World Development Indicators database, 1960–1965; International Monetary Fund, World Economic Outlook Database, 2007; Central Intelligence Agency, World Factbook for the relevant years; United Nations Development Program, Human Development Report, 2008; World Food Program, 2010 report, *New York Times,* September 15, 2010; *Southern African Report,* September 24, 2010.
2. Greg Mills, a South African commentator, flatly declared that Africa's peoples were poor because its leaders had "made this choice." Mills, "Why Is Africa Poor?" *Die Burger,* August 26, 2010. Mills drew on his book, *Why Africa Is Poor—and What Africans Can Do about It* (Johannesburg, 2010).
3. Joseph S. Nye Jr., *The Powers to Lead* (New York, 2008), 18–20; Kellerman, *Bad Leadership,* 21–25.
4. Burns, *Leadership,* 117, drawing to some extent on Abraham Maslow's hierarchy of needs.

5. Howard Gardner, *Changing Minds: The Art and Science of Changing Our Own and Other People's Minds* (Boston, 2004), 39, 108; Gardner, *Multiple Intelligences: The Theory in Practice* (New York, 1993), 9; Gardner, *Frames of Mind: The Theory of Multiple Intelligences* (New York, 2004, 2nd ed.), 239.
6. Mark A. Zupan, "An Economic Perspective on Leadership," in Nohria and Khurana, *Handbook*, 287.
7. Daniel Goleman, *Working with Emotional Intelligence* (New York, 1998), 318; Goleman cites the founding work of Peter Salovey and John D. Mayer, "Emotional Intelligence," *Imagination, Cognition, and Personality* 9 (1990), 185–211.The subsequent literature is discussed in Mayer, Salovey, and David Caruso, "Models of Emotional Intelligence," in Robert J. Sternberg (ed.), *Handbook of Intelligence* (New York, 2000), 396–420. Emotional intelligence is akin to Fiedler's "relationship-motivated" leadership. In Goleman's original *Emotional Intelligence* (New York, 1995), 34, 43, "to empathize and to hope" was a fourth element after being able to "motivate" oneself, to control impulses, and to regulate moods. "Emotional aptitude" (36) was closer to what is called "emotional intelligence" here.
8. Tony Blair, *A Journey: My Political Life* (New York, 2010), 608.
9. Dean Williams, *Real Leadership: Helping People and Organizations Face Their Toughest Challenges* (San Francisco, 2005), xiii. The environment constitutes the "chessboard" on which leaders have to play. See Blondel, *Political Leadership*, 30, 45.
10. Quoted in Dexter Filkins, "After the Uprising: Can Protesters Find a Path between Dictatorship and Anarchy?" *New Yorker*, April 11, 2011, 41.
11. These behavioral attributes are similar to those detailed in a corporate context by Warren G. Bennis, *On Becoming a Leader* (New York, 1989), 161, 192–198, summarized and organized in Elcock, *Political*, 81–83.
12. Conger and Kanungo, *Charismatic Leadership*, 195.
13. Jay A. Conger, *The Charismatic Leader: Behind the Mystique of Exceptional Leadership* (San Francisco, 1989), 43. See also Gayle C. Avery, *Understanding Leadership* (London, 2004), 24–26, 99–102. Avery has much of interest to contribute to nearly all of the discussions of competencies in this chapter.
14. Ibid., 41.
15. Conger and Kanungo, *Charismatic Leadership*, 59. Keohane is skeptical about the need for leaders to have a vision. *Thinking*, 87.
16. See Nye, *Powers to Lead*, 88. The use here of the navigator metaphor echoes Plato.
17. Jay A. Conger, Gretchen M. Spreitzer, and Edward E. Lawler III (eds.), *The Leader's Change Handbook: An Essential Guide to Setting Direction and Taking Action* (San Francisco, 1999), xliii.
18. Rosabeth Moss Kanter, "Leadership for Change: Enduring Skills for Change Masters," a Harvard Business School class note, November 17, 2005, 5.
19. Burns, *Leadership*, 20; Avery, *Understanding Leadership*, 22–23. Blondel, *Political Leadership*, 22, 27, challenges this dichotomous approach to leader-

ship, arguing that the range within the categories of heroic and ordinary leadership is more instructive than the postulated two-way distinction.

20. J. M. Kouzes and B. Z. Posner, *The Leadership Challenge: How to Get Extraordinary Things Done in Organizations* (San Francisco, 1987), reported in Bass, *Handbook*, 625. See also Abraham Zaleznick, "Managers and Leaders: Are They Different?" *Harvard Business Review* 55 (1977), 67–80; Philip M. Podsakoff, S. B. Mackenzie, R. H. Moorman, et al., "Transformational Leader Behaviors and Their Effects on Followers' Trust in the Leader, Satisfaction, and Organizational Citizenship Behaviors," *Leadership Quarterly* 1 (1990), 177–192.
21. Burns, *Leadership*, 4, 33, 254–265, 322, 425–426. Burns says that Machiavelli's mordant maxims in *The Prince* (1532) teach transactional, not transformational, leadership (447). On transformational leaders, see also Nye, *Powers to Lead*, 7–9, 61–65, 126, 130; on transformational and transactional leadership, see also Conger and Kanungo, *Charismatic Leadership*, 58–59, 69; Bernard M. Bass and Bruce J. Avolio, "Transformational Leadership: A Response to Critiques," in Martin M. Chemers and Roya Ayman, *Leadership Theory and Research: Perspectives and Directions* (San Diego, 1993), 52, 56; Bass, *Handbook*, 41, 623.
22. Lee, 1989, quoted in James Minchin, *No Man Is an Island: A Portrait of Singapore's Lee Kuan Yew* (London, 1990, orig. pub. 1986), 343. See also chapter 5 in this book, 92.
23. Ronald A. Heifetz and Donald L. Laurie, "Mobilizing Adaptive Work: Beyond Visionary Leadership," in Conger, Spreitzer, and Lawler, *Leader's Change Handbook*, 63.
24. Ibid., 81.
25. Ronald A. Heifetz, *Leadership without Easy Answers* (Cambridge, Mass., 1994), 23.
26. Mandela's inclusive actions are discussed at greater length in chapter 3, 59–65.
27. Lucian W. Pye, *Mao Tse-tung: The Man in the Leader* (New York, 1976), 238.
28. Quoted in Kanter, "Globalizing World," 589. The speaker was a Latin American corporate executive.
29. Bass, *Handbook*, 260.
30. Nye, *Powers to Lead*, 30. See also Nye, "Power and Leadership," 305. On 306 and 307 in the same chapter, Nye provides a sensible understanding of what "power" means in practice and in leadership usage.
31. Huntington, *Third Wave*, 46.
32. Richard E. Neustadt, *Presidential Power: The Politics of Leadership from FDR to Carter* (New York, 1980, 2nd ed.), 48.
33. Stephen Breyer, *Making Our Democracy Work: A Judge's View* (New York, 2010), 214.
34. See also Michael A. Toth, *The Theory of the Two Charismas* (Washington, D.C., 1981), 29, drawing heavily on Max Weber (Guenther Roth and Claus Wittich, eds.), *Economy and Society: An Outline of Interpretive Sociology* (Berkeley, 1978), 1:212–213, 2:941.

35. Quoted in Rachel Donadio, "Italy's Political Houdini May Not Escape This Time," *New York Times*, November 18, 2010. On Thatcher, see Keohane, *Thinking,* 206.
36. For a limited discussion of some of these issues, see Terence R. Mitchell, "Leadership, Values, and Accountability," in Chemers and Ayman, *Perspectives*, 113–115. The standard handbook on leadership has disappointingly little to say about "legitimacy." See Bass, *Handbook*, 283–286. Likewise, the index to Keith Grint (ed.), *Leadership: Classical, Contemporary, and Critical Approaches* (Oxford, 1997), an acclaimed reader, has (like many standard leadership texts) no mention of legitimate or legitimacy. Instructive for the discussion here is Kenneth F. Janda, "Towards the Explication of the Concept of Leadership in Terms of the Concept of Power," in Glenn D. Paige (ed.), *Political Leadership: Readings for an Emerging Field* (New York, 1972), 56; Easton, *Systems Analysis*, 302–307.
37. For an early set of studies supporting this conclusion, see Burns, *Leadership*, 431–432.
38. President Kennedy, addressing the Great and General Court of Massachusetts, September 9, 1961, speech reprinted in *Boston Globe,* January 9, 2011.
39. Williams, *Real Leadership*, 7. Howard Gardner's "integrity" is much closer to "self-mastery," below. Gardner, *Changing Minds*, 110–111. Likewise, Bass' "integrity" is a combination of what this book calls "intellectual honesty," "prudence," and "self-mastery." Bass, *Handbook*, 222–223.
40. For some of these questions, see Ruth W. Grant, *Hypocrisy and Integrity: Machiavelli, Rousseau, and the Ethics of Politics* (Chicago, 1997), 3–31; see also Niccolo Machiavelli (Robert M. Adams, ed. and trans.), *The Prince* (New York, 1992, 2nd ed.), 47–49, 65. For other views of *The Prince,* and the likelihood of it being satire, see Burns, *Leadership,* 445. Machiavelli is pragmatic and without guile, according to Kellerman, *Leadership,* 40. Machiavelli advocated the appearance of being good, not goodness. "Men in general judge more by their eyes than by their hands . . . Everyone sees how you appear, few touch what you are . . ." in Niccolo Machiavelli (Harvey C. Mansfield, ed. and trans.), *The Prince* (Chicago, 1998, 2nd ed.), 71.
41. This moral model is not the heroic leadership model of Joseph Badaracco. See Ellen Pruyne (ed.), *Conversations on Leadership* (Cambridge, Mass. 2002), 44–46. See the lengthy discussion of ethical and moral leadership in Bass, *Handbook*, 200–212.
42. Conger and Kanungo, *Charismatic Leadership,* 213.
43. Heifetz, *Leadership without Easy Answers*, 191.
44. Mohandas K. Gandhi, *Satyagraha* (Ahmedabad, 1951), 233, quoted in Erik H. Erikson, *Gandhi's Truth: On the Origins of Militant Non-Violence* (New York, 1969), 444, 446. See also Judith M. Brown, "Gandhi as Nationalist Leader, 1915–1948," in Brown and Anthony Parel (eds.), *The Cambridge Companion to Gandhi* (New York, 2011), 59–67.

45. J. Patrick Dobel, "Political Prudence and the Ethics of Leadership," *Public Administration Review* 58 (1998), 78.
46. For Botswana, see Robert I. Rotberg, *Governance and Leadership in Africa* (Philadelphia, 2007), 18–19, 37–38.
47. Dobel, "Ethics of Leadership," 76.
48. See Chatman and Kennedy, "Psychological Perspectives," 161–162.
49. Richard E. Neustadt and Ernest R. May, *Thinking in Time: The Uses of History for Decision Makers* (New York, 1986), xix-xx.
50. As in Geoffrey Vickers, *The Art of Judgment: A Study of Policy Making* (New York, 1965), 195; or Machiavelli (Adams), *The Prince*, 64, 87–89.
51. For character and proportion, see Keohane, *Thinking*, 206, 212.
52. Terry L. Cooper, "Hierarchy, Virtue, and the Practice of Public Administration: A Perspective for Normative Ethics," *Public Administration Review* 47 (1987), 328. See also David K. Hart, "The Virtuous Citizen, the Honorable Bureaucrat, and Public Administration," *Public Administration Review* 44 (1984), 116–117. Prudence is close in definitional terms to Weber's "ethic of responsibility"—the evaluation of diverse values, interests, and attitudes, and the consequences of choosing wisely while taking those many considerations into account. See Weber, "Vocation," 77–128.
53. See J. Patrick Dobel, "William D. Ruckelshaus: Political Prudence and Public Integrity," in Terry L. Cooper and N. Dale Wright (eds.), *Exemplary Public Administrators: Character and Leadership in Government* (San Francisco, 1992), 252–253, 262–263.
54. Kennedy, speech on January 9, 1961, *Boston Globe.*
55. Adam Smith (D. D. Raphael and A. L. Macfie, eds.), *The Theory of Moral Sentiments* (Oxford, 1976), 237. See also Dobel, "Ethics of Leadership," 75.
56. For Turkmenistan, see Gregory Gleason, "Turkmenistan under Niyazov and Berdymukhammedov," in Robert I. Rotberg (ed.), *Worst of the Worst: Dealing with Repressive and Rogue Nations* (Washington, D.C., 2007), 115–134.
57. Elcock, *Political*, 97; Kellerman, *Followership*, 69–70. The term itself comes from Irving Janis, *Groupthink: Psychological Studies of Policy Decisions and Fiascoes* (Boston, 1982), especially 148–158. Gardner, *Changing Minds*, 40–42, 108, 109, 111. "Intrapersonal" intelligence also is central to "self-mastery."
58. Kennedy, speech on January 9, 1961, *Boston Globe.*
59. Machiavelli (Adams), *The Prince*, 65, 87–89. For the "isolation from reality" leadership trap, see Kets de Vries and Engellau, "Clinical Approach," 198.
60. Williams, *Real Leadership*, 5.
61. For a game-theoretic examination of how followers behave when leaders convey information about the state of the world in both "agreement" and "disagreement" states, see Eric A. Dickson, "Leadership, Followership, and Beliefs about the World: An Experiment," accessed January 4, 2011, http://www.nyu.edu/gsas/dept/politics/faculty/dickson.
62. Conger and Kanungo, *Charismatic Leadership*, 56, 59, 190. See also Bass, *Handbook*, 223–224.

63. Bennis, *On Becoming a Leader*, 153. See also the discussion in Bass, *Handbook*, 258–260, where trust is the "authenticity" of a leader.
64. Machiavelli (Adams), *The Prince,* 29, 38. Mansfield translates "resource" as "remedy," which seems more apt. Machiavelli (Mansfield), *The Prince,* 41.
65. See R. B. Bernstein, *The Founding Fathers Reconsidered* (New York, 2009), 42–43. But see also Nye, "Power and Leadership," 313.
66. President Kennedy, Inaugural Address, January 20, 1961, accessed May 29, 2009, www.bartleby.com/124/pres56.
67. David McClelland, *Power: The Inner Experience* (New York, 1975), 260. McClelland drew for this concept on R. deCharms, *Personal Causation* (New York, 1968).
68. John W. Gardner, "The Antileadership Vaccine," in *Annual Report of the Carnegie Corporation* (New York, 1965), 3, 12; Gardner, *On Leadership* (New York, 1993; orig. pub. 1990), 191.
69. For the full story, see Jiang Yonglin, *The Mandate of Heaven and the Great Ming Code* (Seattle, 2011), 4–6.
70. Manfred Kets de Vries, "The Leadership Mystique," *Academy of Management Executive* 8 (1994), 73–92, in Grint, *Leadership*, 253.
71. See the congruence established in Bass, *Handbook*, 606, 616–617. An earlier expression of the same possible overlap is Bass and Avolio, "Transformational Leadership," 52, 62.
72. Conger and Kanungo, *Charismatic Leadership*, 59, 62–63, 204, 211–218. For a very helpful exegesis of Max Weber's "charisma," and of the subsequent critique of Weber by the likes of Carl Friedrich, Edward Shils, and many others, see Alan Bryman, *Charisma and Leadership in Organizations* (London, 1992), 22–40. Bryman comments wryly, but not dismissively, that "in the concept of charisma we find a seductive but irritatingly intangible way of discussing leadership," 41.
73. Conger, *Charismatic Leader*, 140, 153–158.
74. I asked Suu Kyi in October 1996 to describe the sources of her charisma. That week in 1996 was one of the few during the 1990s when she was not under house arrest or in jail. For Suu Kyi after her release in 2010 from house arrest, see chapter 7 in this book, 153–156.
75. Barbara J. Kellerman, comment on Weber, in Kellerman (ed.), *Leadership: Essential Selections on Power, Authority, and Influence* (New York, 2010), 79, 80. Charismatic leaders "implicate the self-concept of followers." See Boas Shamir, Robert J. House, and Michael B. Arthur, "The Motivational Effects of Charismatic Leadership: A Self-Concept Based Theory," *Organization Science* 4 (1993), 590.
76. Weber, *Economy and Society*, 2:1116.
77. Some of this hesitation echoes Bass, *Handbook*, 580–581.
78. Alexei Barrionuevo, "Brazil's New Leader Starts in Shadow of Predecessor," *New York Times*, January 1, 2011.

CHAPTER THREE

1. Quoted in Tom Lodge, *Mandela: A Critical Life* (New York, 2006), 179–180.
2. Quoted in Stanley B. Greenberg, *Dispatches from the War Room: In the Trenches with Five Extraordinary Leaders* (New York, 2009), 145; cf. Nelson Mandela, *Long Walk to Freedom: The Autobiography of Nelson Mandela* (Boston, 1994), 538.
3. Mandela, *Long Walk,* 8.
4. See Richard Stengel, "Mandela: His 8 Lessons of Leadership," *Time,* July 9, 2008.
5. Quoted in Lodge, *Mandela,* 6. See also Mandela, *Long Walk,* 12.
6. Lodge, *Mandela,* 5.
7. Quoted in Stengel, "8 Lessons."
8. Lodge, *Mandela,* 40. For this period in Mandela's political awakening, see also Ahmed Kathrada, *No Bread for Mandela* (Lexington, Ky., 2011), 55–56.
9. For details, see Robert I. Rotberg, *Suffer the Future: Policy Choices in Southern Africa* (Cambridge, Mass., 1980), 28–60.
10. See Anthony Sampson, *Mandela: The Authorized Biography* (New York, 1999), 83–91. But cf. Lodge, *Mandela,* 57.
11. Lodge, *Mandela,* 60.
12. Ibid., 62.
13. Ibid., 61.
14. Sampson, *Mandela,*143; Lodge, *Mandela,* 86.
15. Quoted in Lodge, *Mandela,* 90, but the footnote in Lodge to Mandela, *Long Walk,* 242, lacks that quotation.
16. Quoted in Nelson Mandela, *The Struggle Is My Life* (London, 1978), 155–175.
17. Mandela, *Long Walk*, 424. Mandela was even willing to meet with the leaders of "government-sponsored organizations," such as the official homelands. Mandela favored "participation" rather than boycotts, but his colleagues refused to let Mandela become, in such a manner, a "collaborationist," 441.
18. Ibid., 428.
19. See Robert I. Rotberg, "Mandela's Prisoner," *Boston Globe*, August 29, 1988.
20. Sampson, *Mandela*, 294–295.
21. Quoted in Allister Sparks, *The Death of Apartheid* (film), in Sampson, *Mandela,* 331.
22. Mandela, *Long Walk,* 455–456.
23. Ibid., 458–459.
24. Quoted in John Carlin, *Playing the Enemy: Nelson Mandela and the Game That Made a Nation* (New York, 2008), 24.
25. Mark Gevisser, *A Legacy of Liberation: Thabo Mbeki and the Future of the South African Dream* (New York, 2009), 190–198.

26. This paragraph and the next draw on Robert I. Rotberg, *Ending Autocracy, Enabling Democracy: The Tribulations of Southern Africa 1960–2000* (Washington, D.C., 2002), 415–417, and the op-eds by the same author listed therein.
27. Mandela, *Long Walk*, 480.
28. Robert I. Rotberg, "Has South Africa Found Its Nixon?" *New York Times*, March 14, 1989; Rotberg, "South Africa's Tide Shifts," *New York Times*, August 3, 1989. De Klerk and I talked about these conclusions at Ditchley Park in Britain, in 2003, and at the Harvard Kennedy School, in 2007.
29. Quoted in Rotberg, *Ending Autocracy*, 420, 445–448.
30. Mandela, *Long Walk*, 485.
31. Ibid., 495. Several foreign observers felt that this speech (in Cape Town) was less than stirring. Indeed, Mandela often spoke woodenly, but his sincerity and clarity apparently was enough for local listeners. For the critics, see Lodge, *Mandela*, 168; Patti Waldmeir, *Anatomy of a Miracle: The End of Apartheid and the Birth of the New South Africa* (Harmondsworth, 1997), 201; Sampson, *Mandela*, 403; Carlin, *Playing the Enemy*, 84.
32. Sampson, *Mandela*, 450.
33. Ibid., 415.
34. Mandela, *Long Walk*, 530; cf. Sampson, *Mandela*, 461–462; Carlin, *Playing the Enemy*, 120.
35. Rosabeth Moss Kanter, *Confidence: How Winning Streaks and Losing Streaks Begin and End* (New York, 2004), 318.
36. This paragraph and the previous one draw on Rotberg, *Ending Autocracy*, 461–462, and the articles cited therein.
37. Mandela, *Long Walk*, 536; Sampson, *Mandela*, 478.
38. Quoted in the *Guardian*, in Sampson, *Mandela*, 484.
39. For details, see Rotberg, *Ending Autocracy*, 460–461.
40. See Gevisser, *Legacy*, 247.
41. Quoted in ibid., 249.
42. Carlin, *Playing the Enemy*, 4, 16, 17, 95, 113, 163, 193. See also Kanter, *Confidence*, 291–292.
43. Stengel, "8 Lessons," elaborates on Mandela's conscious effort in the 1960s to learn Afrikaans so that he could understand Afrikaners and meet them on their own ground in their own language. At his presidential inaugural in 1994, Mandela spoke a few sentences in Afrikaans, but those sentences gave reassurance to Afrikaners. "What's done is done," he said in Afrikaans. Quoted in Gevisser, *Legacy*, 265.
44. Quoted in Gevisser, *Legacy*, 261.
45. Quoted in Kanter, *Confidence*, 315.

CHAPTER FOUR

1. Rotberg and Gisselquist, *Index of African Governance*, 9.
2. *CIA World Fact Book*, March 2010.

3. This sentence is not meant to overlook Botswana's dispute with BaSarwa regarding the Central Kalahari Reserve, or the occasional abridgments of free speech that have occurred.
4. For a good discussion of the kgotla's place in Ngwato history, and additional references, see Diana Wylie, *A Little God: The Twilight of Patriarchy in a Southern African Kingdom* (Hanover, N.H., 1990), 100–107.
5. Quett Ketumile Joni Masire (Stephen R. Lewis Jr., ed.), *Very Brave or Very Foolish? Memoirs of an African Democrat* (Gaborone, 2006), 35.
6. Charles Rey, *Monarch of All I Survey: Bechuanaland Diaries 1929–37* (Gaborone, 1988), 29.
7. See Thomas Tlou, Neil Parsons, and Willie Henderson, *Seretse Khama, 1921–80* (Gaborone, 1995), 49, 53.
8. See Wylie, *Little God,* 184.
9. Tlou, Parsons, and Henderson, *Seretse,* 100, 101. See also Anthony Sillery, *Botswana: A Short Political History* (London, 1974), 149, who writes that Britain should have been "braver, more honest." Sillery was a leading administrator at the time in Botswana.
10. Peter Lewis, of the Commonwealth Relations Office, quoted in Tlou, Parsons, and Henderson, *Seretse,* 113.
11. Quoted in ibid., 120.
12. Quoted in ibid., 147.
13. Quoted in ibid., 148.
14. Quoted in ibid., 193.
15. Quoted in ibid., 195.
16. But see Festus Mogae, "A Review of the Performance of Botswana's Economy," in M. A. Oommen, F. K. Inganji, and L. D. Ngcongco (eds.), *Botswana's Economy since Independence* (New Delhi, 1983), 19.
17. See Edwin S. Munger, *Bechuanaland: Pan-African Outpost or Bantu Homeland?* (London, 1965), 68–71.
18. For a review of educational statistics, see Keetla Masogo, "Education a Fundamental Right or to Meet Manpower Requirements?" and Taufila Nyamadzabo, "Will Botswana Attain Manpower Self-Sufficiency by the Year 2000?" in Sue Brothers, Janet Hermans, and Doreen Nteta (eds.), *Botswana in the 21st Century* (Gaborone, 1994), 425–446. See also Masire, *Very Brave,* 220.
19. Robin Palmer and Neil Parsons, "The Roots of Rural Poverty: Historical Background," in Palmer and Parsons (eds.), *The Roots of Rural Poverty in Central and Southern Africa* (Berkeley, 1977), 7. See also David Denoon and Balam Nyeko, *Southern Africa since 1800* (Harlow, 1984), 225.
20. See also Masire, *Very Brave,* 47.
21. Quoted in Tlou, Parsons, and Henderson, *Seretse,* 223.
22. Khama, quoted in Munger, *Bechuanaland,* 2.
23. See Sillery, *Botswana,* 151–154.
24. Tlou, Parsons, and Henderson, *Seretse,* 235.

25. Quoted in Masire, *Very Brave,* 48. See also ibid., 103.
26. Ibid., 56.
27. Tlou, Parsons, and Henderson, *Seretse,* 61.
28. Quoted in Tlou, Parsons, and Henderson, *Seretse,* 252. By condemning autocracy, Khama was alluding to the practices of his fellow African presidents. But he was also saying that his government would not tolerate the autocratic practices of chiefs.
29. Ibid., 280, 282, 335.
30. Tlou, Parsons, and Henderson, *Seretse,* 271, but note the absence of quotes in the original.
31. Masire, *Very Brave,* 103.
32. Quoted in Tlou, Parsons, and Henderson, *Seretse,* 364.
33. Khama, speaking in New York, quoted in ibid., 360.
34. See E. Y. Ablo and D. J. Hudson, "Monetary Policy of Botswana," in Oommen, Inganji, and Ngcongco, *Economy,* 93–123.
35. Lewis G. Nchindo, "Diamonds in Botswana," in Oommen, Inganji, and Ngcongco, *Economy,* 233–234.
36. Masire, *Very Brave,* 209.
37. Tlou, Parsons, and Henderson, *Seretse,* 334.
38. Masire, "Economic Opportunities and Disparities," in Masire, *Very Brave,* 239. Also in Robert I. Rotberg, "Leadership Alters Corrupt Behavior," in Rotberg (ed.), *Corruption, Global Security, and World Order* (Washington, D.C., 2009), 352–353.
39. Masire, *Very Brave,* 240. Also in Rotberg, "Leadership Alters Corrupt Behavior," 351–354, from which these paragraphs are derived.
40. Subsequent analysis of corruption in Botswana suggests that Khama and Masire were successful in dampening or retarding the spread of venal corruption, and therefore in limiting petty corruption. See Andrew Briscoe and Quill Hermans, *Combating Corruption in Botswana* (Gaborone, 2001), 10–12, 123–124. But see Masire's lament in his *Very Brave,* 245.
41. Transparency International website, accessed July 5, 2011, http://www.transparency.org. Singapore tied first and the United States ranked twenty-second on the Corruption Perceptions Index for 2010.
42. Daron Acemoglu, Simon Johnson, and James A. Robinson, "An African Success Story: Botswana," in Dani Rodrik, *In Search of Prosperity: Analytic Narratives on Economic Growth* (Princeton, 2003), 85–88, 104–106.

CHAPTER FIVE

1. http://www.transparency.org, October 26, 2010. See also Jon S. T. Quah, "Combating Corruption in Singapore: What Can Be Learned?" *Journal of Contingencies and Crisis Management* 9 (2001), 29. In 1960, Singapore's GNP per capita was about $443.
2. Unlike the ideas in the second chapter in this book, Lee believed that lead-

ership consisted of "integrity, drive, verve, intelligence, physical and mental discipline." See Lee, quoted in Han Fook Kwang, Warren Fernandez, and Sumiko Tan, *Lee Kuan Yew: The Man and His Ideas* (Singapore, 1998), 95. The quotations in the text come first from Michael D. Barr, *Lee Kuan Yew: The Beliefs behind the Man* (Richmond, Surrey, UK, 2000), 124, and Han, Fernandez, and Sumiko, *Lee*, 101, 231. The business of a leader, Lee also avers, is "not to follow the crowd." Ibid, 229. The last quotation is from Minchin, *Island*, 343. Lee's notion that persons are "born to lead" is supported by new research explored in Shane, *Born*, 122–136. See also above, 182n6, where good leadership is described as a capable of being learned and nurtured.

3. Lee, interview with David Gergen, Ronald Heifetz, and John Thomas, October 17, 2000, unpublished transcript. This chapter also draws upon six hours of partially taped interviews between Lee and me in his Singapore offices on January 13–14, 2006. For Blair, on Brown, see above 20.
4. Thomas Bellows, book review, in *Third World Quarterly* 7 (1985), 1096.
5. Cited in Barr, *Lee*, 10. For details about Lee's upbringing, see Han, Fernandez, and Sumiko, *Lee*, 26. For Lee at Raffles, see the reminiscences of Eddie Barker in Lam Peng Er and Kevin Y. L. Tan (eds.), *Lee's Lieutenants: Singapore's Old Guard* (St. Leonards, NSW, Australia, 1999), 83.
6. See Maurice Baker, in Barr, *Lee*, 11; Lee, *The Singapore Story* (Singapore, 2000), 1:42.
7. Lee, quoted in Han, Fernandez, and Sumiko, *Lee*, 29.
8. Lee, speech in Padang, 1963, in *Prime Minister's Speeches*. See also Barr, *Lee,* 14.
9. Lee, quoted in Han, Fernandez, and Sumiko, *Lee, 31.*
10. Michael Lever, quoted in Barr, *Lee,* 16.
11. Lee, *Singapore Story,* 1:132.
12. Lee, quoted in Han, Fernandez, and Sumiko, *Lee*, 45.
13. Lee, *Singapore Story,* 1:151.
14. Ibid., 229.
15. Ibid., 251.
16. Ibid., 263. The most revealing contemporary study of communism and the tactics of the communists in Singapore in this period is Dennis Bloodworth, *The Tiger and the Trojan Horse* (Singapore, 1986), 55–136, 202–221.
17. Philip Moore to Lord Head, September 22, 1963, quoted in Lee, *Singapore Story,* 508.
18. Lee, *Singapore Story,* 1:475, 1:542. See also Diane K. Mauzy and R. S. Milne, *Singapore Politics under the People's Action Party* (New York, 2002), 22.
19. Albert Winsemius, quoted in Barr, *Lee*, 37.
20. Quoted in Lee, *Singapore Story*, 1:640.
21. Ibid., 1:22.
22. Lee, speaking in 1980, quoted in Barr, *Lee*, 81–82.
23. Lee, *Singapore Story,* 1:663. The "life and death" quote is Lee in Han, Fernandez, and Sumiko, *Lee,* 128.

24. Lee Kuan Yew, *From Third World to First: The Singapore Story, 1965–2000* (Singapore, 2000), 76–77. See also Ang Cheng Guan, "The Global and the Regional in Lee Kuan Yew's Strategic Thought: The Early Cold War Years," in Derek Heng and Syed Muhd Khairudin Aljunied (eds.), *Singapore in Global History* (Amsterdam, 2011), 244–245.
25. For a nearly contemporary study of Singapore's composition, ethnic politics, and communism, see Chan Heng Chee, *Singapore: The Politics of Survival, 1965–1967* (Singapore, 1971), 14–25.
26. Ezra F. Vogel, "A Little Dragon Tamed," in Kernial Singh Sandhu and Paul Wheatley (eds.), *Management of Success: The Moulding of Modern Singapore* (Singapore, 1989), 1057–1058. See also Sharon Siddique, "Singaporean Identity," ibid., 563–576. For Lee's own explanation of what he did to mandate English as Singapore's key language, see Han, Fernandez, and Sumiko, *Lee,* 134.
27. Nirmala Puu Shotam, "Language and Linguistic Policies," in Sandhu and Wheatley, *Success,* 511. See also Mauzy and Milne, *Singapore Politics*, 99–107.
28. For details, see Cedric Pugh, "The Political Economy of Public Housing," in Sandhu and Wheatley, *Success*, 841–853. But see Lee, quoted in Han, Fernandez, and Sumiko, *Lee*, 96.
29. Lee, *Singapore Story*, 127–128.
30. For a glimpse at Lee's tree-growing micromanagement, see Cherian George, *Singapore: The Air-Conditioned Nation* (Singapore, 2000), 12–13.
31. Robert O. Tilman, "The Political Leadership: Lee Kuan Yew and the PAP Team," in Sandhu and Wheatley, *Success*, 60; Lee, *Third World*, 226.
32. Carnes Lord, *The Modern Prince: What Leaders Need to Know* (New Haven, 2003), 105.
33. Tan Cheng Bock, quoted in Jonathan E. D. Richmond, "Transporting Singapore: The Air-Conditioned Nation," *Transport Reviews* 28 (2008), 359. Lee preferred a "spectator society." See David Gibbons, "The Spectator Culture: A Refinement of the Almond and Verba Model," *Journal of Commonwealth Political Studies* 9 (1971), 19–35.
34. Mauzy and Milne, *Singapore Politics*, 53–54.
35. David Brown, *The State and Ethnic Politics in Southeast Asia* (London, 1994), 69.
36. Vogel, "Dragon," 1053. On the administrative state, see Chan Heng Chee, "Politics in an Administrative State: Where Has the Politics Gone?," in Ong Jin Hui, Tong Chee Kiong, and Tan Ern Ser, *Understanding Singapore Society* (Singapore, 1997), 294–306. That chapter originally appeared in Seah Chee Meow (ed.), *Trends in Singapore* (Singapore, 1975), 51–68.
37. Dennis Bloodworth to Louise Williams, quoted in Minchin, *Island,* 359.
38. Quoted in Han, Fernandez, and Sumiko, *Lee,* 127.
39. Quoted in ibid., 91.
40. See Quah, "Combating Corruption," 31–32.
41. Quoted in Han, Fernandez, and Sumiko, *Lee,* 205.
42. In his Harvard interview, Lee spoke proudly about the engineering in-

novations that he used, along with punishments, to deter such antisocial behavior. The quotation is from the interview.

43. Lee, *Singapore Story*, 163.
44. Lee, *Third World*, 157.
45. Ibid., 163.
46. Lee, quoted in Han, Fernandez, and Sumiko, *Lee*, 239. See also Quah, "Combating Corruption," 33.
47. Francis T. Seow, *To Catch a Tartar: A Dissident in Lee Kuan Yew's Prison* (New Haven, 1994), 20.
48. Quoted in Syed Hussein Alatas, "The Problem of Corruption," in Sandhu and Wheatley, *Management of Success*, 993.
49. For a sensible critique, see George, *Air-Conditioned*, 76–78. For details, see Quah, "Combating Corruption," 33–34. See also, on corruption and public sector accountability, Hilton L. Root, *Small Countries, Big Lessons: Governance and the Rise of East Asia* (Hong Kong, 1996), 47.
50. This paragraph benefited from conversation with Ben W. Heineman Jr. See also Robert I. Rotberg, "Creating Robust Institutions: Preparing Secure Foundations," unpublished paper (Cambridge, Mass., 2006). Further see Eric M. Uslaner, *Corruption, Inequality, and the Rule of Law: The Bulging Pocket Makes the Easy Life* (New York, 2008), 204. Singapore could have survived and attracted investment, Uslaner reminds us, only if it conquered corruption (208). But he applauds institutions and says nothing about the critical role of political culture (213).
51. Barr, *Lee*, 126; T. J. S. George, *Lee Kuan Yew's Singapore* (London, 1973), 97; Minchin, *Island*, 253. All three authors are otherwise extremely critical of Lee, his legal shortcuts, and his autocratic leadership.
52. Seow, *To Catch a Tartar*, 46–52. Subsequently, in 1988 when he was in private legal practice, Seow was arrested and held for seventy-two days in a detention center and subjected to harsh interrogation procedures that amounted to torture. He had allegedly contravened a provision of the Internal Security Act, but Seow suggests that Lee had taken affront because of his legal defense of political protestors. For the details and a sharp commentary, see Seow, 106ff. and the thirty-page foreword by C. V. Devan Nair to Seow's book. Nair had been a close associate of Lee (and the nation's President) and a freedom campaigner who had been imprisoned by the British colonial authorities. In the foreword, Nair calls Lee's behavior "loutish" and treacherous.
53. Quoted in Han, Fernandez, and Sumiko, *Lee*, 212.
54. For Lee's proud explanation of his legal successes against defamers, see Lee, *Third World*, 151–155. For a perceptive discussion of Lee's use of the law of defamation, see Mauzy and Milne, *Singapore Politics*, 132–139.
55. Ibid., 218. See also George, *Air-Conditioned*, 65–72; Bloodworth, *Trojan*, 324–327.
56. For Lee's selection of judges, see Lee, *Third World*, 248–249.

57. Minchin, *Island,* 349.
58. Seth Mydans, "Days of Reflection for the Man Who Defined Singapore," *New York Times*, September 11, 2010.
59. Chan, "Administrative State," 302.
60. See Chia Siow Yue, "The Character and Progress of Industrialization," in Sandhu and Wheatley, *Success,* 250–279; Lawrence B. Krause, "Government as Entrepreneur," ibid., 436–451. For Lee's explanation of why air-conditioning was imperative, see Lee, *Singapore,* 316.
61. George, *Air-Conditioned*, 17–18.
62. Lee's New Year's message, quoted in Minchin, *Island,* 299.
63. Quoted in Han, Fernandez, and Sumiko, *Lee,* 117, 119.
64. For Lee's considered cynicism about one man, one vote, see his responses to questions by Fareed Zakaria, in Zakaria, "Culture Is Destiny: A Conversation with Lee Kuan Yew," *Foreign Affairs* 73 (1994), 119.
65. Minchin, *Island,* 317.

CHAPTER SIX

1. A British official military historian, quoted in Lord Kinross, *Ataturk: A Biography of Mustafa Kemal, Father of Modern Turkey* (New York, 1965), 111. British forces evacuated the Gallipoli Peninsula early in 1916.
2. Ataturk's speeches, quoted in Andrew Mango, *Ataturk: The Biography of the Founder of Modern Turkey* (Woodstock, N.Y., 2000), 420.
3. For details, see Mark Mazower, *Salonica, City of Ghosts: Christians, Muslims and Jews* (New York, 2004); M. Sukru Hanioglu, *Ataturk: An Intellectual Biography* (Princeton, 2011), 18, sheds doubt on the likelihood that Mustafa Kemal's father ever was a soldier. Hanioglu's first chapter, 8–30, also shows how Ataturk's subsequent attitudes toward the West and to various kinds of reforms stemmed plausibly from the influence of his early years in Salonica.
4. Vamik D. Volkan and Norman Itzkowitz, *The Immortal Ataturk: A Psychobiography* (Chicago, 1984), 27. The authors draw on the theories of D. W. Winnicott, Heinz Kohut, and others. Volkan and Itzkowitz are also interviewed extensively in a compelling documentary about Kemal by Tolga Ornek, "Ataturk," 1998. Tuncay Babali kindly lent me a copy of this film.
5. See Bernard Lewis, *The Emergence of Modern Turkey* (New York, 2002, 3rd ed.), 244.
6. For Kemal's subversive organizing in Damascus and his limited role in the CUP, see M. Sukru Hanioglu, *Preparation for a Revolution: The Young Turks, 1902–1908* (New York, 2001), 211–212.
7. For this period, see Rachel Simon, "Prelude to Reforms: Mustafa Kemal in Libya," in Jacob M. Landau (ed.), *Ataturk and the Modernization of Turkey* (Boulder, 1984), 17–24; Hanioglu, *Ataturk*, 41, says that Mustafa Kemal was smuggled into Cyrenaica in order to organize a local militia insurgency against the Italians, who had invaded Libya.

8. Kinross, *Ataturk*, 153.
9. Dankwart A. Rustow, "Ataturk as Founder of a State," in Rustow, *Philosophers and Kings*, 210.
10. Volkan and Itzkowitz, *Ataturk*, 143. Interestingly, Kemal was scathing about Wilsonian idealism: "Poor Wilson, he did not understand that lines which cannot be defended by the bayonet, by force, by honor and dignity, cannot be defended by any other principle." Quoted in Rustow, "Ataturk as Founder," 215.
11. Kinross, *Ataturk*, 269.
12. Halide Edib Adivar, quoted in Kinross, *Ataturk*, 271–272.
13. Rumbold, quoted in Martin Gilbert, *Sir Horace Rumbold: Portrait of a Diplomat, 1869–1941* (London, 1973), 229.
14. On the relevance of height and physical looks to leadership attainments, see Nye, *Powers to Lead*, 15, 61.
15. Kemal to Ismet, April 1, 1921, in Gilbert, *Rumbold*, 238.
16. Volkan and Itzkowitz, *Ataturk*, 179.
17. Steven I. Davis, *Leadership in Conflict: The Lessons of History* (New York, 1996), 17.
18. But see, in terms of "relatively easy," the account of tense times and possible all-out combat in Gilbert, *Rumbold*, 263–279.
19. According to the 1936 Treaty of Montreux, Turkey gained full possession of the Straits, including the right to fortify it and to maintain troops along its littoral. The free passage of commercial shipping was also guaranteed.
20. Mango, *Ataturk*, 351.
21. Ibid., 362.
22. Ataturk's speeches, quoted in Mango, *Ataturk*, 368–369.
23. Ataturk's speeches, quoted in Mango, *Ataturk*, 364. See also Lewis, *Modern Turkey*, 264. For a commentary on the reforms embedded within a documentary about Kemal's life, see Can Dundar, "'Don't Give Up': Mustafa Kemal Ataturk's Biography" (2008), in Turkish with English subtitles, on YouTube.
24. Ibid., 370.
25. Ataturk's speeches, quoted in Mango, *Ataturk*, 413.
26. See Dundar, "Ataturk" documentary, part 8. But Ataturk flatly refused to become the new caliph, as Indian Muslims petitioned. Hanioglu, *Ataturk*, 152. On images, representations on currency and stamps, and the Ataturk "personality cult," see ibid., 186–187.
27. Ataturk's speeches, quoted in Mango, *Ataturk*, 435.
28. The fez had been adopted for the Ottoman army only in the nineteenth century, and was derived from Greek usage.
29. Quoted in Mango, *Ataturk*, 435; Volkan and Itzkowitz, *Ataturk*, 255. See also Lewis, *Modern Turkey*, 269–270.
30. Mango, *Ataturk*, 436.
31. Quoted in Volkan and Itzkowitz, *Ataturk*, 255; Mango, *Ataturk*, 434. Kemal's wife wears a modest black chador, but without a veil, in the "Ataturk" film.

32. Quoted in Mango, *Ataturk*, 438.
33. Albert Einstein, then based in France as the head of the Organization for the Protection of the Jewish Population, was instrumental in helping to save the lives of numerous Jewish scholars and physicians. In 1933, he asked the Turkish government to receive forty such émigrés, and promised to pay their salaries for the first year. The government refused the offer. But Ataturk intervened and welcomed the refugees. Eventually, more than 1,000 lives were thus saved. Vamik Volkan, plenary address, 99th Annual Meeting of the American Psychoanalytical Society, Washington, D.C., June 11, 2010.
34. Joseph C. Grew (Walter Johnson, ed.), *The Turbulent Era: A Diplomatic Record of Forty Years, 1904–1945* (Boston, 1952), 2:786; dispatch of July 20, 1928.
35. Rustow, "Ataturk as Founder," 221.
36. Volkan and Itzkowitz, *Ataturk*, 292.
37. Mango, *Ataturk*, 443.
38. Ataturk's proclamations and telegrams, quoted in Mango, *Ataturk*, 427.
39. See also Stanford J. Shaw and Ezel K. Shaw, *History of the Ottoman Empire and Modern Turkey* (New York, 1977), 2:378.
40. Grace Ellison, *Turkey Today* (London, 1928), 24.
41. But see Shaw and Shaw, *Modern Turkey*, 2:393.
42. But see William M. Hale, "The Traditional and the Modern in the Economy of Kemalist Turkey: The Experience of the 1920s," in Landau, *Modernization*, 156.
43. Quoted in Hasan Riza Soyak, *Reminiscences of Ataturk* [in Turkish] (Istanbul, 1973), 2:405.
44. Grew to Secretary of State Henry L. Stimson, December 3, 1930, in Grew, *Turbulent Era*, 2:875.
45. See also Metin And, "Ataturk and the Arts, with Special Reference to Music and Theater," in Landau, *Modernization*, 219–223.
46. Quoted in Lewis, *Modern Turkey*, 287. See also Z. Y. Hershlag, "Ataturk's Etatism," in Landau, *Modernization*, 177–178.
47. O. Faruk Logoglu, *Ismet Inonu and the Making of Modern Turkey* (Ankara, 1997), 92, 94.
48. Ibid., 95.
49. Quoted in Y. K. Karaosmanoglu, *Ataturk* (Istanbul, 1971, 4th ed.), 123, cited in Volkan and Itzkowitz, *Ataturk*, 318.
50. Dundar, "Ataturk" documentary.
51. Grace Ellison, *An Englishwoman in Angora* (New York, 1923), 162, 166, 167.
52. Volkan and Itzkowitz, *Ataturk*, 358.
53. Rustow opens his acute analysis of "Ataturk as the Founder of a State," 208–209, with an extended discussion of Ataturk's charismatic attainments. He makes the important point that charismatic legitimacy must be reasserted over and over again by the repetitive performance of political and other miracles. Charismatic leadership is crisis leadership, filling voids in people's mental needs.

54. On the importance of organizational skills, see Nye, *Powers to Lead*, 77.
55. Rumbold, quoted in Gilbert, *Rumbold*, 240.
56. Louis Browne, of *Chicago Daily News,* quoted in Kinross, *Ataturk*, 193.
57. Rustow, "Ataturk as Founder," 221.

CHAPTER SEVEN

1. "Personal" legitimacy is Easton's term, following Talcott Parsons. See Easton, *Systems Analysis*, 303–304.
2. Lee "retired" from the Singaporean cabinet in May 2011, but kept his parliamentary seat.
3. See Masire, *Very Brave*, 239.
4. Ibid., 241–242. This paragraph closely follows the argument in Rotberg, "Leadership Alters Corrupt Behavior," 353–354.
5. Archbishop Tutu, at the University of the Western Cape, quoted in *Southern African Report*, February 25, 2011.
6. Andrew Feinstein, *After the Party: Corruption, the ANC and South Africa's Uncertain Future* (New York, 2009), 185–195; Gevisser, *Legacy*, 256–260.
7. Helen Zille, quoted in *Southern African Report*, February 18, 2011.
8. See Burns, *Leadership*, 18, 439.
9. For the concept of state failure, and definitions, see Rotberg, "The Failure and Collapse of Nation-States: Breakdown, Prevention, and Repair," in Rotberg, *When States Fail: Causes and Consequences*, 1–45.
10. Re "counterfeit," see Williams, *Real Leadership*, 13–21. Kellerman analyzes the varieties of "bad" leadership, but has almost too little to say about what she calls "the Heart of Darkness" and "Evil" leadership. Her index has no entry for "venal." But the tyrants and despots described in this section are very Stalinist in being pathologically repressive of their own people, power-mad, paranoid, excessively corrupt, and vicious. Nearly all are "effective" if "irresponsible" leaders. They cause pain. Kellerman, *Bad Leadership*, 47–48, 191–192, 212, 225.
11. Benedict Rogers, *Than Shwe, Unmasking Burma's Tyrant* (Chiang Mai, Thailand, 2010), 95–99; Emma Larkin, *Everything Is Broken: A Tale of Catastrophe in Burma* (New York, 2010), 119, 130, 160–163.
12. For details, see Priscilla A. Clapp, "Burma: Poster Child for Entrenched Repression," in Rotberg, *Worst of the Worst*, 135–165.
13. Personal conversation with the author, Rangoon, 1996. For a tracing of the roots of charisma and grace from Linear B tablets at Mycenae to its introduction into English in the seventeenth century, see Stephen Minta, "Byron, Death, and the Afterlife," in Edward Berenson and Eva Gilon (eds.), *Constructing Charisma: Celebrity, Fame, and Power in Nineteenth-Century Europe* (New York, 2010), 120–121.
14. Karen Connelly, *Burmese Lessons* (New York, 2009), 68.
15. Sai Zom Hseng, "Main Ethnic Parties Plan to Sit in New Parliament,"

November 20, 2010, http://www.Irrawaddy.org. For details of the new rulers and discussion of the fraudulent election, see International Crisis Group, "Myanmar's Post-Election Landscape," *Asia Briefing* 118, March 7, 2011, http://www.crisisgroup.org.

16. Seth Mydans, "Myanmar Dissident, Reunited with Son, Speaks of Leading a 'Revolution,'" *New York Times,* November 24, 2010.
17. See the horrifying account of Sanjar Umarov, an opposition leader and physicist who was imprisoned and tortured systematically from 2005 to 2009. C. J. Chivers, "An Uzbek Survivor of Torture Seeks to Fight It Tacitly," *New York Times,* September 25, 2010.
18. Robert I. Rotberg, "Repressive, Aggressive, and Rogue Nation-States: How Odious, How Dangerous?" in Rotberg, *Worst of the Worst,* 30. See also Martha Brill Olcott, "Uzbekistan: A Decaying Dictatorship Withdrawn from the West," ibid., 250–268.
19. United Nations Development Program, *Human Development Report,* 2006. The rankings of venality come from Rotberg, *Worst of the Worst,* where they are explained in detail. The list is topped by North Korea, Turkmenistan, Burma, Zimbabwe, Belarus, Equatorial Guinea, Togo, Uzbekistan, Syria, and Tunisia, in that order.
20. U.S. State Department, "Tunisia," in *Country Reports on Human Rights Practices–2003* (February 25, 2004).
21. See also Rotberg, "Repressive, Aggressive," 32–33; Clement Henry, "Tunisia's 'Sweet Little' Regime," in Rotberg, *Worst of the Worst,* 300–324.
22. Rotberg, *Ending Autocracy,* 228; Robert I. Rotberg, "Signs of Trouble Lurking in Zimbabwe," *Boston Globe,* April 18, 1983.
23. Robert I. Rotberg, "Africa's Mess, Mugabe's Mayhem," *Foreign Affairs* 79 (2000), 47–61.
24. See Robert I. Rotberg, "Corruption and Torture in Mugabe's Zimbabwe," *Boston Globe,* February 14, 2009; Hartnack, "Mugabe Rails"; Donald G. McNeil Jr., "President of Zimbabwe Defies Court Order to Free 2 Journalists," *New York Times,* February 8, 1999.
25. For a coruscating, detailed account of Mugabe's atrocities and depredations, see Peter Godwin, *Fear: Robert Mugabe and the Martyrdom of Zimbabwe* (New York, 2011).
26. For details, see Robert I. Rotberg, "Winning the African Prize for Repression: Zimbabwe," in Rotberg, *Worst of the Worst,* 166–192; Rotberg, "Mugabe Über Alles," *Foreign Affairs* 89 (2010), 11–12.
27. For Nguema and his nephew, and for Eyadema and his son, see John R. Heilbrunn, "Equatorial Guinea and Togo: What Price Repression?" in Rotberg, *Worst of the Worst,* 223–249. For Siaka Stephens, see William Reno, "Sierra Leone: Warfare in a Post-State Society," in Rotberg (ed.), *State Failure and State Weakness in a Time of Terror* (Washington, D.C., 2003), 71–100.
28. Press statement by Tsvangirai, Oct 7, 2010. See also Robert I. Rotberg,

"Mugabe Doesn't Need an Excuse," Foreign Policy, http://www.foreignpolicy.com, December 29, 2010.

29. For Banda, see Philip Short, *Banda* (London, 1974).
30. Maxton Grant Tsoka, "Spot the Difference: A Comparison of Presidents' and Governments' Performance since 1999," *Afrobarometer Briefing Paper* 74.
31. Rotberg and Gisselquist, *Index of African Governance*, 18.
32. *Southern African Report*, February 18, 2011.
33. Fergus Cochrane-Dyet to Foreign Minister William Hague, in a leaked cable to London, quoted in the *Daily News* (Harare), April 22, 2011.
34. See J. Oloka-Onyango, "Constitutional Transition in Museveni's Uganda: New Horizons or Another False Start?," *Journal of African Law* 39 (1995), 156–172. The disenchanted voter, quoted in Josh Kron and Jeffrey Gettleman, "Of Irish Soil and Seeking to Take Root in Ugandan Politics," *New York Times*, March 2, 2011.
35. Gerald Bareebe, "Peers Pin Museveni on Bad Governance," *The Daily Monitor* (Kampala), March 24, 2009.
36. Daniel Edyegu, "I Am Ready to Live by Sacrifice—Museveni," *The New Vision* (Kampala), February 26, 2009.
37. "Rambo Reigns," *Economist*, February 26, 2011.
38. Godber Tumushabe, director of Advocates Coalition for Development and Environment, Kampala, in Michael J. Wilkerson, "Heads I Win, Tails You Lose," Foreign Policy, February 20, 2011, http://www.foreignpolicy.com.
39. See A. B. Assensoh, "Kenyatta of Kenya," in Assensoh, *African Political Leadership* (Malabar, Fla., 1998), 33–67.
40. Africa Research Institute, "Kenya: A Nation Fragmented," briefing note 0801, February 2008; Robert I. Rotberg, "Is Ethnic Strife Inevitable in Africa?" Global Post, November 7, 2010, http://www.GlobalPost.com.
41. There is an extensive literature, but see J. D. Legge, *Sukarno: A Political Biography* (North Sydney, NSW, 1972), 279–310; Michael R. J. Vatikiotis, *Indonesian Politics under Suharto: The Rise and Fall of the New Order* (London, 1998, 3rd ed.), 190–202; James T. Siegel, *A New Criminal Type in Jakarta: Counter-Terrorism Today* (Durham, 1998), 19–28, 107–116; Adam Schwarz, *A Nation in Waiting: Indonesia's Search for Stability* (London, 1999, 2nd ed.), 310–325.
42. For the notorious warlord turned senator named Prince Johnson, see Glenna Gordon, "You Can't Look Back," Foreign Policy, July 7, 2009, http://www.foreignpolicy.com. Johnson-Sirleaf won The Nobel Prize for Peace in 2011. She was also re-elected president in 2011, after a tough campaign and a run-off against a competitor.
43. *Economist,* August 23, 2008; All Africa News, June 30, 2009, http://www.allafricanews; The Fund for Peace, "Unlock (Universal Network of Local Knowledge)," June–August, 2010, September–November, 2010, reports on Liberia, accessed January 5, 2011, http://www.fundforpeace.org. According

to "Hold Your Breath," *Economist*, September 10, 2011, Johnson-Sirleaf's "zero-tolerance" policy on corruption had not succeeded. "Nepotism still abounds. . . . Visitors can be forgiven for thinking the police's sole function is to extract money."

44. Helene Cooper, "Iron Lady: The Promise of Liberia's Ellen Johnson Sirleaf," World Affairs, December 22, 2010, http://www.WorldAffairsJournal.org.
45. Johnson-Sirleaf is the only female leader mentioned by name in this book. There have been others who might have been discussed, especially the Asian female leaders of very mixed reputation and accomplishment in Pakistan (Benazir Bhutto), Bangladesh (Sheikh Hasina and Khaleda Zia), Sri Lanka (Sirimavo Bandaranaike and Chandrika Kumaratunga, mother and daughter), the Philippines (Corazon Aquino and Gloria Arroyo), and India (Indira Gandhi). We could also include Michelle Bachelet of Chile, Janet Jagan of Guyana, Laura Chinchilla of Costa Rica, and the formidable Mary Eugenia Charles of tiny Dominica. I do not mean to slight them but, except for Bachelet, Aquino, and Charles' better-than-average integrity, none in their day led as transformationally as Johnson-Sirleaf. Several were wildly corrupt. Several were authoritarian. Only Bachelet was an effective leader in the manner outlined in this book or displayed the competencies expected of such a leader. For Johnson-Sirleaf demonstrating male-female leadership behavior, see Keohane, *Thinking*, 137.
46. Stephen Kinzer, *A Thousand Hills: Rwanda's Rebirth and the Man Who Dreamed It* (New York, 2008), 236.
47. *Economist*, September 27, 2008.
48. Quoted in Kinzer, *Thousand Hills*, 235–236; Transparency International 2010, http://www.transparency.org; Rotberg and Gisselquist, *Index of African Governance*.
49. For important foreign policy decisions impinging on peace and war and made by dominant political leaders, see Margaret G. Hermann, Thomas Preston, Baghat Korany, and Timothy M. Shaw, "Who Leads Matters: The Effects of Powerful Individuals," in Hermann (ed.), *Leaders, Groups, and Coalitions: Understanding the People and Processes in Foreign Policymaking*, special issue of *International Studies Review* (2001), 104–110.
50. Instructive, in this context, are Bronwen Manby, "Principal Human Rights Challenges," and William Reno, "The Roots of Sectarian Violence, and Its Cure," both in Robert I. Rotberg (ed.), *Crafting the New Nigeria: Confronting the Challenges* (Boulder, 2004), 175–198, 219–238.
51. On the criminalized state, see Robert Legvold, "Corruption, the Criminalized State, and Post-Soviet Transitions," in Rotberg, *Corruption*, 194–238.
52. Barr, *Lee*, 124. For a fascinating set of suggestions on how best to nurture leaders, see the final section of Nohria and Khurana, *Handbook*.

Index

Abdulhamid II (Ottoman sultan), 122, 123
Aceh insurgency (Indonesia), 168
Adams College (Turkey), 70
Adana, Turkey, 127
adulation, 28
Aegean Sea, 127, 128
Afghanistan, 142
Africa: GDP per capita, 17; governance rankings, 13; leadership in, 1; unified stand, 83
African Advisory Council, 75
African National Congress (ANC), 40–41, 151; clashes with Inkatha Freedom Party, 57, 61; laying down arms, 57; militancy, 45–47; not favored by Khama, 71; shift away from Marxism, 63; and Truth and Reconciliation Commission, 65; Umkhonto we Sizwe, 48, 49, 50; Youth League, 44
African nationalism, 72
African Peer Review Mechanism, 165
Afrikaans (language), 64, 65, 192n43
Afrikaner Broederbond, 56
agency: human, 10, 15, 160, 175, 182n5; individual, 6, 7; leaders, 89, 152
agreement, state of, 189n61
agriculture, 139, 141, 157, 162
alcoholism, 149
Aleppo, Syria, 127
Allies, 144; assault, 120, 124; defiance against, 125; evacuations, 128; news notices, 94; treaties regarding Ottoman Empire, 119, 124, 127, 129
All-in-Africa Convention, 48
alphabets, and Ataturk, 137
American political culture, 13–14
Amin, Idi (Uganda), 8, 84, 160, 165, 184n15
amnesty, 57, 60
amoral leadership, 31
Anatolia, 119, 125, 127, 129; statues, 132
ANC. *See* African National Congress
Andaman Sea, 154
Andijan, Uzbekistan, 156
Angola, 54
Angora. *See* Ankara, Turkey
Ankara, Turkey, 125, 127, 128, 132; law school, 134
Ankara University, 134
Anti-Corruption Commission (Liberia), 170
anti-pass movement (South Africa), 47
Aquino, Corazon (Philippines), 204n45
Arabic (language), 24, 130, 132, 137, 138
Armenia, 127
Arroyo, Gloria (Philippines), 204n45
Asia Minor, 119–20, 127
assassinations, and Hani, 59
Ataturk, M. Kemal, 3; charisma, 37, 125, 126; compared with Khama, 117, 127, 144; compared with Lee, 127, 144; compared with

Ataturk (*cont.*)
Mandela, 117, 127; conspiracies against, 136; democracy, 26, 146; economic leadership, 129–30, 138–41, 147; education, 121–22; emotional intelligence, 126; integrity, 127, 144; legitimacy, 27, 121, 125, 146; material accomplishments, 129–30, 138–41, 147; military service, 120–21, 122–23, 124–25; mobilization of followers, 24, 35, 128, 144; narcissism, 143; no personal dynasty, 142–43; origin, 7; parents, 121; prescience, 124; president of republic, 131; schools, 121–22; trappings of office, 33; vision, 22, 23, 143–44
Attlee, Clement (U.K.), 73
authoritarianism: Angola, 8; Ataturk, 132, 135, 146; and charisma, 37; despots, 153–61; eschewing, 69; Europe, 140; female leaders, 204n45; Kagame, 172; Lee, 146, 148; Museveni, 165; Zimbabwe, 14
autocrats, 81, 153; vs. democracy, 11, 25–26, 84, 167, 173–74; despots, 152, 153, 161; examples, 8, 152, 184n15; Indonesia, 167; Khama vs. 69, 81, 84, 194n28; lack of attraction, 174; Lee as, 117, 197n51; Mutharika as, 164; Saleh, 20

baba class, in Singapore, 93
Bachelet, Michelle (Chile), 204n45
bad leadership, 18, 183n13, 201n10
balancing the budget, 85, 86
Balkan Wars, 123
Balliol College, Oxford, 71
Bamangwatoland, 72, 74
Banda, Hastings Kamuzu (Malawi), 84, 163, 184n15
Bandaranaike, Sirimavo (Sri Lanka), 204n45
Bandaranaike, Solomon West Ridgeway (Sri Lanka), 14
Bangladesh, 204n45
Bantu (language), 165
Bantu education, 46
Barisan Sosialis party (Singapore), 105
Barre, Siad (Somalia), 8
BaSarwa (Botswana), 193n3
Basutoland, 74
Bay of Bengal, 154
Bechuanaland, 74
Bechuanaland Democratic Party (BDP; Botswana), 76, 79, 80, 83
Bechuanaland Independence Party (Botswana), 80
Bechuanaland People's Party (BPP; Botswana), 76, 80, 81
Bechuanaland Protectorate, 68
beef, 77, 85
beer, 149
Ben Ali, Zine El Abidene (Tunisia), 27, 156–57
Berlusconi, Silvio (Italy), 28
Bhutto, Benazir (Pakistan), 204n45
"big man," 14–15, 28, 29, 32
Black Consciousness Movement, 51
Black Pimpernel (Mandela), 48, 61
Blair, Tony (U. K.), 20
Bokassa, Jean-Bedel (Central African Empire), 8, 160
Bongo, Omar (Gabon), 8, 184n15
Bosphorus Strait, 93, 120, 127, 129, 199n19
Botha, Pieter W. (South Africa), 52–53, 54–55, 63–64
Botswana, 193n3; balancing the budget, 85, 86; boycotts, 79; cattle, 77, 78; constitution, 66, 75, 77, 79–80; corruption, lack of, 86–88, 89, 148–49, diamonds, 77, 84, 85–86, 87, 88, 89, 90, 148, 149; education, 66, 77, 78, 79, 84; employment, 86; farming, 79; Index of African Governance, 66; institutions, 89–90, 148; mineral deposits, 74, 77; nationalist movements, 75, 76; nepotism, lack of, 88; Police Mobile Unit, 82; political parties, 76, 79, 80, 81, 83; professionals, lack of, 77–78; proposed transfer of territory to South Africa, 74, 76; socioeconomic disparity, 80; taxes, 85, 149; unemployment, 86
bourgeoisie, hegemonic, 9
boycotts: Botswana, 79; consumer, 79; elections, 43, 155, 159; international, 55, 64; rugby, 64; schools, 46, 51, 57, 62; against South Africa, 55, 64; in South Africa, 43, 46, 62, 191n17; Zimbabwe, 159
Brazil, 39
Breyer, Stephen (justice), public trust, 27
bribes, 111, 112
Britain: Japanese invasion of Singapore, 94; occupation of Istanbul, 126, 127; repulsion at the Dardanelles, 120; Treaty of Lausanne, 129; Treaty of Sèvres, 127
British empire, dismantling, 72, 73
British High Commissioner, 164

British Raj, 8
British South Africa Company, 68
Brown, Gordon (U. K.), 20
budget, balancing (in Botswana), 85, 86
Bulgaria, 124
Burma, 153–56
Burnham, Forbes (Guyana), 72
Burns: on leaders vs. power wielders, 10–11; on short-term vs. long-term goals, 12
Bursa, Turkey, 127–28
Bush, George W., opinion polls, 27, 28
Buthelezi, M. Gatsha (South Africa), 60, 61

Cabral, Amilcar (Guinea), 54
caliphate, 130, 131–32
Cambridge Senior Examinations, 93
Cape Verde, 54
cattle, 77, 78
Central Kalahari Reserve, 193n3
Central Provident Fund (Singapore), 104
chador, 199n31
charisma, 36–38, 190n72, 190n74, 192n31, 200n53, 201n13; Ataturk, 125, 126; Mandela, 58, 61; Suu Kyi, 154
Charles, Mary Eugenia (Dominica), 204n45
Chavez, Hugo (Venezuela), 8
child mortality, in Uzbekistan, 156
Chile, 204n45
China: aid to Burma, 154; aid to Liberia, 171; Ming dynasty, 35; public meeting mode, 25
Chinchilla, Laura (Costa Rica), 204n45
Chinese gangs (Singapore), 107
Churchill, Winston, 33, 73
Circassians, 136
city-level leadership, 182n7
civil disobedience, 31, 45, 46
CiZulu (language), 70
clothing: fezzes, 133, 199n28; hats, 124, 133; headscarves, 134; turbans, 133; Turkey, 121, 124, 130, 133–34, 199s31; veils, 121, 124, 134, 199n31; women, 133–34
coal, 88
coercion, 26, 183n13
Coetsee, Kobie (South Africa), 52, 53–54
collaborationists, 191n17
colonial experience, 8–9
colonial legacy, as unimportant, 8–9
Committee of Union and Progress (CUP) Ottoman Empire, 123
common good, 12
Communist Party (Malayan), 95–96
communists, 58, 142; Barisan Sosialis party (Singapore), 105; Malaya, 95–99; manipulation of Lee, 96–97
competency, 28, 29
conformity, 103–4
confrontation vs. cooperation, 76–77
Confucian society, 116–17
Congo, 54, 158
Congregationalism, 69
Conservative Party (South Africa), 55
consistency, and Lee, 92
Constantine, King (Greece), 128
constituents, consulting, 24
constitution(s): America, 13, 14, 35; Botswana, 66, 75, 77, 79–80; insufficient on its own, 107, 163; Kenya, 166; Malawi, 163; Ottoman Empire, 123; safeguards, 14; South Africa, 57, 60, 61; Turkey, 126, 137, 147; Zimbabwe, 14, 159, 160–61
consultation, 24–25
contextual intelligence, 22
"contribution to change," 184n20
cooperation vs. confrontation, 76–77
co-optive power, 26
copper, 77
core competencies: enlarged enterprise, 35–36; legitimacy, 26–34; mobilization, 23–26; trust, 34–35; vision, 21–23
Cornwall, England, 95
corporate leadership: instruction, 24; Leadership Practices Inventory, 22–23; political leadership vs., 2
corruption, 107, 108–12, 194n40, 194n41, 197n50; Botswana's lack of, 86–88, 89, 148–49; Indonesia, 167–68; institutions vs., 112–13; Lee, 114; Liberia, 170; Mali, 163–64; Ottoman Empire, 122, 123; Rwanda, 171–72; South Africa, 150–51; Turkey, 135, 143; Uzbekistan, 156; zero tolerance, 203n39; Zimbabwe, 158
Corruption Perceptions Index, 89, 91, 172, 194n41
Corrupt Practices Investigation Bureau, 111–12
Costa Rica, 204n45
counterfeit leadership, 153, 157
courage, 31, 32
crime: Singapore, 92, 107, 108; South Africa, 50, 60, 62, 151

crisis leadership, 200n53
Cuban missile crisis, 33

Dalindyebo, Jongintaba (South Africa), 42
Damascus, Syria, 122
Dardanelles Strait, 93, 120, 127, 129, 199n19
days of week, names of, 56
De Beers Company, 86
Debswana Company, 86
Defense of Rights congress, 125
Defiance Campaign of 1952 (South Africa), 45–46
de Klerk, Frederik W. (South Africa), 41, 55–57; after Hani's death, 59; partial power transfer, 58; relationship with Mandela after release, 59–61
democracy, 83–84; adherence to, 146
democratic values, 69, 146, 165, 167, 175
democrats vs. autocrats, 25–26
depression, 139, 159–60
dervishes, 123, 132
despots: Ben Ali, 156–57; defining, 152–53; Karimov, 156; Mugabe, 157–61; and schools, 152; Than Shwe, 153–54, 155–56
destiny, 145; Botswana, 80, 82, 117; Khama, 71; Lee, 93; Mandela, 42, 43; Singapore, 117, 118; South Africa, 56, 58; Turkey, 120, 137, 141
Development Bank of Singapore, 115
diamonds: Botswana, 77, 84, 85–86, 87, 88, 89, 90, 148, 149; South Africa, 68; Zimbabwe, 158, 159
disagreement, state of, 189n61
dishonoring opponents, 43
divorce, 133, 134
Doing Business surveys, 91
Dominica, 204n45
Dumlupinar, Turkey, 128
Dutch Reformed Church, 64

"eastern question," 127
economic leadership: Ataturk, 129–30, 138–41; Johnson-Sirleaf, 170–71; Khama, 80–81, 85–86; Lee, 104, 106, 115; Mandela, 62–63; Yudhoyono, 168
Economist, 1, 171–72
Edirne, Turkey, 127
education: Ataturk, 121–22; Botswana, 66, 77, 78, 79, 84; boycotts, 46, 51, 57, 62; despots and, 152; English-speaking, 103; integration, 60, 79; Khama, 69, 70, 71; law schools, 44, 134; Lee, 93; Liberia, 170, 171; madrassas, 121, 131–32; Mandela, 42, 43, 44; military, 122; part of governance, 12, 13, 26, 37, 162, 173; secular, 121–22; Singapore, 92, 93, 102–3, 115; South Africa, 46, 51, 57, 60, 62, 151; Turkey, 130, 131–32, 134, 135, 137, 138; women, 130; Zimbabwe, 157, 159
Einstein, Albert, 199n33
elections: biased, 172; rigged, 29, 155, 157, 159, 166, 201n15; South Africa, 61
elitism, 105–6
emancipation of women, 134, 140
emotional intelligence, 19–20, 92; Ataturk, 126; defining, 186n7; Mandela, 59
empathy, 19–20
employment: Botswana, 86; Turkey, 129
end results, as measure of effectiveness, 184n20
English (language), 103, 196n26
enlarged enterprise, 35–36
Enver Pasha (Ottoman Empire), 123, 124
environmental leadership, 104–5, 116
ethical leadership, 30
"ethic of responsibility," 189n52
ethnic cleansing, 158
ethnic neighborhoods, elimination of, 103–4
ethnic preferentiality, 165, 166
exclusionists, 25
Eyadéma, Gnassingbé (Togo), 8, 160

farming, 79, 162; Malawi, 163; Mali, 15; Turkey, 139, 141; Zimbabwe, 157, 159
Faustian model, 117, 148
female leaders, 204n45
fezzes, 133, 199n28
First World oasis, 104–5, 115–16
Fitzwilliam House, Cambridge, 94
flamboyance, 32
followers: interests of, 36; mobilization of, 23–26; necessary, 10–11; types of, 11
followership, 19, 147, 184n15, 189n61; and charisma, 37; legitimacy of leadership, 27; Mandela, 51
foreign direct investment, 16, 103, 109, 141, 169
foreign policy decisions, 204n49
Fort Hare University College (South Africa), 43, 71
Fourteen Points, 125
France, 120, 126, 127, 129

Francistown, Botswana, 77, 79
Free Republican Party (Turkey), 139–40
freedom of press, 114; lack of, 134–35, 136, 158; Malawi, 164
freedom of speech: lack of, 134–35; Malawi, 164
Freemasons, 140

Gaborone, Botswana, 79, 80
Gallipoli Peninsula, 120, 124, 144
Gandhi, Indira (India), 204n45
Gandhi, Mohandas K., 30–31
gangs, 107
GDP per capita. *See* gross domestic product (GDP) per capita
General Auditing Commission (Liberia), 170
genetic predisposition, 7
Germany: accumulation of power, 142; Turkish alliance with, 124
Ghana: acknowledgement of BPP, 76; leadership styles contrasted, 18
Gini coefficient ratios, 91–92
Girton College, Cambridge, 94
Giuliani, Rudolph (U. S.), 59
Goh Chok Tong (Singapore), 111
gold mines, 77
Gordimer, Nadine, 51
governance, 12–13
governance models: guided democracy, 70; *kgotla*, 68, 75, 87; militaristic, 70; indigenous, 75
grace, 201n13; Mandela, 58; Suu Kyi, 154
Grand National Assembly (Turkey), 126, 128, 131; abolition of caliphate, 131–32; abolition of sultanate, 130; controlled by People's Party, 135; rubber stamp of edicts, 137, 143
Great Depression, 139
Greece: claims to Asia Minor, 120; Izmir, 125, 127; treaty of friendship with Turkey, 142; Treaty of Sèvres, 127–28; war of 1921, 128, 144
Grew, Joseph (U. S. ambassador), 134–35
gross domestic product (GDP) per capita, 17; Botswana, 66, 77; Indonesia, 169; Liberia, 170–71; Singapore, 91, 102, 115, 117; Uzbekistan, 156; Zimbabwe, 159–60
group rights, 56
groupthink, 33
Guinea-Bissau, 54
Guyana, 204n45

Habibie, Jusuf (Indonesia), 168
Hakka, in Singapore, 93
Hani, Chris (South Africa), 59
hard truths, 33
Hasina, Sheikh (Bangladesh), 204n45
Hatay, Turkey, 142
hats, 124, 133
headscarves, 134
Healdtown, South Africa, 42, 43
health: Botswana, 66, 77; of cattle, 77; despots and, 152; improved outcomes, 2, 9, 12, 13, 37; Singapore, 172; Uzbekistan, 156; Zimbabwe, 157
heroes, 132; need for, 130
Hindemith, Paul, 140
Hitler, 140, 142
HIV/AIDS epidemic, 149, 150
Holden, Roberto (Angola), 54
Home, Lord (U. K.), 74
Houphouet-Boigny, Felix (Côte d'Ivoire), 184n15
housing, in Singapore, 103–4
Huddleston, Fr. Trevor (South Africa), 46
Huggins, Godfrey (S. Rhodesia/Zimbabwe), 73
human agency, 10; related to governance, 13
human capacity, 17
human development, in Uzbekistan, 156
human rights violations: Burma, 154; Tunisia, 156–57; Zimbabwe, 158, 159
humiliation, 43
Hutu people (Rwanda), 171, 172
hypocrisy, 29–30

Ibrahim Prize, awarded to Festus Mogae, 66
illiteracy, 17, 102, 137, 169
improvisation, need for, 20
inclusivity, 24–25, 174; Johnson-Sirleaf, 170; Khama, 83; Mandela, 41, 51, 63–64, 191n17; Uganda lacking, 165. *See also* tolerance
incrementalists, 23
Independence Tribunals, 136
Index of African Governance, 13, 66; Malawi, 164; Rwanda, 172
Index of Economic Freedom, 91
India, 8, 72, 204n45
individual action, importance of, 185n24
individual rights, 56, 118
Indonesia, 18, 102, 167–69
infant mortality, 17, 156, 173

inflation, 104; Singapore, 104; Zimbabwe, 160
infrastructure: Liberia, 170, 171; Malawi, 164; Singapore, 104; Turkey, 138–39
Inkatha Freedom Party (South Africa), 57, 60, 61
Inner Temple (Inns of Court, London), 71
Inns of Court (London), 71, 95
institutions, 106–7; accretion of power, 14–15; Botswana, 89–90, 148; vs. corruption, 112–13; origin of, 11–12; Singapore, 148; South Africa, 148; Turkey, 147; Zimbabwe, 158
integration, 60, 79, 103
integrity, 19, 20, 31, 161, 174; Ataturk, 127, 144; Ben Ali, 157; defining, 29–30, 188n39; female leaders, 204n5; Johnson-Sirleaf, 169–70, 204n45; Kagame, 171, 172; Khama, 70, 84, 90; Lee, 106, 110, 112, 115, 117, 195n2; Mandela, 40, 54, 58, 61, 65; Masire, 148; Mbeki, 150; Suu Kyi, 155; Yudhoyono, 168, 169
intellectual honesty, 19, 29–30, 33–34, 188n39; Khama, 70; Lee, 107; Mandela, 58; Mbeki, 150
intelligence, 184n20; contextual, 22; emotional intelligence, 19–20, 59, 92, 126, 186n7; intrapersonal, 189n57
Internal Security Act (Singapore), 197n52
interracial marriage, 45, 72–73, 155
Iran, 142
Iraq, 142
Irrawaddy River (Burma), 154
Islam: Indonesia, 102, 168, 169; Malaysia, 102; Singapore, 102; Turkey, 121, 124, 129, 130, 131, 132, 133, 134, 135, 137, 138, 147; Uzbekistan, 156
Ismay, Lord (U. K.), 74
Ismet (Turkey), 148; military service, 127, 128; prime minister, 131, 135, 141–42, 143; surname Inonu, 138
Inonu, Mustafa Ismet. *See* Ismet
Istanbul: Ataturk, 122, 123, 125; British occupation, 120, 126, 127; CUP, 124; newspapers, 134; reaction to statues, 132; shipping trade, 141; sultan's escape from, 130; Turkish authority, 129
Istanbul University, 134
Italy, 120, 126, 127; accumulation of power, 142; Treaty of Lausanne, 129
Izmir, Turkey, 125, 127, 128, 129
Jagan, Janet (Guyana), 204n45
Japan, occupation of Singapore, 94
Jewish emigration, 199n33
jobs: Botswana, 86; creation, 115; Turkey, 129
Johnson, Prince (Liberia), 170
Johnson-Sirleaf, Ellen (Liberia), 169–71, 204n5
Johor, Sultanate of, 102
Joint Advisory Council (all-Botswana), 75
Joseph, James (U. S. ambassador), 65
Jwaneng, Botswana, 86

Kabila, Laurent (Congo), 158
Kagame, Paul (Rwanda), 7–8, 171–72
Kalahari Desert, 77
kalpak, 124
Karimov, Islam A. (Uzbekistan), 156
Katanga Province, Congo, 158
Katlehong speech by Mandela, 40–41
Kaunda, Kenneth (Zambia), 33, 82, 83, 84, 173
Kemal, Mustapha. *See* Ataturk, M. Kemal
Kennedy, John F.: on courage, 32; Cuban missile crisis, 33; inaugural address, 35; "men of dedication," 12
Kenya, 156, 166–67
Kenyatta, Jomo (Kenya), 166, 184n15
kgotla, 68–69, 75, 87
Khama III (Seretse Khama's grandfather), 67
Khama, Ian (Seretse Khama's son), 149
Khama, Seretse, 3, 7; athletics, 70; on autocrats, 194n28; comparisons, 117, 118, 127, 144; democracy, 26, 83, 146; economic leadership, 80–81, 85–86; educator, 84; exile to Britain, 73–74; illness, 89; inclusivity, 83; integrity, 70, 84, 90; intellectual honesty, 69, 70; interracial marriage, 72–73; legal studies, 71–72; legitimacy, 26, 27, 83, 146; material accomplishments, 146–47, 148; paramount chieftaincy of Ngwato, 69, 71, 72–73; preference for multiracial organizations, 71; president, 80; prime minister, 80; punctilious, 31; renunciation of chieftainship, 74; schools, 69, 70, 71; tolerance, 148; tuberculosis, 70; vision, 81
Khama, Tshekedi (Seretse Khama's uncle), 70, 72, 74–75
Khrushchev, Nikita (Soviet Union), loss of legitimacy, 27

Kibaki, Mwai (Kenya), 166
Kikuyu people (Kenya), 166
Kimberley diamond mines, 68
Kufuor, John A. (Ghana), 18
Kumaratunga, Chandrika (Sri Lanka), 204n45
Kurds, 127, 129, 136
Kutuzov, General, 51–52
Kwa Geok Choo (Singapore), 94–95, 111
Kwa-Zulu, 61

Labour Party (Singapore), 96
language: Afrikaans, 64, 65, 192n43; Arabic, 24, 130, 132, 137, 138; Bantu, 165; CiZulu, 70; English, 103, 196n26; Mandarin, 103; Setswana, 70; Shona, 158; Sindebele, 158; Singapore, 103; Tswana, 74; Turkish, 132, 136, 137–38; Xhosa, 43
laws, in Singapore, 108, 113
law schools, 44, 71, 134
Laz (Turkey), 136
leader quality, 182n4
leaders: female, 204n45; impact on country performance, 6–7; vs. power wielders, 10–11, 153
leadership: bad, 18, 183n13, 201n10; city level, 182n7; corporate, 2, 22–23, 24; counterfeit, 153, 157; effective, 19–20, 201n10; environmental, 104–5, 116; good, 18–19; inborn, 195n2; moral, of Mandela, 64; not dichotomous, 186n19; positive, 17–19; real, 36; responsible, 3, 4, 16, 37, 148, 173; tactical, of Mandela, 58–59; transactional, 161–67; as variable, 10
leadership, economic: Ataturk, 129–30, 138–41; Johnson-Sirleaf, 170–71; Khama, 80–81, 85–86; Lee, 104, 106, 115; Mandela, 62–63; Yudhoyono, 168
Leadership Practices Inventory, 22–23
leadership types, 184n15
Lee Hsien Loong (Singapore), 114, 147–48
Lee Kuan Yew, 3; abuse of power, 114; accusations of corruption, 114; anticommunist, 95–97; Ataturk compared with, 127, 144; birth, 7; consulting constituents, 24, 25; contrasted with Mandela and Khama, 117, 118; debater, 93; defining leadership, 195n2; democracy, 26, 146; economic leadership, 104, 106, 115; environmental leadership, 104–5, 116; honorable behavior, 97; impatience, 118; integrity, 106, 110, 112, 115, 117, 204n5; intellectual honesty, 107; Kagame compared to, 172; on leadership, 92; legal studies, 94–95; legal work, 95–96, 108; legitimacy, 27, 146; material accomplishments, 104, 106, 115, 146–47; mobilization, 35, 116–17; non-self-aggrandizing, 32; ruthless, 106; schools, 93; unpopular decisions, 106; vision, 22, 23, 92, 98–100, 103–4, 107, 116–17
legacies, building on, 147, 148–50
legitimacy, 26–34, 146, 188n26; Ataturk, 27, 121, 125, 146; Ben Ali, 157; and corruption, 109; erosion of, 150; Johnson-Sirleaf, 170; Kagame, 171; Khama, 83; Lee, 109; loss of, 174, 27; Mugabe, 160; Muluzi, 163; Museveni, 165; Suu Kyi, 154–55
Lembede, Anton (South Africa), 44
Lesotho, 68. *See also* Basutoland
Liberia, 169–71
Libya, 123
life expectancy, 152, 173; Singapore, 92; South Africa, 17; Uzbekistan, 156; Zimbabwe, 17
Lim Yew Hock (Singapore), 97
listening, 25, 33
literacy, 9, 13, 17, 38, 162; Liberia, 169; Singapore, 102–3; Tunisia, 156; Turkey, 137–38
Livingstone, David, 67
Lobatse, Botswana, 77; segregation, 79
London, Britain, 71–72, 73–74
London Missionary Society, in Botswana, 67, 70
Lord's Resistance Army, 165
Lovedale School (South Africa), 70, 71
Lukashenko, Alexsandr (Belarus), 152
Lula da Silva, Luiz Inacio (Brazil), 39
Lumumba, Patrice (Congo), 54
Luo people (Kenya), 166
Luthuli, Albert (South Africa), 45, 46
Luzhkov, Yuri (Russia), 182n7

Macedonia, 122
Machel, Samora (Mozambique), 82
Machiavelli, Niccolò, 29–30, 33, 34, 187n21, 188n40
Macmillan, Harold (U. K.), 28
madrassas, 121, 131–32
Mahathir, Muhammad (Malaysia), 173

Maintenance of Order law (Turkey), 136
maize (corn), 164
Malan, Daniel (South Africa), 73
Malawi, 84, 163–64
Malay, nationalist movements in, 100
Malaya: communist insurrection, 97; federation of states, 95; Malaysian Federation, 98–100; political parties, 95–96
Malayan Communist Party, 95–96
Malaysia, 173
Malaysian Federation: attitude toward Chinese, 99–100; proposed, 98–99; Singapore's expulsion, 100–101, 107; Singapore's place within, 99
Malaysian Singapore Airlines, 110, 114
Mali, farming in, 15
malnutrition, 17
management, leadership vs., 3
Mandarin (language), 103
mandate of heaven, 35
Mandela, Nelson, 3, 7; Afrikaans, 192n43; ANC militancy, 45–47; arrests, 45; athleticism, 43, 44; Black Pimpernel, 48, 61; charisma, 37, 58; commitment to British legal system, 47, 50; comparisons, 18, 117, 118, 127; courage, 64; democracy, 26, 146; economic leadership, 62–63, 147; emotional leadership, 59; enlarged enterprise, 35; feelings of others, 36; followership, 51; grace, 58; hope for reconciliation, 47; inclusivity, 41, 51, 63–64, 191n17; integrity, 40, 54, 58, 61, 65; intellectual honesty, 33, 58; Katlehong speech, 40–41; law firm work, 44, 47; legitimacy, 27, 146; material accomplishments, 62–63, 147; Methodist, 42; mobilization of followers, 61, 65; moral leadership, 64; nonviolence, 53; not collaborationist, 191n17; ordinary man, 58; prudence, 42, 58; relationship with de Klerk after release, 59–61; responsibility for actions, 43; rugby jersey, 64; schools, 42, 43, 44; self-mastery, 58, 59; solidarity, 57; South Africa's jailor, 52, 54; symbolic acts, 25, 41, 46, 64, 65; tactical leadership, 58–59; vision, 23; wooden speech, 192n31
Mao, and public meeting mode, 25
Mao Tse-Tung (China), 25, 95
Marshall, David (Singapore), 96, 97
Marshall, John (chief justice; U. S.), 13
martial law, 136
Marxism, 51, 55, 63, 101
Masire, Quett (Sir Ketumile; Botswana), 76, 78, 81, 85, 87–88; integrity, 148; repaying debt, 87; vice president and finance minister, 80; vision, continuation of, 148–49
Maun, Botswana, 77
Mauritius, 8, 152, 173, 175; Corruption Perceptions Index, 89, 113; inclusivity, 25; Index of African Governance, 13, 66; Transparency International, 89, 113
Mbeki, Govan (South Africa), 7, 56
Mbeki, Thabo (South Africa), 18, 28, 54, 56, 61–63, 65, 150–51
Mda, Peter (South Africa), ANC militancy, 45
Meadowlands, South Africa, 46
means and ends, 31
medical insurance, 104
mediocrity, 181n5
Mediterranean Sea, 128
Mehmed VI (Ottoman sultan), 123, 124, 125, 127, 130
"men of dedication," 12
meritocracy, 106–7
Methodists, 42
metropoles, and oppression, 8
Middle Temple (Inns of Court, London), 95
military victory, 57
mineral deposits, 74, 77, 86, 158
Ming dynasty, 35
mobilization of followers, 23–26, 116–17; Ataturk, 24, 35, 128, 144; Lee, 105; Mandela, 61, 65
Mobutu Sese Seko (Congo/Zaire), 8, 160, 184n15
Moffat, John (Botswana), 67
Mogae, Festus (Botswana), 66, 149
Moi, Daniel arap (Kenya), 166
Mokhehle, Ntsu (Lesotho), 71
Monastir (Macedonia), 122
Monrovia, Liberia, 169
Morales, Evo (Bolivia), 8
moralistic, 30
moral leadership, 30, 64
Mosul, Iraq, 127, 129
motivators, underlying, 9
Movement of Democratic Change (Zimbabwe), 159, 161
Mubarak, Hosni (Egypt), loss of legitimacy, 27

Mudros peace agreement, 124
Mugabe, Robert Gabriel (Zimbabwe), 8, 14, 82, 83, 149, 150, 157–61
Muluzi, Bakili (Malawi), 163–64
Museveni, Yoweri (Uganda), 8, 165–66
Mussolini, Benito (Italy), 140, 142
Mutharika, Bingu wa (Malawi), 163, 164
Muzorewa, Bishop Abel (Zimbabwe), 82, 83
mwalimu (teacher), 25
Myanmar. *See* Burma

Nanyang University, 103
Napoleon, 122, 143
Nasser, Gamal Abdel (Egypt), 75
Natal, South Africa, 61
national identity, 101, 103–4, 145; Ataturk, 129; Liberia, 170; Singapore, 101, 103; Turkey, 129
nationalist movements, 174, 183n8; African, 72; Botswana, 75, 76; Kenya, 156; Malay, 100; Singapore, 94, 96; Turkey, 126, 127, 131; Zimbabwe, 82, 83
nationalization of industries, 141
National Pact, 125
National Party (South Africa), 44–45, 55
National University of Singapore, 103
National Wages Council, 115
nation rebuilding, 7–8
nation-states, worst, 156
needs, authentic, 36
Nehru, Jawaharlal (India), 8
nepotism, 113–14, 203n39; Ben Ali, 157; Kagame's stand against in Rwanda, 171; lack of, 88; Mugabe, 158; Museveni, 165; Singapore, 113; Suharto, 167–68; Tunisia, 157
Ne Win (Burma), 27, 153, 160
newspapers, in Turkey, 134–35
Nguema, Macias (Equatorial Guinea), 160, 184n15
Nguema, Teodoro Obiang (Equatorial Guinea), 8, 160
Ngwato people (Botswana), 67, 68, 74
Nixon, Richard M. (U.S.), 56
Njonjo, Charles (Kenya), 71, 72
Nkomo, Joshua (Zimbabwe), 8, 54, 71, 82
Nkrumah, Kwame (Ghana), 76, 184n15
Nkumbula, Harry (Zambia), 54, 72
nonracialism, 57, 71, 79, 82
nonviolence, Mandela asked to pledge, 53
Numeiri, Gaafar (Sudan), 184n15
Nutford House (London), 72
Nyerere, Julius (Tanzania), 82, 83, 84, 184n15

Obama, Barack, 11, 27, 35
Obote, A. Milton (Uganda), 165
OECD, 91
oil, and Chinese pipeline, 154
opinion polls, 26–27
Orania, South Africa, 64
Orapa, Botswana, 85–86
Organization for the Protection of the Jewish Population, 199n33
Organization of African Union, 81
ostentation: Ataturk, 33; Lee, 32; Masire, 148
Ottoman Empire: constitution, 123; division of, 119–20

Paine, Thomas (U. S.), 81
Pakistan, 8, 72, 204n45
Pan Africanist Congress (PAC) of South Africa, 47, 49–50
Pan-Islamism, 130
Pan-Turanianism, 130
participation, 191n17
partition, India and Pakistan, 8
patronage, 150
pensions, 104
People's Action Party (PAP; Singapore): elections, 97–98; formation; 96, hold on power, 113, 114; recruiting, 107
People's Party (Turkey), 131, 135, 140
persuasion, 11
Phey Yew Kok (Singapore), 110
Philippines, 204n45
physical stature, 127
pitso, in Lesotho, 68
police, in Singapore, 111
Police Mobile Unit, in Botswana, 82
policy-making, ignoring, 184n16
political culture, 13–15, 185n24
political leadership: dynamics of, 10–12; task of, 19
political parties: Botswana, 76, 79, 80, 81, 83; Burma, 155; Malawi, 163; Malaya, 95–96; Singapore, 95–96, 97–98, 105, 107, 113, 114; South Africa, 44–45, 47, 49, 53, 55, 57, 60, 61; Turkey, 131, 135, 140; Zimbabwe, 159, 161
Pollsmoor prison (South Africa), 52
Pol Pot (Cambodia), 160

polygamy, 134
pondokkies (squatter settlements), 62
Postal and Telecommunications Uniformed Staff Union, 96
power abuse, 114
power wielders, vs. leaders, 10–11, 153
Prince, The (Machiavelli), 187n21, 188n40
princes, 184n15
"prisoner of conscience," 52
professionals, lack of, in Botswana, 62, 77–78
Progressive Federal Party (South Africa), 55
Progressive Party (Singapore), 95–96
Progressive Republican Party (Turkey), 135
property rights, in Singapore, 113
prophets, 184n15
prudence, 31–32, 189n52
public trust, 27. *See also* legitimacy
pula currency, in Botswana, 85
purpose, sense of, 35–36

Qaddafi, Muammar (Libya), 8, 27
quotas, 103

racial riots, 100
Raffles College (Singapore), 93–94
Raffles Institution (Singapore), 93
Rahman, Tunku Abdul (Malaysia), 98, 99–101
railways: Botswana, 71, 77, 79; Liberia, 171; Rhodesia Railway, 79, 87; South Africa, 68; Turkey, 138, 139, 141
rain, necessity of, 77
Raj, 8
Ramgoolam, Sir Seewoosagur (Mauritius), 8, 174
Rand currency, in South Africa, 85
Rawlings, Jerry (Ghana), 18
reelection: Ben Ali, 157; focus on, 162; Kagame, 172; Lee, 99 106; mark of voter approval, 106; Mugabe, 159; Museveni, 165, 166; Mutharika, 164; Than Shwe, 155; Yudhoyono, 168
relationship skills, 184n20
religion, 81; London Missionary Society, 67, 70; madrassas, 121, 131–32; Methodists, 42. *See also* Islam
religious disaffection, 123
relocation during apartheid in South Africa, 46
rent seeking, 163, 166
repression, 201n10
Republican People's Party (Turkey), 131, 135, 140
Rey, Charles (Bechuanaland), 70
Reza Khan (Persia), 142–43
Rhodes, Cecil (South Africa), 68
Rhodesia, 14, 68, 73, 76, 80, 82–83. *See also* Zimbabwe
Rhodesian African National Congress, 76
Rhodesia Railways, 71, 79, 87
rights, group vs. individual, 56
Rivonia political prisoners (South Africa), 50
roads: Liberia, 170, 171; Malawi, 164; Turkey, 138–39
Roan Selection Trust (Botswana), 77
Robben Island, South Africa, 50, 51, 52, 64
Romania, 142
Roosevelt, Franklin D., 35
rugby, 25, 39, 64, 71
Russia, 63, 124, 128. *See also* Soviet Union
Ruwenzori, Uganda, 165
Rwanda, 171–72

Sabah (Malaysia), 98, 101
sabotage, 48, 49, 50
Sabotage Act (South Africa), 49
Sakarya, Turkey, 128
salaries, 112
Saleh, Ali Abdullah (Yemen), 20, 27
Salisbury, Lord (U. K.), 74
Salonika, 121, 122, 123
Salt Satyagraha, in India, 30
Samsun, Turkey, 125
Sanusi dervishes, 123
Sarawak (Malaysia), 98, 101
schooling: Ataturk, 121–22; Botswana, 66, 77, 78, 79, 84; boycotts, 46, 51, 57, 62; despots and, 152; English-speaking, 103; integration, 60, 79; Khama, 69, 70, 71; law schools, 44, 134; Lee, 93; Liberia, 170, 171; madrassas, 121, 131–32; Mandela, 42, 43, 44; military, 122; part of governance, 12, 13, 26, 37, 162, 173; secular, 121–22; Singapore, 92, 93, 103, 115; South Africa, 46, 51, 57, 60, 62; Turkey, 130, 131–32, 134, 135, 137, 138; women, 130; Zimbabwe, 157, 159
Sea of Marmara, 127, 128
secular religion, 81
security, in Liberia, 170
segregationists, in South Africa, 44–45

Selassie, Haile (Ethiopia), 184n15
Selebi-Pikwe, Botswana, 77
self-confidence, 146
self-mastery, 32, 189n57
Senegal, 173
Seow, Francis T. (Singapore), 114, 197n52
Setswana (language; Botswana), 70
Shan Nationalities Democratic Party (Burma), 155
Sharpeville, South Africa, 47
Shona (language; Zimbabwe), 158
shrines, 132
Sidelsky, Lazar (South Africa), 44
Sierra Leone, 14
Sindebele (language; Zimbabwe), 158
Singapore: baba class, 93; corruption, 107, 108–12; crime, 92, 107, 108; Crown Colony, 95–96; demographics, 101–2, 102–3; education, 102–3, 115; expulsion from Federation, 100–101, 107; First World oasis, 104–5, 115–16; GDP, 102; housing, 103; infrastructure, 104; institutions, 148; Japanese occupation, 94; laws, 108, 113; life expectancy, 92; literacy, 102–3; medical insurance, 104; national defense, 102; nationalist movements, 94, 96; official languages, 103; pension, 104; police, 111; political parties, 95–96, 97–98, 105, 107, 113, 114; property rights, 113; racial riots, 100; referendum on joining Federation, 98–99; Rwandan similarities, 172; schools, 92, 93, 103, 115; taxes, 100, 111, 115; trade, 102; unemployment, 102, 115; values, 97, 113; vision, 22, 23; wages, 115–16; water, 102
Sisulu, Walter (South Africa), 7, 43, 45, 53, 56
Sithole, Ndabaningi (Zimbabwe), 82
situational dynamics, 20
Sivas, Turkey, 125–26, 127
Slovo, Joseph (South Africa), 48, 57
slums, 62, 103–4, 116
Smith, Ian (Rhodesia), 80, 82, 83
Smuts, Jan Christiaan (South Africa), 44–45, 73
Sobukwe, Robert (South Africa), 47, 49–50, 71
social contract, implied, 20
social discipline, 103–4
social intelligence, 19
Society for the Fatherland and Freedom, 122
socioeconomic disparity, in Botswana, 78
Sofia, Bulgaria, 124
Sophiatown, South Africa, 46
South Africa: anti-pass movement, 47; appeasement of, 73–74; boycotts, external, 55, 64; boycotts, internal, 43, 46, 62, 191n17; civil disobedience, 45, 46; constitution, 57, 60, 61; corruption, 150–51; crime, 50, 60, 62, 151; demographics, 55; diamonds, 68; education, 151; institutions, 148; lack of professionals, 62; leadership role, 1; leadership styles contrasted, 18; legitimacy, 28; life expectancy, 17; ministry of education, 60; planning of new government, 59–61; political parties, 44–45, 47, 49, 53, 55, 57, 60, 61; proposed transfer of territory from Botswana, 74, 76; relocation, 46; sabotage, 48, 49, 50; Sabotage Act, 49; schools, 46, 51, 57, 60, 62; segregationists, 44–45; simple majority, 60; strikes, 48; Suppression of Communism Act, 45, 49; truth and reconciliation commission, 60–61, 65; unemployment, 55, 62, 151; Union of South Africa, 68; vision, 23
South African Communist Party, 47, 49
Southern African Development Community, 83
Soviet Union, 27, 141, 142. *See also* Russia
Soweto, South Africa, 46, 51, 57
Soweto school uprising (boycott), 51, 57
sports, and Khama, 70
Springboks (rugby team), 64
squatter settlements, 62
Sri Lanka, 14, 204n45
stakes, importance of, 35–36
stare decisis, 13–14
statues, 130, 132
Steinbeck, John, 51
Stevens, Siaka (Sierra Leone), 14, 160
stewardship, 28
Straits, 93, 120, 127, 129, 199n19
Strijdom, Johannes G. (South Africa), 74
strikes, 96, 100
Suharto (Indonesia), 167
Sukarno (Indonesia), 18, 102, 167
Sukarnoputri, Megawati (Indonesia), 168
sultanate abolished, in Turkey, 130
Sultanate of Johor, 102
Suppression of Communism Act (South Africa), 45, 49
surnames, 138

Suu Kyi, Daw Aung San (Burma), 37, 153, 154–55, 190n74
Swaziland, 68, 74
symbolic gestures, 25, 41, 46, 64, 65

Tambo, Oliver (South Africa), 7, 44, 47, 53
Tamerlane, 122
Tan Kia Gan (Singapore), 110
Tanzania, 84
taxes: beer, 149; Botswana, 85, 149; loss of control, 100; Singapore, 100, 111, 115; Turkey, 139
Taylor, Charles (Liberia), 160, 170
Teh Cheang Wan (Singapore), 110
telegraph, 138, 144
Than Shwe (Burma), 153–54, 155–56
Thatcher, Margaret (U. K.), 28
Thein Sein (Burma), 155–56
Thembu chieftaincy (South Africa), 41
Thrace, 119, 123, 127, 129
Tiger Kloof, South Africa, 70–71
tobacco, 163
tolerance: Kenyatta, 166; Khama, 146, 148; Mandela, 40, 146. *See also* inclusivity
Tolstoy, Leo, 51
Tomlinson, Frederick (South Africa), 74
torture, 31
traditional values, 42, 88, 113
traffic jams, 182n7
transactionalists, 3, 22, 23, 150, 151, 152, 161–67, 174, 187n21
transformationalists, 3, 22–23, 39, 152, 187n21, 204n45
transparency, 33; Churchill, 33; essential, 12, 170; Khama, 88; sought, 162, 173
Transparency International, 89, 91, 172, 194n41
Transvaal Republic, 68
Treaty of Lausanne, 129
Treaty of Montreux (1936), 199n19
Treaty of Sèvres, 127
triads, 107
Tripoli, Libya, 123
trust, 34–35
Tsvangirai, Morgan (Zimbabwe), 159, 160–61
Tswana, 67; cabinet members, 80; and cattle owning, 78; language, 74; as process oriented, 69
tuberculosis, 70
Tunisia, 156–57
Tunku Abdul Rahman (Malaysia), 98, 99–101
turbans, 133
Turkey: alliance with Germany, 124; constitution, 126, 137, 147; corruption, 135; coup against sultan, 123; education, 130, 132; farming, 139, 141; foreign relations, 142; Grand National Assembly, 126; Independence Tribunals, 136; infrastructure, 138–39; institutions, 147; Islam, 130, 131, 132, 137, 138; Jewish emigration, 199n33; jobs, 129; literacy, 137–38; minorities, 136; national identity, 129; nationalist movements, 126, 127, 131; National Pact, 125; schools, 130, 131–32, 134, 135, 137, 138; secularization, 131–32, 134, 135; surnames, 138; taxes, 139; Treaty of Lausanne, 129; Treaty of Sèvres, 127; vision, 22, 23; war of independence, 128, 144
Turkish (language), 132, 136, 137–38
Turkish Linguistic Society, 138
Tutsi people (Rwanda), 171
Tutu, Desmond (South Africa), 150
twin studies, 7
typecasting, 184n15
tyrants, 184n15

Uganda, 84, 165–66
Umkhonto we Sizwe (South Africa), 48, 49, 50, 58, 59
underemployment, 62
undernourished, 17
unemployment: Botswana, 86; reducing, 20, 86; Singapore, 102, 115; South Africa, 55, 62, 151; Zimbabwe, 159, 160
Union of South Africa, 68. *See also* South Africa
unions, 96, 115
Union Solidarity and Development Party (Burma), 155
United Democratic Front (Malawi), 163
United Democratic Front (UDF; South Africa), 53
United Party (South Africa), 44–45
United States, 127; constitution, 13, 14, 35; political culture, 13–14; Supreme Court, 27
University of Botswana, 78
University of Cambridge, 94–95
University of Singapore, 103
University of Witwatersrand, 44, 71

unpopular decisions, 106
U.S. Supreme Court, 27
Uzbekistan, 156

values, 14, 35, 189n52; democratic, 69, 146, 165, 167, 175; political culture, 13; Singapore, 97, 113; spiritual, 42; traditional, 42, 88, 113; vision, 21, 23, 88
veils, 121, 124, 134, 199n31
venality, 201n10, 202n19
Verwoerd, Hendrik (South Africa), widow of, 64
Victor Verster prison (South Africa), 54, 57
vision, 21–23; Ataturk, 22, 23, 143–44; Johnson-Sirleaf, 169–70; Lee, 92, 98–100, 103–4, 107, 116–17; Mandela, 23; necessity of, 1; selling of, 23–26; simplicity of, 21; and values, 21, 23, 88; Yudhoyono, 168
voter appeal, 28
voting fraud, 29, 155, 157, 159, 166, 201n15; South Africa, 61

Wade, Abdoulaye (Senegal), 173
wage gap, 151
wages, in Singapore, 115–16
Wahid, Abdurrahman (Indonesia), 168
War and Peace (Tolstoy), 51–52
war, and prudence, 31
Washington, George, 13, 34–35
water, potable, 102
Wee Toon Boon (Singapore), 110
white veto, 60
Williams, G. Mennen (U. S.), 76
Williams, Ruth (Botswana), 72
Wilson, Woodrow (U. S.), 120, 125
Wilsonian idealism, 199n10
women: leaders, 204n5; schools, 130; in Turkey, 130, 133–34
Workers' Party (Singapore), 98
World Bank *Doing Business* surveys, 91
World Bank loans, 77
World Economic Forum, 91
World War I, end of, 119–20

Xhosa (language; South Africa), 43
Xuma, Alfred B. (South Africa), 44, 45

Young Turks, 123
Yudhoyono, Susilo Bambang (Indonesia), 18, 168–69
Yugoslavia, 142

Zambia, 54, 84, 173
ZANU-PF (Zimbabwe African National Union–Patriotic Front), 161
Zenawi, Meles (Ethiopia), 8
Zia, Khaleda (Bangladesh), 204n45
Zimbabwe, 14, 54, 149, 150, 157–61; life expectancy, 17; nationalist movements, 82, 83; schools, 157, 159; unemployment, 159, 160. *See also* Rhodesia
Zimbabwe African National Union–Patriotic Front (ZANU-PF), 161
zinc, 77
Zulus, 67
Zuma, Jacob (South Africa), 1, 18, 150, 151
Zwane, Ambrose (Swaziland), 71